JUN 0 8 2011

D1118610

Officially Withdrawn

IN THE
FASCIST
BATHROOM

IN THE FASCIST BATHROOM

Punk in Pop Music
1977–1992

Greil Marcus

HARVARD UNIVERSITY PRESS

CAMBRIDGE, MASSACHUSETTS
LONDON, ENGLAND

Copyright © 1993 by Greil Marcus
All rights reserved
Printed in the United States of America
Second printing, 2001
First Harvard University Press paperback edition, 1999

Library of Congress Cataloging-in-Publication Data
Marcus, Greil.
[Ranters & crowd pleasers]
In the fascist bathroom : punk in pop music, 1977–1992 /
Greil Marcus.
p.   cm.
Originally published: Ranters & crowd pleasers. New York :
Doubleday, 1993.
Includes bibliographical references and index.
ISBN 0-674-44577-5
1. Punk rock music—History and criticism.
2. Popular culture. I. Title.
ML3534.M362   1999
781.66—dc21   98-43708
CIP
MN

To Janet Duckworth,
David Frankel
and Doug Simmons

CONTENTS

INTRODUCTION

News item from the Associated Press, covered in the *Seattle Times*, 8 October 1987:

WHY DID THE MARKET PLUNGE SO WILDLY?

New York—Wall Street's latest plunge has been partly attributed to the rumored pessimism of a 38-year-old Yale psychology graduate and former rock drummer who has emerged as one of the leading gurus of 1980s stock forecasting.

Robert Prechter is the author of The Elliott Wave Theorist, an idiosyncratic investment newsletter that holds that the market reflects mass psychology and that moods go from good to bad in waves.

The former Merrill Lynch analyst has attracted a wide following because of what traders call his remarkably accurate forecasts based on seemingly inconsequential trends ranging from skirt lengths to rock lyrics.

Rumors were widespread Tuesday that Prechter had issued a short-term bearish market forecast on the private telephone hotline for the 16,000 subscribers to his newsletter, which costs $233 annually.

Traders said those rumors contributed to a massive selloff on Wall Street that erased more than 90 points from the Dow Jones industrial average, the biggest one-day loss in the history of the well-known indicator.

Prechter's fame grew in the late 1970s when he recommended buying stocks, partly because of an anguished song by the punk-rock group the Sex Pistols.

He reasoned that the song's gloom indicated a low point in the public mood and meant an emotional and market improvement would follow. A few months later the market lifted. . . .

You have to wonder just what Sex Pistols song it was that ultimately led to the erasure of ninety points off the Dow Jones average—or that, after biding its time for a decade or more, finally wreaked its revenge on the paper boom of the go-go eighties. Was it the Sex Pistols' first single, the November 1976 "Anarchy in the U.K.," where Johnny Rotten led off with the strange announcement, "I am an antichrist," and for a few minutes made it seem as if the rage issuing from his mouth could level London? Was it their next record, the May 1977 "God Save the Queen," with its sneering final chant of "NO FUTURE— NO FUTURE—NO FUTURE"? Or did one fan hear, from inside the storm of that song, the Sex Pistols' hardest prophecy of the end of the world, and take it as a sign that nothing worse would be forthcoming, from anywhere?

> God save history
> God save your mad parade
> Lord God have mercy
> All crimes are paid

Whatever Robert Prechter heard, a lot of other people heard something just as consequential. Very quickly, pop music changed—and so did public discourse. A NIGHT OF TREASON, promised a poster for a concert by the Clash in London in 1976, and that might have summed it up: a new music, called "punk" for lack of anything better, as treason against superstar music you were supposed to love but which you could view only from a distance; against the future society had planned for you; against your own impulse to say yes, to buy whatever others had put on the market, never wondering why what you really wanted was not on sale at all.

Punk was a new music, a new social critique, but most of all it was a new kind of free speech. It inaugurated a moment—a long moment, which still persists—when suddenly countless odd voices, voices no reasonable person could have expected to hear in public, were being heard all over the place: sometimes as monstrous shouts in the marketplace, sometimes as whispers from an alleyway. There was an absolute denial of self-censorship in the Sex Pistols' songs that gave people who heard them permission to speak as freely. If an ugly, hunched-over twenty-year-old could stand up, name himself an antichrist, and make you wonder if it wasn't true, then anything was possible.

When the Sex Pistols broke apart after a show in San Francisco in January 1978, people flocked to pronounce the moment dead. Johnny Rotten himself was among them. "It was good at the time," he said in 1986, looking back. "It could have gone anywhere at one point. It kept people on edge. It kept me on edge, I know that. I was scared to walk down the street half the time. At the end there was a pointless rerunning of a B movie, packed with the obvious. It shouldn't have been. It could have been something very courageous, and an absolute change." It wasn't an absolute change—but the truth is that as punk could have gone anywhere, it did. It was a movie rerun again and again—sometimes pointlessly, sometimes not. Pop music had claimed new territory, new subject matter, new kinds of humor, new kinds of noise, all based in that first refusal, the complexity and drama of the Sex Pistols' first no.

The pop marketplace swiftly re-formed, and exiled punk to cult stations scattered along its borders. But especially in backwaters, where the glare of publicity was not much in evidence, when Johnny Rotten's movie arrived at the bottom of a double bill, when it was unspooled once more, the movie changed as it ran, and its characters stepped out of the screen. An example, as typical as any could be: in 1983, five long years after the official death of punk, the news arrived in Aberdeen, Washington, a town of 19,000 about one hundred miles southwest of Seattle. One person in Aberdeen, Buzz Osborne, had a tape which he played only for those he thought deserved to hear it; on this tape were punk songs, transferred from records that were hard to find, and he passed them on as secret knowledge. Osborne then formed the first punk band in town: "They started playing punk rock and had a free concert right behind Thriftways supermarket where Buzz worked," Kurt Cobain of Nirvana told Gina Arnold in 1991, looking back as his band rode their punk album *Nevermind* to number one, but not looking down. "They plugged into the city power supply and played punk rock music for about 50 redneck kids. When I saw them play, it just blew me away. I was instantly a punk rocker. I abandoned all my friends, 'cause they didn't like any of the music. Then I asked Buzz to make me that compilation tape of punk songs. . . ."

You can follow such a story as something very small, or as something very big. However you follow it, it is a story that was played out, lived out, more times than anyone knows in the years after the Sex Pistols vanished—in a village in Andalusia, after class at the University of Leeds, in a warehouse in Prague. The story was always the same: the music made a promise that things did not have to be as they seemed, and some brave people set out to keep that promise for themselves. The story was always different: each version left behind its own local legends, heroes, casualties, a few precious documents, a tale to tell.

This book is a collection of pieces on punk and related matters written from 1977 through 1992. Most of the material is drawn from columns I wrote for *New West* (which became *California Magazine*), *Artforum*, and the *Village Voice*, with occasional pieces from *Rolling Stone* and elsewhere. One piece—the very last in the book, following its formal conclusion—comes from *RAW*, Art Spiegelman and Françoise Mouly's graphics magazine. For what became "I Am a Cliché," I was given a set of

lurid drawings by artist Scott Gillis, already laid out with vary-
ing amounts of white space for each one, and asked to produce a
specific number of words to accompany each picture. The result
was fiction, a violent fantasy that doesn't fit anywhere else: my
most extreme version of punk as a force with the capacity to
change, or simply momentarily redeem, a life that all unknow-
ing was waiting for it.

Before that last note, in some ways this book is what I left
out of an earlier book, *Lipstick Traces*, which also began with
the Sex Pistols: that is, music. This book is mostly about
records, performances, twists of the radio dial. Readers of *Lipstick Traces* will find here some of what I left in there, mainly
quotations—for me, talismans—that occur in these pages in
very different contexts. More dubiously, there is also some of
my own writing that ended up cannibalized for *Lipstick Traces*
—as little as I could manage. Most of the pieces in this book
have been rewritten to some degree, not to change judgments,
but to correct factual errors, improve clarity, or flesh out passages originally cut for reasons of space or editors' incompre-
hension. Most of the titles are not original, because most of the
original titles were terrible puns.

Because this book is no kind of history of punk, but rather
notes from a life renewed by it and yet still lived within the
confines of pop music, international capitalism, and revanchist
politics, it begins in 1969, with the Rolling Stones' *Let It Bleed*,
an album that at the time sounded to me like the last music of
the 1960s, and has sounded more like that ever since. Save for
"I Am a Cliché," the book ends with a 1991 column on an odd,
momentary reappearance of what I suppose ought to be called
"the sixties," as a concept more than a time. The book begins
and ends this way because the shadow of that period, of its
utopianism and failure—its curse coding a wish for the impossible into pop music—hangs over punk from "Anarchy in the
U.K." through *Nevermind*, a secret yes the punk no has never
banished. "Still the spirit of '68," Johnny Rotten sang in 1979,

then trading as John Lydon with his band PiL. Spreading confusion and alarm: that, he sang, was his albatross, his fated vocation.

In between those spectral sixties borderlines is what I found to write about punk. I made no attempt to write about everything; I missed a lot, and now it is too late to catch what made the Vktms' "Midget" so funny or the Avengers' "We Are the One" so spooky, and anyway I caught up with them only years after the fact. I tried, in the moment, to write about what moved me, scared me, disgusted me, made me and so many other people feel so privileged to be present when, in some nightclub now long gone, rumor turned into fact.

I played favorites, devoting a lot of space to bohemian bands from the U.K. and scabrous groups from Los Angeles, ignoring New York, where most punks seemed to be auditioning for careers as something else. I wrote about a good deal *as* punk that to other people was not punk at all, stuff that sullied the very purity of the concept—anything from Fleetwood Mac's *Tusk* to Laurie Anderson's "O Superman" to a Bruce Springsteen career move to David Lynch's film *Blue Velvet* to a particularly bizarre rendition of Billy Joel's "Uptown Girl"—not because to me punk is an attitude more than a musical style, but because I think it is infinitely more than a musical style, period. Among other things, as an event in cultural time it was an earthquake, and it changed the landscape, throwing all sorts of once-hidden phenomena into stark relief. "O Superman" would have been an obscure, art-world curio before the Sex Pistols, before the Gang of Four, before the Slits; after them, it could invade the center of pop life. A born ranter like Elvis Costello, despite whatever musical style he might favor at a given moment, is unthinkable without punk, and he probably would have been unhearable, too—just as, after punk, the likes of George Harrison's $354 autobiography, Julian Lennon's "Too Late for Goodbyes," or USA for Africa's "We Are the World" charity record seemed much funnier, or much uglier, than they ever would have seemed before. Changing the rules of pop, insisting on new values, smashing old pieties, punk revealed its opposite as surely as it turned up allies.

Within those boundaries, I've gathered together pieces that I hope have something to say to each other. Sometimes I wrote about a band once and never again, nothing more to say. Sometimes I followed careers: the Clash, the Mekons, Margaret Thatcher and Ronald Reagan, Elvis Costello and Bruce Springsteen. Costello and Springsteen work as parallel figures in these pages: one always nibbling at the boundaries of the mainstream, the other seemingly at home nowhere else. In the 1980s, under Thatcher and Reagan, they were headed toward the convergence of Springsteen's *Nebraska* and Costello's "Pills and Soap" and *King of America*. They were three of the quietest punk records ever made, and three of the truest—negations as complete and unflinching, in their way, as hard and cruel, as any of the explosions in "God Save the Queen." The Sex Pistols' first achievement was to burn rock 'n' roll down to essentials of noise; if punk ever really ended, it was in the middle of its tale, when two singers from whom most punk chroniclers would withhold the name burned punk down to something close to silence.

—Greil Marcus, Berkeley
10 June 1992

PROLOGUE
The End of the 1960s

Let It Bleed is the last album from the Rolling Stones we'll see before the sixties, already gone really, become the seventies; it has the crummiest cover art since *Flowers* and a credit sheet that looks like it was designed by a government printing office. The tones of the music are at once dark and perfectly clear; the words are slurred and often buried. The Stones as a band, and Mick Jagger, Keith Richards, Mary Clayton, Nanette Newman, Doris Troy, Madelaine Bell, and the London Bach Choir as singers sometimes carry the songs far past their lyrics. There's a glimpse of a story—not much more.

With "Live With Me," "Midnight Rambler," and "Let It Bleed," the Stones prance through familiar roles with their masks on. On "Monkey Man" they submit grandly to the image they've carried for almost the whole of the decade: "All my friends are junkies! (That's not *really* true . . .)." Hidden between the flashier cuts are tunes waiting for a listener to catch up with them: a revival of Robert Johnson's "Love in Vain," Keith Richards's "You Got the Silver." But it's the first and last of *Let It Bleed* that tell what story there is.

"Gimmie Shelter" and "You Can't Always Get What You Want" give the lie to the brutalism of "Midnight Rambler" and the easy riches of "Live With Me." Years kick in: it's a long way from "Get Off My Cloud" to "Gimmie Shelter," from "(I Can't Get No) Satisfaction" to "You Can't Always Get What You Want." A new map is being drawn; the old stance of arrogance and contempt isn't erased, but it is blurred. Once the Stones were known as the group that would always take a good old-

fashioned piss against a good old-fashioned gas station. Now
Jagger sings it this way: "I went down to the demonstration/ To
get my fair share of abuse. . . ."

"Gimmie Shelter" is a song about fear; it probably serves
better than anything else as a passageway straight into the
next decade. The band builds on the best melody they've ever
found, slowly adding instruments and sounds until explosions of
bass and drums ride on over the first crest of the song into
howls from Jagger and Mary Clayton, a black session singer
from Los Angeles. It's a full-faced meeting with all the terror
the mind can summon, moving fast and never breaking, so that
men and women have to beat the terror at its own pace. When
Clayton sings alone, so loudly and with so much force you think
her lungs are bursting, Richards frames her with measured,
pressured riffs that blaze past her emotionalism and toss the
song back to Jagger's distanced judgment: "It's just a shot
away, it's just a shot away. . . . It's just a kiss away, it's just a
kiss away." You know a kiss won't be enough.

You remember the Stones' girls—say, the common, flirty (or
was it "dirty"?) machine operator in "The Spider and the Fly,"
or for that matter the girl back home who told the singer
"When you've done your show go to bed"? They're still around
for *Let It Bleed*, with their own masks on—all the cooks and
maids, upstairs and downstairs, all the Crazy Horse strippers
and London socialites in "Live With Me," or the mangled victims of the Midnight Rambler. But the true women in this music seem to be people who can shout like Mary Clayton—
tougher than any of the skirts jumping out of the old Stones
orgy, knowing something the rakes don't know. That's what
makes "Gimmie Shelter" so shocking—it hits from both sides,
with no laughs, no innuendo, nothing held back. It's a search for
the future contained in the present; the Stones have never done
anything better.

Meanwhile, as the band closes out the decade, a book of pictures by David Bailey (once the Stones' photographer) has ar-

rived in the stores, a panorama of the celebrities who meant something in London these past ten years: *Goodbye Baby & Amen: A Saraband for the Sixties*. In words and staged portraits it tries to capture the liberation London found when the last symbols of empire were jettisoned, when Christine Keeler cut the boards out from under the British establishment, when John Lennon, Pete Townshend, and Mick Jagger drove out old speech with new noise, when movie stars, directors, models, photographers, architects, painters, playwrights, and poets took art out of museums and took their clothes off at the same time. With a tombstone on its jacket, the book reaches for a sense of freedom already past, urging images of one long party lasting through the years, some still looking for it.

There's a strange quote from filmmaker Bryan Forbes, pictured with his wife, actress and *Let It Bleed* backup singer Nanette Newman: "The curious thing is that ideas float in the air and a lot of us explored the same territory; there was no collusion. We weren't committing adultery with each other's permission. We never knew, in fact, that we were sleeping with the same girl." Forbes calls up an excitement and a creativity that were unconsciously shared, and the sex that pervades his talk merely adds realism to his utopianism. In London, in the sixties, when styles on Carnaby Street changed by the day, when each new group was *thrilling*, when America looked to London with envy, joy, and, really, wonder, what one saw was a mad pursuit of every next day, and what one saw looked like the most complete freedom the world had ever known.

Yet as you stare at the pictures in *Goodbye Baby & Amen*— Marianne Faithfull pure against the sunset, Susannah York falling out of her dress, the Beatles and the Stones posing as kings, and the weird, scary spread of Christine Keeler vamping the book to a close—you see that the book cannot really bring the era into focus. It's as if these people and the years they lived through were never there at all, like the fantasy of an American writer, Gerard van der Leun, of rock 'n' roll London at its peak:

Tonight, to the consternation of the duly delegated authorities, an unkempt mob of anarchists clad in body paint and fright wigs stormed the Houses of Parliament following their frenzied participation in the Intergalactic Sonic Sit-In at the Royal Albert Hall. After laying siege to the speaker's podium, they used their cigarette lighters to fuse the works of Big Ben into a bronze statue of Smokey Robinson. . . .

But following that fantasy—rather, as it happened: van der Leun was writing in the summer of 1968—America's own sixties, the final sixties of assassination, riot, war, and the cold gloom of Richard Nixon, caught up with London's party, foreshadowing its end, exposing its hometown marvelousness. The French rising of 1968 gave the very idea of Carnaby Street a ludicrous tinge—even if, in some way, the freedoms of Carnaby Street might have been what the French students and workers were fighting for—while those same Paris street fights pushed the Rolling Stones into "Street Fighting Man," their admission that they were no longer where it's at, that Swinging London was now Sleepy London Town. Then Jean-Luc Godard tossed out *Weekend*, proof British directors were second-rate. It was all over. It was no fun.

It became hard for Americans to think of London as a *city*, as a circuit of possibilities—for most it was simply where pop stars lived. Not long before, when Michelangelo Antonioni came to town to make his London movie, he made his hero a photographer—and though *Blow-Up* was a lousy movie, Antonioni's argument that the photographer's picture was more real than the thing itself was at the heart of both the movie's lousiness and, for the moment, its truth. As an era faded Godard made his own English film—with the Rolling Stones. He tried to undercut their status, to demystify their power, and, interestingly, he failed. The Rolling Stones and a few more have lasted, and if the rest have lost whatever they had, that is why *Goodbye Baby & Amen*, and David Bailey's own self-dating style of photography—heavy black and white, focus pressed down to the pores, opening them, taking off the clothes of even his most stylishly dressed subjects—carries such a pathetic message. "We were there! *We were!* And it was a grand time. . . ."

This era and the collapse of its bright and flimsy liberation are what the Rolling Stones leave behind with the last song of *Let It Bleed*. Dreams of having everything, right now, are gone; the record ends with a song about compromise with what you want, with a celebration of learning to take what you can get, maybe even what you deserve, because time has passed, and the rules have changed. Back a few years, London's new working-class, middle-class pop aristocracy were out for just what they wanted, and they got it—but no one can live off a memory, a memory of that sense of mastery of, when was it, '65, '66? If "Gimmie Shelter" is a song about terror, "You Can't Always Get What You Want" looks for satisfaction in resignation. *That* sort of goal isn't what made "Satisfaction" the unanimous nationwide poll-winning choice as the greatest song of all time a few years ago—but then radio stations don't hold those sort of polls anymore. Today the comforts of unanimity are missing. You have to reach for this song yourself.

It is one of the most extreme productions ever staged by a rock 'n' roll band, and every note of it works: the stately, virginal introduction by the Bach Choir; the slow movement of sessionman Al Kooper's French horn and organ, a reminder of his push in Bob Dylan's "Like a Rolling Stone" (four years ago, but it seems like eons); a strum from Keith Richards; then the first verse and chorus from Jagger, singing almost unaccompanied. From there the music dissolves and builds again in surges, begins over and over in a mood of tragedy and fatigue, and ends with complete optimism and exuberance. It's as much a movie as *Blow-Up*—beginning and ending with a party in a

Chelsea mansion, the singer meeting a strung-out woman he apparently knows from earlier times, when things were different all around. The tune moves from there to street fighting, to street fighting and political revolt as just another show, and then to the strangest scene of all. The singer is in the Chelsea drugstore, waiting in line for his prescription. He strikes up a conversation with a man much older—it sounds as if it's someone he's seen around but never really spoken to. The older man is nervous, in bad shape. He could be sixty years old, or he could be thirty-five. The singer tries to be nice, to be polite; maybe he sees himself in the old man's face, maybe he doesn't. But the old man wants something from the singer. He whispers. You can't tell if he's said "bed" or "death," but suddenly there's a smile in Jagger's voice, as if he's waited years for this moment. The singer turns to the old man with a lift that summons one more chorus: "I said, you can't always get what you want—"

From there, of course, it's back to the party.

On *Let It Bleed* you can find every role the Rolling Stones have ever played—swaggering studs, rebel criminals, harem keepers, fast-life riders—a decade's worth of poses. But at the beginning and the end there is an opening into the seventies—harder to take, and stronger wine. "You Can't Always Get What You Want" echoes back into "Gimmie Shelter"; these songs no longer reach for mastery over other people, but for an uncertain mastery over the more desperate situations the coming years are about to enforce.

—*Rolling Stone*,
27 December 1969

Two Late

Beginnings

Johnny Rotten
and Margaret Drabble

You only have to think back to the music of the time to recall how open the possibilities of British life seemed ten or twelve years ago. You only have to read the papers, or note the terror the Sex Pistols have struck in some British hearts, to understand how closed those possibilities are today. British society seems to have come to a dead end, to have turned back on itself. Though they were more than naïve illusions, the promises of the British sixties—particularly the promise that easy money, a spirit of adventure, and a revitalized popular culture shared by all would finally make the killing strictures of the British class system irrelevant—now seem like less: a con game people ran on themselves. Today there is no easy money, there is little adventure, and popular culture, to the extent that it's alive, is divisive, not unifying. The country feels as if it is shrinking. The pervasive sleaziness of the center of London today, the way Piccadilly has turned into one great den of pornography, seems to speak for a country that can no longer raise an image of itself that it wants to look at. England seems like a vacuum, and ugliness, physical and spiritual, is filling it. Resentment is everywhere and for the moment blind, without satisfying objects. Time has stopped.

Both the Sex Pistols, with "God Save the Queen," and Margaret Drabble, with her new novel, *The Ice Age*, have confronted this new world; their subject is the attempt of people in present-day England to live without a belief in the future. Certainly there are differences between Johnny Rotten and Margaret Drabble. He's a twenty-one-year-old punk from the lower middle class, formerly employed as a rat exterminator in the

London sewers; she's thirty-eight, a celebrated and widely read novelist writing for, and mostly about, educated people in their thirties or older. But both are scared, and both are responding to an overwhelming sense that their culture—political, economic, and aesthetic—has collapsed around them, leaving them stranded in a society that seems not only without prospects but without meaning.

The Ice Age is a rich book, full of characters that come to life in a page and grow throughout the novel: a building contractor who in the sixties bids to escape his class and in the seventies finds himself in prison for fraud; a spoiled, angry teenager eager for oblivion; a classics professor retreating not only from the present but from all signs of life in the past. But the richness of *The Ice Age* is not in its plot, which centers on two people in their late thirties, Alison Murray and Anthony Keating, who are trying to build a relationship in the midst of personal disasters and public decay. The richness of the novel has to do with the way Drabble connects the private lives of her characters to the public miasma they are forced to share with everyone else.

What's at stake here is Drabble's ability to catch what it means to try to live with some vague, necessary sense of virtue in a society that no longer understands the word; a society which, while more or less randomly punishing some who transgress against it, can no longer afford to protect the sick or the old, or to reward those who have lived according to the values in which they were taught to believe. "All over the nation," Drabble writes,

families who had listened to the news looked at one another and said, "Goodness me," or "Whatever next," or "I give up," or "Well, fuck that," before embarking on an evening's viewing of color television, or a large hot meal, or a trip to the pub, or a choral society evening. All over the country, people blamed other people for all the things that were going wrong—the trades unions, the present government, the miners, the car workers, the seamen, the Arabs, the Irish, their own husbands, their own wives, their own idle good-for-nothing offspring, comprehensive education. Nobody knew whose fault it really was, but most people managed to complain fairly forcefully about somebody: only a few were stunned into honorable silence. Those who had been complaining for the last twenty years about the negligible rise in the cost of living did not, of course, have the grace to wish that they had saved their breath to cool their porridge, because once a complainer always a complainer, so those who had complained most when there was nothing to complain about were having a really wonderful time now.

When a society reaches such a pass, Drabble says, people freeze up, and that is what she slowly dramatizes in *The Ice Age.* On the sleeve of the Sex Pistols' latest 45, "Pretty Vacant," you see two buses, destinations clearly marked: BOREDOM and NOWHERE. In *The Ice Age* these are not destinations, because Drabble's characters have already arrived. People who can afford it are "more ironic, more cynical, more amused by more things and less touched by anything"—and that is as true and hard a statement about the seventies as the seventies have produced. People like Anthony Keating do not merely suffer from boredom, they cultivate it, as an escape from anxiety. One man feels himself "turning into a tree," and he's grateful, because he no longer has to think. Alison Murray returns from a country that may as well be Albania—a place that seems like nowhere—but it's when she reaches London that she understands nowhere is where she lives, and where she comes from. The place is shabby—a word that recurs throughout *The Ice Age*—shabby, mean-spirited, selfish, unfriendly, brutalized. Hideous new buildings have broken up communities that took centuries to form; people, Alison Murray among them, can no longer connect to the landscape in which they grew up, because it speaks for things that no longer really exist, or that they don't want to know about. Personal horrors—an IRA bomb attack that kills a friend and mutilates another, a child with cerebral palsy, a financial disaster, a friend in prison—all come to seem fated, signs of a greater loss of efficacy and will: a common price some of which everyone will have to pay sooner or later, in money or in blood.

Hanging over every page of the book is the contrast between the sixties and the seventies: between narcissism and self-pity, delight and despair, fast money and depression, a lust for good times and good ideas and the willingness to settle for what, in the seventies, is called survival. It's a chill on the soul, and Drabble perhaps renders it best in the name she invents for a tranquilizer given to children with physical defects: "Oblivine."

Most novelists today—especially in America, where social bonds have always been looser than in England—write as if to disengage their characters, and by implication their readers, from the society in which they live. Margaret Drabble writes to connect her characters to a reality larger than their own, and to discover what can be made of that connection—how it works, what it promises, what it costs. In *The Ice Age* she is saying that post-industrial society, the corrupt welfare state, has passed beyond its ability to order itself, to posit values worthy of respect, and to maintain the kind of community that binds people rather than separates them. What is shared is a feeling of sordidness, and each person finds his or her own way to turn away from it; both Drabble and the Sex Pistols are working to turn their audiences back upon that sordidness, because that is the only honest thing to do. When things are as Drabble describes them in *The Ice Age* or as the Sex Pistols describe them in "Anarchy in the U.K." and "God Save the Queen," that is the only way to hang on to a sense of what it means to live without lying, without betraying yourself and everybody else.

—*Rolling Stone*,
20 October 1977

The End of an Antichrist:
Sex Pistols, Winterland,
San Francisco,
14 January 1978

O n the last stop of the Sex Pistols' first American tour they took on almost as many people—over five thousand —as they faced in Atlanta, Memphis, Baton Rouge, Dallas, San Antonio, and Tulsa put together. They held the stage for an hour; four days later, they blew apart. It may be that their only alternative to the future the rock 'n' roll world had imagined for them—a future devoid of imagination, a future made up of the rock 'n' roll rewards and penalties they had set out to deny—was to quit the scene; that, or a plane crash.

The Sex Pistols left behind more history than music, but on their final night the music lived up to the history. The first thing that struck me, not a minute into the show, was how much stronger they sounded onstage than on their records. The music was all bite: you could reach out and touch every jagged note.

It was drummer Paul Cook and Steve Jones—somehow revitalizing every stance in the English book while sounding as if he were playing a guitar factory instead of a guitar—who made the noise, and together they were likely the only great two-man band in the history of rock 'n' roll. Sid Vicious used his bass as a prop; spraying the crowd with spit, beer, and mucus, he looked like an English Charley Starkweather. With one arm taped from wrist to biceps (Vicious was to OD twice that week), he was there to bait the crowd.

What was most surprising about Johnny Rotten was the way you could read his intelligence not only in his eyes—he might have been a kid out of *Village of the Damned* seventeen years later—but in the way he used his body. He slumped like Quasimodo; he cut through the curtain of objects hitting the stage and the band (ice, cups, shoes, coins, pins, and probably rocks) with a twist of his neck. He hung onto the mike as if he were caught in a wind tunnel, about to be blown off the stage.

"There's not enough presents," Rotten yelled after a belt flew over his shoulder. "You'll have to throw up better things than that." A perfectly rolled British umbrella landed at his feet. "That'll do," he said. The crowd wasn't young—most were older than anyone in the band—and they were mean, either by pose, choice, or necessity. A man in a football helmet butted his way through the crowd until he smashed a cripple out of his wheelchair; the band went its own way. "Bodies" broke the show open with the same intensity with which "No Fun"—the single encore—finished it off: Rotten and Jones bore down as if they had nothing left to lose. There was the unrecorded "Belsen Is a Gas" ("Belsen is a gas, I heard the other day/ Saw the open graves where the Jews all lay"), the careening momentum of "Liar," the dead-end-kid sputter of "Problems," and, finest of all, the hate and delight Rotten put into the chorus of "Pretty Vacant": "AND WE DON'T CARE!" Finest of all, because the force of his negation brought such pleasure: a thin edge of affirmation.

Just before the band left the stage—carefully gathering up everything of value (there were four umbrellas by the end)—Rotten rang a change on his music. It was that famous line from "Anarchy in the U.K.": "Don't know what I want/ But I know how to get it." This night, the negative was gone. He knew what he wanted, Rotten shouted, and he meant it. But whatever it was, those of us who were there couldn't give it to him—and he knew that too. So, minutes later, he left, and we will see nothing like him again.

—Rolling Stone,
9 March 1978

1977–1979

Elvis Costello:
The Old Waldorf,
San Francisco,
16 November 1977

Elvis Costello, the British pheenom, could hardly have picked a better place to open his first American tour than San Francisco. As an import, his debut lp, *My Aim Is True*, had been airing for months on KSAN, the area's leading FM outlet; avant-garde record stores like Berkeley's Rather Ripped had sold every copy they could get hold of. By the time Costello touched these shores, Columbia, the bonus baby's new label, had his album in the shops and other FM stations were falling into line. Costello himself did his best to make his presence felt, materializing at a Randy Newman concert, at the Mabuhay Gardens, a punk venue, and on KSAN, where in the course of an interview he claimed both that "Elvis" is his given name and that his organist had never listened to ? and the Mysterians. And his legend had preceded him: this twenty-two-year-old former computer operator, everyone seemed to know, was the man who had told Nick Kent of *New Musical Express* that his songs are motivated solely by "*revenge* and *guilt*," the only emotions he understands; who hates the music business so much he's keeping a blacklist against the day he seizes power; who wants to die before he gets old: "I'd rather kill myself. . . . I'm not going to be around to witness my artistic decline." There is genius in the wording of that last line, and it was already in the songs ("I said I'm so happy I could die/ She said drop dead and left with another guy"), an acrid rockabilly sound and a punk point of view reduced to a dead stare. The sold-out crowd of six hun-

dred that squeezed into the Old Waldorf was ready for whatever it was Elvis Costello had to offer, or inflict.

Playing rhythm and attempting lead guitar, Costello onstage is serious, impersonal, and not quite all there; his band—
organ, bass, and drums—is straight out of the Electric Prunes'
"I Had Too Much to Dream." "Psycho music," a friend said with
approval, as Costello ate the mike and launched into "Night
Rally," a doomstruck, as-yet-unrecorded attack on Britain's
neofascist National Front. "They're putting your name in the
forbidden book," he spat out. "I know what they're doing, but I
don't wanna look." The man doesn't exactly exude equanimity.

The crowd was mad for Costello—and any number of his
performances, from "Alison" to "(The Angels Wanna Wear My)
Red Shoes," were direct and hard—but I think there was a
certain amount of autohype involved. The band, punk in looks
and to a fair degree musically, is weak—at one point their
sound suggested the seminal punk rocker was not, say, "Search
and Destroy," but "Batman Theme"—and Costello ran across
his faster numbers, such as "Mystery Dance," so hurriedly his
phrasing dissolved and the rhythmic punch of his arrangements
collapsed. The coldness of his demeanor—he never cracked a
sneer, let alone a smile—made the black humor of his lyrics
inaccessible, or irrelevant.

Costello's confidence, however, is not in doubt. He changed
his songs radically from set to set, always including a lot of
tunes no one had heard before; a sense of repression, perversity, or simply fury was always present. The most striking difference between Costello on record and Costello in the flesh is
that the contradictions of his persona stand out much more
starkly under the lights: all at once, he communicates the arrogance of the next big thing and the fear of the imposter who's
sure he'll be shot before he gets through his third number.

—*Rolling Stone*,
12 January 1978

The Clash

One version of rock 'n' roll, from the *Official Scrapbook* of the film *Sgt. Pepper's Lonely Hearts Club Band*, produced by Robert Stigwood, directed by Michael Schultz:

We decided that for the ending of *Sgt. Pepper* we should create a moment of spectacular movie magic, and have Peter Frampton and the Bee Gees joined by the collective starpower of scores of famed recording stars. . . . Formal invitations were engraved. . . . The guests were treated royally—first-class transportation to Los Angeles, limousines, luxurious hotels, the finest champagne and food—nothing but the best.

Another version, from a report in the U.K. fanzine *Zig Zag* on a concert that took place last year in Belgium:

Fifteen feet from the stage is the ugliest, most vicious-looking barbed wire fence you ever saw. Ten feet tall, effecting perfectly an arena within an arena, only this inner arena is where the privileged hang out, and behind this monstrosity of a fence the other arena, where the less privileged have been herded like cattle. . . .

Suddenly, Strummer leaps into the inner arena. He streaks straight to the fence, and with his bare hands he is pulling and tugging at the bastard as hard as he can. For a second nobody knows what to do, and then all hell is let loose. Security men grab at Strummer, other people leap from the stage and grab the security men. . . .

Joe Strummer, twenty-five, is the lead singer of the Clash. Along with guitarist Mick Jones, twenty-three, he was in San

Francisco to finish off the recording of the second Clash album, as yet untitled—a record a lot of people have been waiting for. An English punk band formed hard on the emergence of the Sex Pistols, the Clash are now so good they will be changing rock 'n' roll simply by addressing themselves to the form, and so full of the vision implied by their name they will be dramatizing certain possibilities of risk and passion merely by taking a stage.

Meeting Strummer, it's not hard to imagine him ripping down a fence separating his band from its audience. A joyful loathing of such elitism is part of what kicked off the English punk revolt in the first place, and no band has tried harder, or more self-consciously, to live up to that revolt, to keep its spirit whole, than the Clash. Built like Bruce Springsteen (a comparison Strummer, who takes Springsteen for a myth-addled softie, would not appreciate), with a James Dean haircut (no DA), black leather jacket, white T-shirt, suspenders attached with safety pins to buttonless black pegged pants, and the kind of boots they used to say your mother wore, Strummer carries himself like a man who takes nothing for granted. A few hours around him left me sorting out suppressed rage from a quick sense of humor: as in the Clash's music, you feel a wearied, bemused intolerance for frauds large and small, and a biting eagerness to wipe them out.

From the beginning, Strummer, Jones, bassist Paul Simonon, and drummer Topper Headon (briefly replaced by Terry Chimes, according to the born-again spirit of punk renamed Tory Crimes) have appeared as a gang of partisans bent on the defeat of all the right enemies. They've never hedged their hatred of Britain's neo-Nazi National Front (some of Mick Jones's friends are members, as was Strummer's brother), their disgust with what Labour and the Tories have done with their power, or their embrace of reggae and its commitment to righteousness and Judgment Day. "London's Burning," "White Riot," and the rave-up cover of Junior Murvin's reggae hit "Police and Thieves"—all on *The Clash*, their first album, still unissued in the United States because its sound was considered too crude—were part and parcel of a refusal of any version of the barbed-wire fence.

Middle-class in background, working-class in the themes of their songs and in Strummer's crunched accent, the Clash have been understood as "political" for the right reasons: because, more directly than other bands, they saw in punk proof that apparently trivial questions of music and style profoundly threatened those who ran their society. That meant those who ruled were afraid, which implied that their hold on power was not so certain as it seemed. Politics thus became an intensified, eyes-open version of everyday life—but if the Sex Pistols were frankly nihilistic, asking for destruction and not caring what came of it, the Clash are out for community, the self-discovery of individuals as a means to solidarity, a new "I" as the means to a discovery of an old "we."

Just as it was something punks—and everybody else—lived out off-stage, politics was something to dramatize onstage, until the limits and contradictions of one's life could be tensed, revealed, and broken through. This was the clash the band named itself for—and acted out, or played out on record or in front of audiences, what began as a stance, as a pose, was soon no act at all. The Clash didn't seek targets for protest songs, they sought a purchase on reality. They didn't carp about bad jobs—their "Career Opportunities" was about Mick Jones's onetime job as the lowliest letter-opener, which is to say as the opener of suspected IRA letter bombs—they made noise out of their humiliations.

What has been extraordinary about the Clash is their ability to create a sound, an attack, that pushes beyond any here-and-now British specifics of race, class, or culture, details that might dim their power elsewhere. Their strongest record so far, "Complete Control," a U.K.-only single, is on paper nothing more than a petulant denunciation of CBS, their British label, for releasing a 45 without first clearing it with the band. It comes across not as a naïve complaint about artistic freedom but as a cosmic last stand, perhaps the most thrilling, transporting version of the punk impulse to leap from the smallest insult to greatest refusal: a definition of how much anger and determination are worth, and of how good they can feel. It's hard rock that ranks with "Hound Dog" and "Gimmie Shelter" —music that, for the few minutes it lasts, seems to make both seem uncertain, even eager to please.

Some of the almost completed tracks I heard at the Automatt studios in San Francisco were better. Producer Sandy Pearlman, a New Yorker brought in to make the Clash palatable to American audiences, has broadened the sound—"There are," he announced, "more guitars per square inch on this record than in anything in the history of Western civilization"— but he hasn't compromised the Clash's darkness, or their force. "He couldn't," said Strummer. "Though he's been trying for six months to turn us into Fleetwood Mac. I think he just gave up last night."*

The Clash have drawn on the fuck-you sound of the New York Dolls, the Stooges, the early Rolling Stones and the Who, and on the romantic populism of Mott the Hoople, but those influences long ago ceased to be more than footnotes. What you hear now in the storm of their sound is reggae, in the rhythm section, and, in Strummer's furious singing, in Mick Jones's crossing guitar lines, and in the twists and turns of the song structures, Captain Beefheart. One of many rock 'n' roll

---

* He didn't. The album Pearlman produced, *Give 'Em Enough Rope*, came out thinned and distracted, with highs and lows missing; Fleetwood Mac's 1977 "Go Your Own Way" had far more. Mick Jones had picked up the central, explosive guitar riff of "Safe European Home," the album's strongest song, from the live version of Sammy Hagar's "I've Done Everything for You," on the radio constantly as the band worked in San Francisco; Pearlman erased the riff from the final master, fearing it would sound like a cheap cop, and thus erased the voice of the tune.

prophets-without-honor rescued from oblivion by British punks, Beefheart is a Southern Californian who in the late 1960s combined Delta blues (mostly Charley Patton and Howlin' Wolf), bebop, and the sprung rhythms of American speech (out of Mark Twain, Mike Fink, and neighborhood bars) into awesome, and often awesomely difficult, music: caterwauls and clatter, polite greetings that hinted at obscenity, drunken curses breaking up revival meetings, preachers silencing blasphemers. His masterpiece, the 1969 *Trout Mask Replica*, broke every rule in rock 'n' roll except one: move the listener. As Mike Bloomfield once put it, it didn't matter if it was Robert Johnson's most delicate, heartbroken guitar piece, or the Rivingtons declaiming "Papa Oom Mau Mau, Papa Ooo Mau Mau" again and again and again (I know it's "Oom Mow Mow," but "Mau Mau" is what the Rivingtons meant), it had to make you sit up and say, *What? What?*, and Beefheart's music always did.

"When I was sixteen," Strummer mused when I mentioned the *Trout Mask* echoes I thought I heard in the Clash's new tracks, "that was the only record I listened to—for a year." The Clash have taken Beefheart's aesthetic of scorched vocals, guitar discords, melody reversals, and rhythmic conflict and made the whole seem anything but avant-garde: in their hands that aesthetic speaks with clarity and immediacy, a demand you have to accept or refuse. It sounds like a promise rock 'n' roll has waited years to keep. The sense of confusion and doubt in the sound is still there, along with a sense of triumph.

There is also a claim on history, made and unmade. In "English Civil War," which simply by its title both harks back to the seventeenth century and posits a future no one wants to think about, Strummer somehow jumps the years and takes over the voice of a twenty-year-old conscript who's stepped into the no-man's-land trenches of the Great War and now, just for a moment, speaks his piece. "Guns on the Roof," a song that began as an account of the arrest of two Clash members for shooting pigeons, turns into music about terrorism, and Strummer sings as a prisoner in the dock: if the fear and pride he communicates mean anything, he'll never see the streets again. As the band uses the beat from the Who's 1965 "Can't Explain" ("Very traditional, don't you think?" said Mick Jones) to set off bombs in the courtroom, Strummer charges the bench: "I swear by/ ALL MIGHTY GOD/ To tell the WHOLE truth/ And nothing but—the TRUTH!" Guitars rain down on every line: you're taken out into the battle outside the courtroom, back to the courthouse, and, finally, in a grand, bitter fantasy of freedom, all across the world. "I'd like to be in Af-er-ee-ca," jibes the singer at himself. "I'd like to be in the U.S.A./ Pretending that the wars are done."

These songs take the harshness of the sound kicked up by the Sex Pistols and the Clash's first recordings to its limits; "Safe European Home" shatters them. Inspired by a trip the reggae fans made to Jamaica, a pilgrimage that turned up sour ("I went to a place where every white face was an invitation to robb-er-ee," runs the key line), it's a wild, self-mocking testament to the way the attempt to escape your own culture inevitably leads to being thrown back upon it. A high, keening, up-and-down guitar line pushes Strummer's raging vocal; Mick Jones slaps him back with incessant harmonies, taunting: "Wherrrrr'd you go?" The music is almost too strong, the pace too fast; finally it breaks, and the band changes into a new, metallic reggae as Strummer and Jones shift into a Jamaican patois as distant, and as revealing, as Strummer's borrowed cockney, the voices drifting across each other, dub style, until humor and betrayal share the song with anger and delight. The Clash make it home—safe, not exactly where they want to be, but the only place they belong. They may want the world but in the heart of this song it doesn't matter that Lee Perry, Jamaica's finest, produced "Complete Control," or that Bob Marley said yes to the Clash in his "Punky Reggae Party." The Clash, this song says, have to fight their own war, on their own ground.

The wars the Clash are turning into music—wars of class, race, and identity—are all too real. How they turn out will determine what the Clash, and their audiences, will make of their lives. But the war the Clash are actually fighting is, for better or for worse, mostly a rock 'n' roll war: a struggle to define and seize the essence of the music, to take over its history, to refashion its past and future according to what can be done by a few people, now. The Clash seem eager to get on with it. Killing time one day before their nightly sessions in the studio, Strummer and Jones found themselves in a movie theater, face to face with the result of all those engraved invitations and hired limousines—with platinum-coated barbed wire. "It was unbelievable," Jones said of the *Sgt. Pepper* finale. "They had 'em all! Every ligger in L.A.! Tina Turner, Alice Cooper, Dr. John—everyone with nowhere else to go!" The film at least provided an idea for an album cover. "These are the people who've made rock 'n' roll what it is today," Jones said, "and I think we owe them some sort of tribute. We'll put every one of them on the sleeve of our record, just like the faces on the Beatles' *Sgt. Pepper*, every one hanging from—"

"Gallows," offered Strummer.

"No," said Jones thoughtfully. "Lampposts."

The choice was not without meaning: gallows are a sign of authority. Lampposts are what the kids in the Clash's streets would use, if they had the chance, or took it.

—New West,
25 September 1978

Doom Squad

"The political crisis of capitalism reflects a general crisis of Western culture, which reveals itself in a pervasive despair of understanding the course of modern history or of subjecting it to rational direction." So read the liner notes to *Armed Forces*, the third album from Elvis Costello.

Well, not really: Costello would never speak so colorlessly. Those words are from *The Culture of Narcissism*, a new book by Christopher Lasch, but they could appear on the sleeve of *Armed Forces* (originally titled "Emotional Fascism") without misrepresenting its motives. Along with his tight and tricky band, the Attractions—anonymous but not impersonal, drawing on the mid-sixties tinniness of the British Invasion while insisting on a late-seventies punk intensity—Costello is out to define his times.

Far too weird in looks and stance to have had a chance before the Sex Pistols trashed all pop rules in London, Costello drew on punk's spirit but escaped its label. With *My Aim Is True* and the 1978 *This Year's Model* he was tuneful and scabrous, moving from the crouch of a loser to the firmly planted feet of a public rebel. When he said he was driven by revenge and guilt, he made those two emotions poles of a whole world, and within it he mounted a brutal, word-drunk attack on the illusions of romance and the banality and apathy of popular culture. He was an original: bitter, cruel, and funny, as much his own target as anyone else was.

The sound of *Armed Forces* is nowhere near as open as that of Costello's first two lps: it's suppressed, claustrophobic, twitching. Two, sometimes three Costello vocal tracks fight over the songs; the singer may drop to one channel as the band seemingly heads off for foreign lands. But it's soon clear that just below the messy, nervous surface of the music is a very stark and specific vision.

As its title implies, *Armed Forces* is a political album, a set of songs about how we live out the politics of our age whether we want to, mean to, or not. A few cuts make this obvious, but they carry the least weight: "Oliver's Army," a hummable assault on British imperialism, goes little distance for hitting an easy mark. The real burden of this record is in what appear to be conventional Costello numbers about sexual conflict and recrimination—numbers that explode those categories.

On this album, every moment of personal failure or unsatisfied passion is invaded by the cruelty and shamelessness of the political world: the heritage of mass murder our society wants to shrug off and can't; the heritage it pursues, in newspeak. Images of fascist, Stalinist, and free-world crime—and of the crimes of the totalitarian cults that have colonized spaces of doubt in Western society—are dragged from beneath the buzz of the news and out of our collective amnesia. The secret, unspeakable realities of political life, realities we seem to successfully deflect or ignore, rise up to force a redefinition of relationships between men and women, the essential stuff of ordinary life, on these unspeakable terms. Costello isn't after simple culpability: American responsibility for, say, the Iranian secret police. He's after the way the Iranian secret police—and those of other places, and not-distant times—invisibly shape our sense of ourselves.

He offers "Two Little Hitlers," a ditty that may describe a marital struggle, or our shared future ("Two little Hitlers will fight it out until/ One little Hitler does the other one's will"), or our shared past ("I will return," moons the singer, "I will not burn"). "Senior Service" is a vicious mix of sexual jealousy and terror—in fact, *the* Terror, with Costello as Madame Defarge.

There is the amazing "Goon Squad," sung as a letter from a rising young man to his parents. He's full of reassurance ("I'm doing *so* well"), pitching his plea for help between the lines: "But I never thought they'd put me on the/ Goon Squad!" The headlong pace of the song buries most of the story, and you don't know what this man is or who he works for, but finally he swallows his guilt and his squeamishness, and you can hear the victim-turned-thug talking: "They'll never get to make a lamp-shade out of me—"

These are only hints; three stronger numbers can speak for *Armed Forces*. "Green Shirt" seems like just another love song, not some obscure reference to the green shirts worn by Romania's fascist Iron Guard. The singer bites out a defense against his lover's accusation of—impotence, maybe; you can't really tell. It's slow and edgy in a classic Dylan vocal style, all nerves, disturbing but you don't know why. Then terrible things begin to crawl to the surface.

> Better cut off all identifying labels
> Before they put you on the torture table
> Because somewhere in the Quisling clinic
> There's a shorthand typist taking seconds over minutes
> She's listening in to the Venus line
> She's picking out names
> I hope none of them are mine

It's sung as a sensitive, rushed lover's plaint—and despite suggestions of *1984*, or 1934, this is a love song, if love can survive its terms—but then Costello crashes out in hysteria: "Who put these fingerprints on my imagination?" His trembling, breathy voice is the voice of a man watching through a peephole as other people fuck—or the voice of a man desperate to explain exactly why he has to kill you, just before he does.

"Chemistry Class" opens as a typical Costello love/hate opus, itching with blocked lust and fantasies of doom. But you catch a bizarre, horribly acute line—"Snakes and ladders, crawling up her nylons"—and then this:

> Ready to experiment
> Ready to be burned
> If it wasn't for some acci—
> Accidents
> Then some would never learn

The broken pause on "accidents" is disorienting; it's nothing compared to what you might feel when, after a few listenings, you make out the lover's crooning refrain: "Are you ready for the final sol-oo-shun . . . ?"

This merging of our political shadows with our private affairs suggests a secret, shared longing for a real police state: a vengeful, guilty authoritarianism that, in the emotional fascism of everyday life, we are already acting out. Such a tale demands some release, and with "(What's So Funny 'Bout) Peace, Love and Understanding," Costello provides it.

It's the last song on *Armed Forces*, and with it the album cuts loose. This is the disc's one true rocker, a great car song, with the open feel of the early Byrds soaring through "The Bells of Rhymney": even Costello's voice is fuller, less defensive. The performance blows away the murk and gloom of the record: even as the song again tracks across the fears of *Armed Forces*, for a moment it dissolves them.

Written and originally recorded by Nick Lowe in 1974 as the final parody of the naïve hippie,* the tune bears no trace of irony here. It sounds like the last burst of faith from someone who's seen too clearly for his own good—and given the seam-

---

* Costello's version of "Peace, Love and Understanding" was first released as the B-side of Nick Lowe's single "American Squirm" ("I made an American squirm/ And it felt so right. . . .")—and credited to "Nick Lowe and His Sounds."

less irony that surrounds Costello's every move on the rest of
Armed Forces, it makes no sense for him to end with more. The
only reason for Costello to end with this song is that he means
what it says.

> As I walk through
> This wicked world
> Searching for light in the darkness of insanity
> I ask myself
> Is all hope lost
> Is there only pain and hatred and misery
> And each time I feel like this inside
> There's one thing I wanna know
> WHAT'S SO FUNNY ABOUT PEACE LOVE AND
>   UNDERSTANDING?

Costello's voice is thick, dumb, and irresistible; he brings it
off, every hopeless, corny word, perhaps because there is
enough evil on *Armed Forces* to make you need to have those
words come off.

"I am the bastard child of an unholy union between fascism
and Stalinism," writes Bernard Henri-Levy, seeking the source
of the failure and betrayal of the last great rebellion of our
time, that of Paris, May 1968. "Hitler did not die in Berlin.
Conqueror of conquerors, he won the war in the stormy night
into which he plunged Europe. Stalin . . . is here among us, a
stowaway in history. . . . And I am writing in an age of barba-
rism that is already, silently, remaking the world of men." Elvis
Costello and the Attractions will be performing up and down
the West Coast soon; it should be something to see. For in a
different language—more elusive, and more convincing—this is
exactly what Elvis Costello is talking about.

—*New West*,
12 February 1979

From 1979, Remove 7,
Add Zero to 9, Then Wait

"The Drive to 1981 will end on September 11, 1981," said Robert Fripp. "What happens then?" someone called. "Then," Fripp said, "begins the Decline to 1984."

It was a decent joke, and the crowd laughed, but it was clear Fripp wasn't kidding. He was talking pop strategy, and to Fripp, strategy itself can produce aesthetic satisfaction, because he means to be around for the long haul.

Fripp is a thirty-three-year-old Englishman, former guitarist for King Crimson, an early-seventies art-rock band. After it broke up, he retreated from the rock world, spent time with followers of George Gurdjieff, and slowly surfaced within the pop avant-garde, collaborating on albums with Brian Eno, playing on David Bowie's *"Heroes,"* producing records by Peter Gabriel, Daryl Hall, and the Roches—seeking out and spreading new ideas within the commercial and musical forms of rock 'n' roll. On July 30, he was at Tower Records in Berkeley, surrounded by two hundred of the faithful and the curious. Ostensibly, he was there to promote *Exposure*, his first solo album, an aural montage with vocal contributions by Hall, Gabriel, Terre Roche, and J. G. Bennett (a Gurdjieff teacher). In fact, his purpose was to introduce his new music: "Frippertronics."

Frippertronics is wholly instrumental, made on the spot with a guitar that has been altered to produce tones similar to those of a synthesizer, and two tape recorders. Fripp feeds a note into the first recorder, which feeds tape into a second, which feeds a signal back into the first, which rerecords it and feeds the augmented tape back to the second; he adds a second

note, and a third, and so on. As he creates a sort of layered tape
loop, each note in turn loses definition as the tape proceeds
through the next generation; each note changes just before the
same process changes the following note. Sounds are at once
added and lost as the process continues over several minutes,
and you hear it all. Fripp modulates the volume as the piece
takes shape; a panning pedal allows him to channel the tones, or
degrees of the tones, to one or more of four speakers.

It sounds dry, of course, but the result wasn't formal. The
music took over the store. It swept through the room (and
swept the room clean of all prior associations) with a grace that
belied the technology. The molelike man, dressed in a dark suit
and a thin tie, sat on a stool and barely seemed to move. There
was an eerie feeling of completeness to Fripp's music, and an
inexplicably ancient aura: I was sure that druids had come to
the edge of the forest with his second piece and that they had
emerged with the third, though no doubt everyone at Tower
thought of something different. I'd never heard more suggestive sounds—and this on a hot afternoon with people crammed
into the aisles of a chain store! Tones soared through the room
in arcs; they hung in the air, rang like bells, and then retreated
to their boxes. When Fripp raised a guitar and softly soloed
against the tape he'd made, playing blues just a step past (or a
step behind, I don't know) Jimi Hendrix, the question of
whether or not this was rock 'n' roll was both answered and
made irrelevant. What Fripp was insisting on was a glimpse of
possibilities.

Those possibilities were as much economic and social as musical. Fripp spent only about half of his nearly two hours at
Tower playing; the rest of the time he answered questions in
the manner of a very careful lecturer. "The Drive to 1981," he
explained, is his three-part plan (*Exposure* plus forthcoming lps
of Frippertronics and "Discotronics") to redefine elements of
popular music, gain himself an audience, and produce a body of
work against which he can describe "the new"; "The Decline to

1984" will be a tactical retreat in the face of worsening economic and political conditions, a wave of reaction, and endemic violence in Europe and America. The economic base of all activities will be cut back drastically; performers who rely on large amounts of capital will be ruined. If I understand Fripp correctly, he thinks authentically new culture will be made only when the eighties are finished; at that point, he expects to be ready—toughened, relatively unscarred, committed to a career as an entertainer in his hometown in Dorset, yet be able to be heard, through a network of independent companies and musical cults, all over the world. "The 1990s will be a time of considerable panic, I suspect," Fripp said. "I'll be in place."

Fripp posits a struggle between "dinosaurs"—the huge record companies and multimillion-dollar rock acts—and "small, intelligent objects" that will be all but invisible amidst the feet of the giants until their day comes. Frippertronics, he suggests, is one version of the small object: music that is not itself minimal made within an economic context that is. Fripp listed "Three Rules for Potential Pop Stars" (the hell with his next two albums; when's the textbook coming out?): do your own grocery shopping; do your own laundry; use public transportation.

"Lord—here comes the flood," Peter Gabriel sings on *Exposure*: "We'll say goodbye/ To flesh and blood." That kind of apocalypse seemed very distant as Fripp, at home in a university town, played the pedagogue with perfect grammar and great gentility, but he was offering his own warnings about the very same thing. There were, he wanted the crowd to understand, interesting times ahead.

—*New West*,
27 August 1979

Dead Air

Director Philip Kaufman may have been more acute than he knew when he set his update of *Invasion of the Body Snatchers*—a movie about the replacement of humans by soulless duplicates born from alien seed pods—in contemporary San Francisco, or else he noticed that the pod people were already on the streets. Released in late 1978, when the rotted bodies of hundreds of San Franciscans were still piled in metal coffins, the movie came off as a version of the story behind Jim Jones's People's Temple massacre in Guyana; in fact, because of the horror of that event, the movie came off as the *prosaic* version. And the season was just getting underway. Dan White, a human, was replaced by a pod just days after assassinating liberal Mayor George Moscone and gay supervisor Harvey Milk; by the time White came to trial a few months later, pods had taken over the prosecution of his case, ensuring that no such motives as the former White's homophobia or his right-wing politics would be put before the jury. Thus were White's crimes reduced to voluntary manslaughter.

Now the pods have seized control of KSAN-FM. For more than ten years, the station had been the heart of rock 'n' roll radio in San Francisco; as the legatee of KMPX, the first non–Top 40 rock station in the country, it had in some ways been the heart of rock 'n' roll radio in America. While other FM outlets moved to the right in the face of the punk challenge—Elvis Costello's tearing "Radio, Radio" tells the story—KSAN DJs Beverly Wilshire, Glenn Lambert, Richard Gossett, and Norm Winer sent probes to the left, opening the airwaves to outrage, farce, and surprise.

KSAN was better in 1979 than it was in 1975, but against

competition from heavily promoted stations with narrow, un-threatening formats, ratings declined; this summer, after a par-ticularly poor showing, Metromedia, KSAN's parent company, deputized David Moorhead, formerly in charge of Los Angeles's KMET, to take care of business. He did: within little more than a month, every KSAN DJ was gone, and the music had turned to lead.

On July 31, the eve of the purge, Moorhead held a press conference. If there were a Ron Ziegler School of Broadcasting, Moorhead would be a valued alumnus; it was sickening to watch his attempts to exploit San Francisco's famous superiority com-plex. Oh no, he said to the assembled writers, he would *never* try to impose his successful KMET format on KSAN: San Francisco was *much* more sophisticated than . . . *Los Ange-les*. New personnel—whoever they might be—would have close ties to "The City." KSAN's target audience would be the same: eighteen-to-thirty-four-year-olds.

Swiftly, Moorhead brought in a new program director, Jackie McCauley, and a new music director, KMET's David Perry, from Los Angeles: people well socialized in the values of the music industry. Anyone who pays attention to radio pro-gramming would have concluded that the target audience had been tightened to eighteen-to-twenty-four-year-old males: the demographic unit that, while not composed exclusively of pods, is most vulnerable to their music. Disc jockeys ("I hate the term 'disc jockey,'" Moorhead said; "I prefer 'air personality'") who were committed to much that was adventurous in late-seventies rock were replaced by those willing to submit to all that was fraudulent. The new air staff spoke in homogenized, professional voices, and, like true pods, they betrayed no per-sonal taste: they played what the computers told their bosses to tell them to play. The result was an almost unrelieved diet of that form of rock 'n' roll that claims its listeners not through imagination and style, but by going through the motions: Van Halen, ELO, Charlie, Styx, Foreigner, Pat Travers. Journey. The Knack.

KSAN's human DJs held out as long as they could before being forced out. For weeks, Beverly Wilshire closed her show with warnings: "Radio, Radio," or Peter Gabriel's "Here Comes the Flood." Glenn Lambert, who responded to word of Mc-Cauley's imminent arrival with a thrown-away reference to "our new program director, the Ayatollah Khomeini" (this a week after Khomeini banned music on Iranian radio), took his leave with a historic segue of Bob Dylan's new "Man Gave Names to All the Animals" straight into "The Teddy Bears' Picnic." But today the station is just another set of call letters. To those for whom it had been more than that, waking up to KSAN now is little different from *Body Snatchers'* Brooke Adams waking up to find that her lover has somehow . . . changed.

Just recently, the ratings came out for July and August, the last period when the former KSAN DJs were on the air. The station's overall audience share leaped from a weak 1.8 to a solid 2.5; KSAN was up with teenagers, up with women, and for the eighteen-to-thirty-four male target audience, it topped all competition. Ratings were up for every individual show. It will be interesting to see how KSAN's new management attempts to take credit for the expanded audience attracted by DJs who are no longer working and by music that is no longer played; it will be even more interesting to see the ratings for September and October. It may be that the kindred spirits on whom Moorhead, McCauley, and Perry counted are simply not as numerous as the computers led them to believe—or that the humans are not quite ready for the garbage truck.

—New West,
22 October 1979

Postscript: The new rock version of KSAN soon failed. Metromedia unloaded the franchise, which retained its call letters and became a country station, which it remains.

Live at the Roxy

On 7 July 1978 Bruce Springsteen and the E Street Band played a show at the Roxy in Los Angeles. KMET-FM broadcast it—from "Rave On" to "Raise Your Hand," twenty-three long songs in all—and bootleg lps and off-the-radio tapes have been circulating ever since. I got hold of third-generation cassettes well over six months ago; since then, I've played them often enough, but in the last weeks a few performances have come off those tapes and taken me over. It's not the only music I've listened to this late spring, but it is the only music I've felt scared to play, and scared not to.

If you're lucky, at the right time you come across music that is not only "great," or interesting, or "incredible," or fun, but actually sustaining. Through some elusive but tangible process, a piece of music cuts through all defenses and makes sense of every fear and desire you bring to it. As it does so, it exposes all you've held back, and then makes sense of that, too. Though someone else is doing the talking, the experience is like a confession. Your emotions shoot out to crazy extremes; you feel both ennobled and unworthy, saved and damned. You hear that this is what life is all about, that this is what it is *for*. Yet it is this recognition itself that makes you understand that life can never be this good, this whole. With a clarity life denies for its own good reasons, you see places to which you can never get.

Such a thing happens when it has to. Springsteen's Roxy performances of "Prove It All Night" and "Racing in the Street" (one followed the other in his set) stood out the first time I heard the tapes, but they mainly confirmed what I'd heard at the Berkeley Community Theater a few nights before

the Roxy show: onstage, these songs exploded the limits of
their recorded versions. It was only after the verdict in the Dan
White trial came down—a verdict so shameful and corrupt it
cheapened the lives of all who were involved, including those
who only paid attention—that this music became undeniable.
Every thought was suddenly vulnerable to a loathsome ugliness, and as I played the tape, the music absorbed that ugliness, took it into account—had, it seemed, been ready for it—
and had more to say.

I listened again and again. Once, the songs made me think of
a story Maxim Gorky told about Lenin's love of Beethoven. Ed-
mund Wilson quotes it in *To the Finland Station*.

"I know nothing [Lenin said] that is greater than the *Appas-
sionata*; I'd like to listen to it every day. It is marvelous superhu-
man music. I always think with pride—perhaps it is naïve of me—
what marvelous things human beings can do!" Then screwing up
his eyes and smiling, he added, rather sadly: "But I can't listen to
music too often. It affects your nerves, makes you want to say
stupid nice things and stroke the heads of people who could create
such beauty while living in this vile hell. And now you mustn't
stroke anyone's head—you might get your hand bitten off. You
have to hit them on the head, without mercy, although our ideal is
not to use force against anyone. Our duty is infernally hard."

Springsteen's music made me think of that story; it also
made me think that Lenin didn't have it quite right. Exactly
what is right, I don't know.

The Roxy show came at the start of a tour that would carry
Springsteen and his band through the next six months. Unlike
most live broadcasts, which are produced by radio station
crews and come off blurred and unbalanced, with two instruments drowning out the rest, this one was handled by Springsteen's producer, Jon Landau, and his engineer, Jimmy Iovine.
The result is one of the most vivid pieces of sound in the re-

corded history of live rock 'n' roll. There's nothing you can't hear; even when the band goes after its harshest, most brutal rave-ups, every note stands out. When Max Weinberg brings his stick down on the rim of his snare drum near the end of "Racing in the Street," you think you can feel the grain of the wood; the thump of the bass drum has slammed doors in my house. The band isn't playing to you, you're inside it, catching cues passed from one musician to another, understanding for the first time the way Roy Bittan's piano leads the music, the way Danny Federici's organ supports it, drawing out a story that would be meaningless without Bittan's frame. Bittan, Federici, Weinberg, bassist Garry Tallent, second guitarist Steven Van Zandt, and even sax man Clarence Clemons on triangle read each other's minds; their sympathy is absolute. They give Springsteen the freedom to cut loose, to send out vocals and guitar that sound heroic, but which, you can now hear, are as much as anything the product of friendship, of trust. Even on the best live albums, the musicians often sound like hired hands; here, they sound like mentors.

The Roxy was a special date on the tour, and the club was packed with music business people (Glenn Frey and Eagles manager Irving Azoff stalked out after the fourth song; Jackson Browne ended the night standing on a table, screaming). The sounds of the crowd are sometimes as exciting as those of the band: even they are preternaturally clear, and the thrill that takes over the audience—a woman's wail as the band drops back in the middle of "Prove It All Night," a whoop that seems to anticipate and then ride a line from Springsteen's guitar—is not like anything I've come across before.

If most of the Roxy performances escaped the limits of their recorded versions, emotionally the Roxy "Prove It All Night" and "Racing in the Street" don't seem to have any limits at all. Both are songs of desperation: "Prove It All Night" is about seizing the last chances life offers, "Racing in the Street" about facing its final defeats. With the first, the band rolls into the melody, stretching it over chorus after chorus, leading you through an instrumental buildup so lovely and painful you don't care if Springsteen ever starts singing. The song seems to have said everything it can possibly say before the first word is sung. The music traces a great circle, widening, moving out—but then Springsteen takes the center and claims it.

> A kiss to seal
> My fate
> Tonight

That this performance should be followed by anything seems strange; that it is topped, taken past itself, is absurd. That's what happens. I know why I had to listen to "Racing in the Street" after a jury told Dan White he was better than the men he murdered; the story this song tells is just as bad.

There has never been an artist so aware of the rock 'n' roll heritage as Bruce Springsteen. In its structure, "Racing in the Street" is Van Morrison's "Tupelo Honey"; in its theme, it is a bitter inversion of Martha and the Vandellas' "Dancing in the Street"; in a very specific lyric reference (the odd construction "you'd best keep away" transformed into "out of our way buddy you'd best keep"), it is Jan and Dean's "Dead Man's Curve." Most of all, it's the Beach Boys' "Shut Down," "409," "Little Deuce Coupe," and "Don't Worry Baby." Springsteen took the Beach Boys' teenagers with their easy, obvious freedom, and dumped fifteen years on them; he made those teenagers grow up. He imagined that they would never really outgrow the freedom they found in their cars and on the road. He made them drive forever toward a dead end that, as a curse, they would always see, that they could never wish away, but that they would never quite reach.

Springsteen finishes the story; he is singing in the first person, and he has understood exactly what has happened to him. The music falls off; then Weinberg begins to tap his stick, and very slowly, the band comes in. After two choruses, Springsteen's guitar, tuned to the soft, high tone that opens "Backstreets," joins the dirge and makes it an elegy. There's no ending. After a time—each change staggering you with a force that is truly awful—Springsteen simply begins to tell a story to introduce the next song, and as the band drops off, Roy Bittan just keeps playing "Racing in the Street" on his piano. You never really hear him stop.

There will, of course, be more shows. Springsteen is twenty-nine, with four albums behind him; that's not many, and I think it's only *Darkness on the Edge of Town* that is mature work. The scary thing about Bruce Springsteen is that he's just starting. Given what his music has done for me these past days, that's also the most positive statement I can summon up, about rock 'n' roll or anything else.

—*New West*,
2 July 1979

Gang of Four

Early this fall I went to hear the Gang of Four, an almost unknown English punk group that had been booked into San Francisco's Temple Beautiful (since renamed—I think I can bring myself to write this—New Wave A Go Go) as an opening act. It took me something under five minutes to decide that these left-wing former university students from Leeds were the most interesting band I'd seen since the Sex Pistols—and the most exciting.

That conviction had little to do with any explicit message. The Gang of Four may announce "We are all socialists" in interviews, or work with England's Rock Against Sexism, but I caught only a snatch of lyrics here and there in the hubbub. It was the pure drama of their music and the way they held the stage that made the difference.

They are something to see—grim, determined, a bit intimidating, as if they truly mean to carry on the work of the people after whom they've named themselves. Singer Jon King is all desperation: arms waving, he rushes across the stage in zigzags, and if he seems like a joke at first, his intensity can soon have you worried. Bassist Dave Allen might appear colorless, a nice guy along for the ride; when he heads for the lip of the stage to hammer down a change, he turns threatening. Drummer Hugo Burnham—short and stocky, his hair cut down to a skinhead burr—could be just a few weeks out of reform school, and it's a shock when he steps out from behind his kit to sing "It's Her Factory," a song about housewives—because he doesn't look as if he could handle a complete sentence.

But it was guitarist Andy Gill who made me afraid to take

my eyes off the stage. Dressed blandly in jeans and a shirt buttoned to the neck, with piercing eyes and a stoic face, he is a performer of unlikely but absolute charisma: his smallest movements are charged with absurd force. He holds himself as if he's seen it all and expects worse. He communicates above all a profound sense of readiness. He's a figure out of countless British sci-fi flicks: caught between powers that are at once impossible to understand and unmistakably evil, he's the everyman who claws his way to the final credits.

On the back of the Gang of Four's first single was a newspaper shot of a matador and a bull; printed alongside was a letter from the group detailing the caption they wanted used. It read: "The matador is saying, 'You know, we're both in the entertainment business, we have to give the audience what they want. I don't like to do this, but I earn double the amount I'd get if I were in a 9-to-5 job.' The bull is saying, 'I think that at some point we have to take responsibility for our actions.' " *Entertainment!*, the Gang of Four's debut album, extends the dialogue and plays with the form; the lyrics change sides from matador to bull with every tune, and the tone throughout is one of ominous, carefully worked out disorder.

The songs are gnomic, situational renderings of the paradoxes of leisure as oppression, identity as product, sex as politics; the theme here is not Armageddon (as, with the same material, it seemed to be onstage), but false consciousness within consumer culture. The performers don't rail against the repression implicit in advertising and mass sexual fantasies; rather, without a hint of condescension, they act out received ideas at just that point where they begin to come apart. Narrative is abandoned, in the music no less than in the lyrics—the tunes are constructed out of jarring off-beats, crooked frames from Gill's guitar—and the process is full of gaps. "Fornication makes you happy," King sings in "Natural's Not in It." He

seems to accept that as the way things are. To follow the story
the band is telling, though, you have to wonder why sex has
turned into "fornication," perhaps make a connection to lines
from "Contract"—"These social dreams/ Put in practice in the
bedroom/ Is this so private/ Our struggle in the bedroom"—and
then wonder why a couple sophisticated enough to describe sex
as "struggle" have turned sex into "a contract in our mutual
interest."

On almost every cut there's the sense that the ability to
speak clearly, to define choices, is slipping away. This is nowhere so evident as on "Return the Gift" and "Anthrax." The
former is the only track on the album with conventional rock 'n'
roll momentum: as King recites a cutup of commercial give-
away slogans, Burnham and Allen find a startling, jerking beat,
and Gill traces it with tiny squeaks—squeaks that, as the music
builds, seem like the pathetic cries of a consumer who will
spend the rest of his life waiting by his mailbox for his package
to arrive. "Anthrax," on the other hand, is anything but impressionistic. It's the band's starkest piece, and rooted in an aesthetic worthy of the group's name: contradiction.

Emerging from a wash of feedback and echo from Gill,
Burnham and Allen punch out a fatalistic, syncopated rhythm.
King comes on, chanting, emotionally frozen—damning himself
for having been so weak as to fall in love.

> And I feel like a beetle on its back
> And there's no way for me to get up
> Love'll get you like a case of anthrax
> And that's one thing I don't want to catch

Aside from some mumbling buried in the mix, that's all you
hear the first time around—and imagery aside, it's fairly standard stuff for punk. That mumbling, however, turns out to be
Gill, delivering a simultaneous critique of King's lyrics. The effect is disorienting and hilarious: Gill speaks in the deadpan

voice of a student called up to read his essay in front of the class.

Love crops up quite a lot as something to sing about; most groups make most of their songs about falling in love or how happy they are to be in love. You occasionally wonder why these groups do sing about it all the time. It's because these groups think there's something very special about it—either that or else it's because everybody else sings about it and always has. You know: to burst into song you have to be inspired and nothing inspires quite like love. [At this point Gill actually pauses to clear his throat.] These groups and singers think they appeal to everyone because apparently everyone has or can love, or so they would have you believe, anyway—but these groups go along with the belief that love is deep in everyone's personality. I don't think we're saying there's anything wrong with love; we just don't think that what goes on between two people should be shrouded in mystery.

Gill, Burnham, King, and Allen are inheritors of Johnny Rotten—their music has the feeling of beginning just where he left off—but perhaps mainly as artists who inhabit the space of freedom he cleared when he proved that anything was possible. He smashed the limits; most are again in place, but I don't think there's any limit to how good the Gang of Four can become.

—New West,
3 December 1979

Logic

In early 1977 London kids followed the word on the street into a club called the Roxy, where they could hear a sound the world at large would soon know all too well as punk rock. The scene was rough: as with all pop movements, it meant to separate those who had a place in it from those who didn't.

One of those with the nerve to take the stage was a schoolgirl who had given herself the wonderful name of Lora Logic. She played saxophone, an unlikely instrument for punk rock, in a group called X-ray Spex; the band was fronted by the even more unlikely Poly Styrene, an overweight teenager with braces, a mixed racial ancestry, and a screech to disinfect the Roxy toilet. Poly went on to fame and a nervous breakdown; Lora went back to school.

The sort of music played at the Roxy became the Next Big Thing—and, just as swiftly, Last Year's Hype. As the scene broke up (buried, the notices would have had one think, by Sid Vicious's timely death) one could almost hear the sigh of relief.

Pushed out of the headlines, punk—in the hands of bands that had sprung up after the official demise of the form—retained its commitment to vulgarity and force, but without a scene to support it or restrict it, punk also became selfconsciously experimental. The lyrics turned impressionistic or flatly abstract; the music began to draw on the technotronic innovations of Brian Eno and Robert Fripp, and on the ghostly, destabilizing effects of Jamaican dub. Punk became an avant-garde, a floating center not only of resistance to mainstream rock but of serious novelty.

This almost secret resurgence has provided a new base for

Lora Logic, who has reappeared as the leader of a five-person band called Essential Logic. A punk founder, she is now just eighteen. That means Deborah Harry is old enough to be her mother, but Lora Logic sounds more in command of her music than Harry, or perhaps any female rock 'n' roller, has ever been.

Lora writes the songs, sings them ("warbles" is her word, and it's apt), and plays tenor and soprano saxophone. She describes her lyrics as "fairly detailed images in a disorderly context," and that will do as a description of her music as such, or as a description of how she perceives the world. Listening to the new *Beat Rhythm News* or to "Essential Logic," an earlier and even stronger four-track EP, you might be reminded of the more radical John Lennon singles ("Instant Karma" or "Cold Turkey"), Roxy Music's *Stranded*, "Telstar," Captain Beefheart, certainly X-ray Spex—but no point of reference holds for more than a moment. You haven't heard this before.

Essential Logic's sound comes at you in pieces, but the pieces aren't quite meant to fit. The band may start out with an enormous rush ("Wake Up," especially in its EP version, has a momentum as complex and lively as "Get a Job"; it's also as plainly ominous as "Anarchy in the U.K."), then cut it off with a discord, double back, and begin again with a ragged, out-of-focus melody that takes new shape. Lora will sing her lyrics in a frantic, up-and-down yelp, as if daring the band to keep up with her, carry the theme forward with a blaring sax, come back singing in a higher register, and then pull the song inside out with a low groan: dead-end-kid bravado in the face of real trouble. What you hear is a statement of absurd confidence shouted out of the disorderly context Lora has enforced.

With no chance to hit the charts in this country, or probably in England, Essential Logic's records rob the charts of their legitimacy. The spirit of pure fun drives the band's music— nothing could be more *gleefully* imaginative—but the woman in the lead is so unusual, so full of nerve and good ideas, that she

can make most everything else on or off the radio seem cow-
ardly and complacent, a failure of will or brains or both, the
result of compromises likely not evident even to those who've
made them.

—New West,
17 December 1979

Rock Death in the 1970s:
A Sweepstakes

I think it was about 1975 when I noticed that the term "survivor" had become the cant word of the seventies. The word was once used to denote a person who had lived through a concrete threat to life—a fire, a natural disaster, a plane crash. (You know the old joke: a plane from Texas crashes in Mexico. Where do they bury the survivors? Ha, ha, ha. They don't bury *survivors*!) As a description of a person's *identity*, the word fit only one who had undergone conditions so harrowing and so remarkable that it could be said with some certainty that the experience had marked the individual's personality irrevocably, to the point where everything else—parentage, intelligence, vocation, etc.—became secondary. Thus the word could be applied fairly to many victims of concentration camps (though not, say, to the Japanese-American victims of internment in the United States during the Second World War, since the threat of immediate death was not present, starvation conditions did not exist, and the relevant victims therefore had nothing specifically to survive save a harsh version of ordinary life), to certain political prisoners, to victims of severe torture, and to some who had escaped famine, epidemics, or wars (though the word would not automatically apply to soldiers: one might say, "He survived the Battle of the Bulge," but one would not, when asked to sum up such a person, respond, "Oh, he's a survivor"). The term implied no particular approbation, let alone celebration. It was a statement of fact, suggesting not so much moral neutrality as a moral limbo.

Today all this has changed. "Survivor," perhaps first corrupted as a reference to those who had taken part in some of

the willful adventures of the sixties, now applies to anyone who
has persevered, or rather continued, any form of activity, including breathing, for almost any amount of time. One who
keeps his or her job for a couple of years is "a survivor." A
woman who has borne a child is "a survivor." A couple who
have celebrated a fifth anniversary are "survivors." An actor or
actress who, though without a current role, can still get booked
onto the *Tonight* show once a year is "a survivor," and will be
identified as such within five minutes of his or her introduction
("You're a real survivor, Elizabeth Ashley!" "You're a survivor
yourself, Johnny!"). Anyone, in fact, who is not legally dead is
"a survivor"—and those who *are* legally dead, but later turn up
among the living, are preeminent survivors.

It must be emphasized that the word now definitely does
imply praise, and that it has been severed from authentic contexts of will and endurance altogether. For that matter, the
word has acquired certain class-bound, racist, and Social Dar-
winist tones. The term is applied to virtually any white, middle-
class person, regardless of lack of achievement or lack of hard-
ship, but it is almost never used anymore to designate one who
has suffered real adversity and surmounted it. To use the word
in such an old-fashioned manner would recall its original moral
connotations—the suggestion that the term "survivor" bespoke
a world in which morality had been defeated, suspended, or
destroyed—and the seventies use of "survivor" has subverted
the reality of morality: the sense that one's life is a product of
choices made within a hard context of conditions one does not
choose and probably cannot change, and that the proper response to such a fact is struggle.

The seventies version of "survival" trivializes struggle,
mocks it. As Bruno Bettelheim wrote in 1976, in an attack on
Lina Wertmuller's concentration-camp film *Seven Beauties* and
Terrence Des Pres's much-touted camp study, *The Survivor*,
the celebration of "survival" is "a self-justification for those
who today do not wish to consider the problems [the camps]

posed, and instead settle for a completely empty survivorship." In these works, survival is elevated above every other value: "Survival is all, it does not matter how, why, what for." Bettelheim might have been writing in a dead language; the use of the term multiplied exponentially after his article appeared.

I became especially interested in the new application of the word in the domain of rock 'n' roll, mainly because it appeared everywhere—as a justification for empty song-protagonists, washed-up careers, third-rate lps, burnt-out brainpans. (This is not even to discuss the use of the word in current fiction, where it has become a surefire way to make vaguely neurotic, white, middle-class characters seem heroic in their depression, inadequacy, and cowardice.) I grew obsessed with the phenomenon: it seemed to me to speak for everything empty, tawdry, and stupid about the seventies, to stand for every cheat, for every failure of nerve. I couldn't get away from the word: week after week, it arrived in the mail. Grand Funk's *Survival*. The Rolling Stones' "Soul Survivor." Barry Mann's *Survivor*. Cindy Bullens's "Survivor" (a great recording, and ruined). Eric Burdon's *Survivor*. Gloria Gaynor's cheesy "I Will Survive." Adam Faith's *I Survive*. Randy Bachman's *Survivor*. Georgie Fame's *Survival*. Lynyrd Skynyrd's *"Street Survivors"* (the only band made to pay for the conceit). Just a couple of weeks ago, the Wailers' *Survival*, and then the *band* Survivor. Every time, a performer covering himself or herself with glory (just as novelists continued to celebrate their hapless autobiographical characters and their lack of anything worth saying). So I railed against it all; I wrote about the word every time I came across it, tried to kill it.

Like Bettelheim, whose efforts were far more prescient and probing than mine, I got nowhere. The word, or its perversion, gathered momentum, and it gathers momentum still. Look through this issue of the *Village Voice*, and you will find it; look through next week's, and you will find it again.

Thus as an envoi to the seventies, I decided that there was

only one appropriate critical response: a piece about those who were certifiably *not* survivors. If the concept cannot be discredited, perhaps it can be turned back on itself.

So let us get down to bones and teeth.

One might think that the enormous toll the rock 'n' roll life has taken in the last decade gives the rock use of "survivor" some credence: when so many have fallen, to continue must be a real accomplishment. But this is not true. What we are faced with is the same old replacement of values and standards by a fraud on both. To perform in the context of the death of one's fellows may be an act of nerve or perseverance, worthy qualities both, although it is more likely a refusal to surrender possibilities of celebrity and financial reward—but in any case such a performance accomplishes nothing by itself. The word "survivor" is used to hide this fact, and to hide the banality, falsity, and enervation of whatever it is a performer's perseverance may actually produce. When Beach Boy Brian Wilson made his famous "return" to public life in 1976, after years of apparent vegetation, he received unanimous acclaim as "a survivor" (of, it turned out, himself); that made it almost incumbent upon fans, and upon the numerous writers flown to Los Angeles to witness the event, not to examine what Wilson had returned with too closely. Today, when writers and fans call Neil Young "a survivor," they don't even know they're insulting him—because Neil Young, so obsessed with rock death, is performing to say that survival is never enough.

If this state of affairs were not reason enough for an anomalous gesture—a study of rock death in the seventies—the evidence is piling up that such a gesture might not be without its commercial possibilities. It was only a few months ago, after all, that a promoter—probably the same one who appears in the last verse of "Highway 61 Revisited"—suggested that he and I collaborate on a book about "all the people in rock 'n' roll who

ever died"; it was only a few weeks after that that I received a
new book called *Those Who Died Young*, which grants almost
the same status to the likes of James Dean and Brian Jones
that your average survivorship journalist might bestow on
James Taylor. Given the obscenity of the survivorship cult,
then, why not an equal, no, a further obscenity: why merely
make a study of rock deaths when one could *rank* them? If, as
the just-issued Jimi Hendrix Christmas EP indicates,
necrophagy in rock is a tradition at least as honorable as that of
the survivor's greatest hits album (heard Jimi's "Little Drummer Boy" yet?), do not the dead deserve an accounting at least
as irreproachable as the survivors receive with each week's edition of *Billboard*?

Rock deaths, therefore, have been rated on a tripartite
scale: nonsurvivor's contribution to rock 'n' roll up to the time
of death; contribution nonsurvivor would have made in the time
after death had death not occurred before the allotted three-
score and ten; and manner of death. Up to ten points could be
scored in each category. Points were awarded generously in the
first category; strictly in the second. Calculations in the third
category were by their very nature somewhat subjective. Information, much of it taken from news clippings and fly-by-
night reference books, was almost always sketchy; coroners are
prone to attribute the mysterious death of any rock-associated
person to "drugs." Still, some standards were maintained: factors taken into account in the awarding of manner-of-death
points included respect for tradition, degree of willfulness, violence, melodrama, imagination, uniqueness, appropriateness,
and divine intervention. Death by travel, an inescapable and
colorful risk of rock life, rated fairly high. Death by heroin, on
the other hand, rated low—it has been called "the common cold
of rock death"—save when special circumstances were involved, such as murder. Death by heroin onstage (see Stephen
Holden's rock-death novel, *Triple Platinum*), as opposed to
death by heroin in a cheap room with a chenille bedspread and,

outside the window, a neon sign flashing "HOTEL," would have scored well, but no such incident has been recorded.

Blues, gospel, country, and authentic folk performers were not included in these calculations unless they had some direct connection to rock 'n' roll, like a hit. Mere influence on rock 'n' roll was generally not sufficient to bring such people the financial rewards available to (if not always secured by) rock 'n' roll performers, and thus it has been decided to withhold the concomitant lack of respect. As for the symbols, PC stands for Past Contribution; FC, Future Contribution; M, Manner of Rock Death; and T, Total Score. Rock deaths are rated in ascending order—but only for suspense.

Have a nice day.

ROCK DEATH	PC	FC	M	T
Miss Chrissie, age unknown, 1972, formerly of GTOs, Frank Zappa-backed "groupie rock" band, heroin.	1	0	1	2
Vinnie Taylor, 25, 1974, Sha Na Na (*The Golden Age of Rock 'n' Roll*) guitarist, drugs.	1	1	1	3
Brian Cole, 28, 1972, former Association ("Along Comes Mary") vocalist, heroin.	3	0	1	4
Steve Perron, 28, 1973, member of Children, composed ZZ Top's "Francene," inhalation of vomit after heroin use.	2	1	1	4

Tommy Bolin, 25, 1976, former James Gang ("Must Be Love") and Deep Purple ("Might Just Take Your Life") guitarist, drugs.	3	0	1	4
Rich Evers, 31, 1978, Carole King lyricist, cocaine.	2	1	1	4
Murry Wilson, 55, 1973, father of Beach Boys Brian, Dennis, and Carl Wilson, recording artist (*The Many Moods of Murry Wilson*), heart attack.	1	0	4	5
Tim Buckley, 28, 1975, singer-songwriter (*Happy Sad*), accidental heroin overdose.[1]	1	0	4	5
Scott Quick, 26, 1976, Sammy Hagar guitarist, "drug seizure."	2	2	1	5
Gary Thain, age unknown, 1976, Uriah Heep (*Return to Fantasy*) bassist, drug use aggravated by trauma of earlier onstage electrocution.[2]	1	1	3	5
Minnie Riperton, 31, 1979, member of Rotary Connection, solo performer ("Lovin' You"), cancer.	1	0	4	5

Jimmy McCulloch, 26, 1979, former
Thunderclap Newman
("Something in the Air") and

---

[1] Three M points added for voluntary manslaughter conviction of person who passed drugs to Buckley.
[2] Two M points added for electricity.

Wings ("Venus and Mars Rock Show") guitarist, drugs.	3	2	1	6
Ray Smith, 45, 1979, rockabilly singer ("Rockin' Little Angel"), suicide.	1	0	5	6
Ross Bagdasarian ("David Seville"), 52, 1972, Chipmunks creator and multivocalist ("Alvin's Harmonica"), natural causes.	3	0	4	7
Billy Murcia, 21, 1972, New York Dolls drummer, drugs.	3	3	1	7
Lowell George, 34, 1979, former leader of Little Feat ("Fat Man in the Bathtub"), drugs.	3	3	1	7
Mike Patto, 36, 1979, singer with Spooky Tooth, Boxer, Patto, throat cancer.	2	1	4	7
Gene Davis, 58, 1970, member of Fats Domino touring band, car crash.	1	1	6	8
Bobby Bloom, 28, 1974, singer ("Montego Bay"), suicide by gunshot.	1	1	6	8
Bill Chase, 39, 1974, leader of jazz-rock band Chase, members of which wore long-hair wigs, plane crash.[3]	0	0	8	8

[3] Though Chase's questionable rock status has the effect of diminishing the overall mythic impact of the eight-point plane-crash rock death, and would otherwise warrant a two-point reduction in the M score, Chase has been

Dorsey Burnette, 56, 1976, Rock 'n' Roll Trio ("Tear It Up," "Train Kept a-Rollin'") bassist, Ricky Nelson songwriter, heart failure.	4	0	4	8
Buddy Johnson, 62, 1977, R&B bandleader, composer ("Since I Fell for You"), brain tumor.	4	0	4	8
Terry Kath, 31, 1978, Chicago ("If You Leave Me Now") guitarist, Russian roulette.[4]	1	1	6	8
Van McCoy, 38, 1979, producer, songwriter, solo performer ("The Hustle"), heart attack.	3	1	4	8
Darrell Banks, 31 or 32, 1970, soul singer ("Open the Door to Your Heart"), shot.	1	1	7	9
Ron "Pig Pen" McKernan, 27, 1973, Grateful Dead ("I Know You Rider") organist, cirrhosis.	3	1	5	9
Cass Elliot, 32, 1974, Mamas & the Papas ("Twelve Thirty") and solo vocalist, choked on sandwich, inhaled vomit.	3	1	5	9
Don Robey, 71, 1974, head of R&B and gospel labels Duke and Peacock (Little Richard, Junior				

awarded two compensatory M points for appropriateness, as the plane in question was on its way to Las Vegas.

[4] As the means to what can be considered the first rock death, that of Johnny Ace in 1954 (but see footnote 5), Russian roulette is worth eight M points. However, as with Chase, because Kath's dubious rock status has the effect of demythologizing the Russian roulette rock death, he is docked two M points.

Parker, Bobby Bland, etc.), natural causes.[5]	8	0	1	9
Phil Reed, age unknown, 1976, Flo & Eddie guitarist, probable suicide in leap from hotel window.[6]	1	1	7	9
Thomas Wayne, 30, 1970, Memphis singer ("Tragedy") and Humes High alumnus, car crash.[7]	4	0	6	10
Charlie "The Redman" Freeman, 31, 1973, Memphis rocker and Dixie Flyers guitarist (see Stanley Booth's "Blues for the Redman"), drug and alcohol abuse.	5	3	2	10
Jerry Lee Lewis, Jr., 19, 1973, drummer, son of rock legend, car crash.	1	3	6	10
William Powell, age unknown, 1977, member of O'Jays ("Love Train"), natural causes after long illness.	6	0	4	10
Harris Womack, age unknown, 1974, member of Valentinos ("It's All Over Now"), stabbed.	3	0	7	10

[5] It has long been rumored that rather than shooting himself while playing Russian roulette, Johnny Ace was in fact shot by Robey. Were this to be proved, it would alter Robey's score, though it is impossible to determine in precisely what manner. It should also be noted here that while death by natural causes or systemic disease before the age of 70 is worth four M points, it is worth one M point thereafter.

[6] First known instance of musician-as-TV-set rock death.

[7] Two PC points added for Elvis association.

Duster Bennett, 29, 1976, U.K. R&B bandleader, car crash.	2	2	6	10

Duster Bennett, 29, 1976, U.K. R&B
  bandleader, car crash.   2   2   6   10
Zenon de Fleur, 28, 1978, member
  of Count Bishops, London pseudo-
  punk band, heart attack after car
  crash.   2   2   6   10
Stacy Sutherland, 31, 1978, former
  13th Floor Elevators ("Budda
  Budda Budda") guitarist,
  shot.   3   0   7   10
Tom Wilson, 47, 1978, former
  Columbia producer ("Like a
  Rolling Stone," "rock" version of
  "The Sounds of Silence"), heart
  attack.[8]   5   1   4   10

Billy Stewart, 32, 1970, soul singer
  ("Summertime"), car crash.   3   2   6   11
John Rostill, 31, 1973, former
  Shadows guitarist (not original
  member), electrocuted by guitar
  in studio.   2   1   8   11
Bobby Darin, 37, 1974, singer
  ("Splish Splash"), heart failure
  during surgery.   5   1   5   11
Ivory Joe Hunter, 60, 1974, R&B
  balladeer ("Since I Met You
  Baby"), lung cancer.   5   2   4   11
Mal Evans, 40, 1976, "Sixth Beatle"
  (road manager), shot to death by
  Los Angeles police ("justifiable

[8] Two PC points added for Dylan association, one PC point deducted for Simon & Garfunkel association.

homicide") while preparing memoirs.[9]	3	1	7	11
Chris Bell, 27, 1978, former Big Star (*Radio City*) guitarist, car crash.	3	2	6	11
Glenn Goines, 28, 1978, Parliament-Funkadelic ("One Nation Under a Groove") instrumentalist, "systemic disorder."[10]	3	4	4	11
Joe Negroni, 37, 1978, Teenager ("Why Do Fools Fall in Love?"), brain tumor.	6	1	4	11
Rick Garberson, 20s, 1979, Bizarros member, suicide by carbon monoxide poisoning.	3	3	5	11
Donny Hathaway, 39, 1979, songwriter, pianist, singer ("Where Is the Love"), defenestration.	2	2	7	11
Alexander Sharp, about 45, 1970, founding member of Orioles ("It's Too Soon to Know"), heart failure.	8	0	4	12
Donald McPherson, 39, 1971, member of Main Ingredient ("Everybody Plays the Fool"), leukemia.	5	3	4	12

Big Maybelle (Mabel Louise Smith), 47, 1972, blues shouter, recorded first version of "Whole Lotta

[9] Two PC points added for Beatles association.
[10] Rumors of ritual murder discounted.

Shakin' Goin' On," diabetic coma after long illness.	8	0	4	12
Graham Bond, 37, 1974, U.K. R&B bandleader, fell or threw self under subway train.	4	1	7	12
Miami Show Bank (Fran O'Toole, Brian McCoy, Tom Geraghty), Dublin pop group, ambushed in van and shot to death on return from show in Belfast.	1	2	9	12
Buster Brown, 62, 1976, R&B vocalist ("Fannie Mae"), natural causes.	7	1	4	12
Sherman Garnes, 38, 1978, Teenager ("I'm Not a Juvenile Delinquent"), heart failure following surgery.	6	1	5	12
Pete Meaden, 35, 1978, first manager of the Who ("The Kids Are Alright"), Mod philosopher, suicide by pill overdose.[11]	4	0	8	12
Jackie Brenston, 49, 1979, Memphis R&B singer ("Rocket 88," so-called "first rock 'n' roll record"), heart failure.	6	2	4	12
Junior Parker, 44, 1971, blues singer ("Mystery Train"), heart disease.	7	2	4	13
John Raynes, 31, 1972, Monotones bassman ("Book of Love"), natural causes.	8	1	4	13

[11] Two M points added for appropriateness, given centrality of pills to Mod lifestyle.

Rory Storm, 32, 1972, former leader of Hurricanes, Ringo Starr's pre-Beatles band, double suicide with mother.[12]	3	0	10	13
Clarence White, 29, 1973, former Byrds (*Sweetheart of the Rodeo*) and Flying Burrito Brothers guitarist, victim of hit and run driver.	3	3	7	13
Nick Drake, 26, 1974, singer-songwriter (*Bryter Later*), accidental overdose of Elavil.[13]	4	5	4	13
Robert Scholl, 37, 1975, leader of Mello-Kings, integrated doo-wop group ("Tonite, Tonite"), boating accident.	5	1	7	13
Tom Donahue, 46, 1975, Top 40 DJ ("Clear Up Your Face and Mess Up Your Mind") and pioneer of FM "freeform" radio (KMPX-FM/SF), heart disease with drug abuse.	8	2	3	13
Florence Ballard, 32, 1976, former Supreme ("Buttered Popcorn"), coronary thrombosis while on welfare.	6	0	7	13
Paul Kossoff, 25, 1976, former Free ("All Right Now") and Back Street Crawler guitarist, heart and kidney failure.[14]	3	2	8	13

[12] Two PC points added for Beatles association.
[13] PC and FC ratings by Ed Ward.
[14] Died once previously, in 1975, but was revived after thirty-five minutes. Four M points added for necrophilia.

Leonard Lee, 40, 1976, member of Shirley & Lee ("Let the Good Times Roll"), natural causes.	8	1	4	13
Peter Laughner, 24, 1977, former Rocket from the Tombs and Pere Ubu founder and composer ("Life Stinks"), alcoholism.	5	5	3	13
Michael Ferguson, age unknown, 1979, pianist in founding "San Francisco Sound" group Charlatans ("Alabama Bound"), Haight-Ashbury visual stylist, diabetes.	7	2	4	13
Bobby Ramirez, 23, 1970, White Trash drummer, beaten to death in Chicago bar because of long hair.	2	2	10	14
Don Drummond, age unknown, 1971, Skatalites ("Al Capone") trombonist, suicide after murdering lover.	6	1	7	14
Ray Jackson, 31, 1972, Stax producer, pianist, and songwriter ("If Loving You Is Wrong"), fire.	5	4	5	14
Berry Oakley, 24, 1972, Allman Brothers ("Blue Sky") bassist, motorcycle crash.[15]	4	3	7	14
Jim Croce, 30, 1973, singer-songwriter ("Operator"), plane crash.	3	3	8	14

[15] One M point added for augmentation of minor tradition of Allman Brothers rock death, inaugurated the previous year.

Robbie McIntosh, 24, 1974, Average White Band ("Pick Up the Pieces") drummer, heroin overdose at hands of another.[16]	3	3	8	14
Louis Jordan, 66, 1975, R&B "jump blues" bandleader ("Open the Door Richard"), natural causes.	10	0	4	14
Freddy King, 42, 1976, blues guitarist ("Hide Away"), heart disease and hepatitis.	6	4	4	14
Jimmy Reed, 50, 1976, R&B legend ("Baby What You Want Me to Do," "Bright Lights, Big City"), alcohol abuse.	8	1	5	14
Slim Harpo, 45, 1979, R&B singer and harp player ("Baby Scratch My Back"), heart failure.	7	3	4	14
Marc Bolan, 29, 1977, former leader of T. Rex ("Bang a Gong"), car crash.	5	3	6	14
Angus McLise, 41, 1979, original Velvet Underground drummer (also La Monte Young group, Primitives, Falling Spikes, Warlocks), malnutrition.[17]	5	0	9	14

Al Wilson, 27, 1970, Canned Heat
     singer and writer ("On the Road

---

[16] Two M points added for Cher proximity.

[17] McLise quit the group on the eve of its first gig upon discovering the band was to be paid for its performance; he then decamped for the East, and died in Nepal. Three PC points added and all FC points deducted for purism.

Again"), suicide by sleeping pills.	7	3	5	15
Les Harvey, 25, 1972, Stone the Crows (*Teenage Licks*) guitarist, electrocuted onstage by microphone.	2	3	10	15
Danny Whitten, 29, 1972, Crazy Horse guitarist ("Cowgirl in the Sand"), heroin.[18]	7	7	1	15
Shirley Brickley, 32, 1977, Orlons ("Cross Fire!") lead singer, shot.	6	1	8	15
George Goldner, 52, 1970, founding rock producer and entrepreneur (Crows, Frankie Lymon & the Teenagers, Chantels, Gee and Red Bird labels), heart attack.	10	2	4	16
Tammi Terrell, 24, 1970, Motown vocalist ("Ain't No Mountain High Enough," with Marvin Gaye), brain tumor allegedly caused by fall down stairs.[19]	6	0	4/10	10/16
Chris Kenner, 45, 1976, New Orleans singer ("Land of 1000 Dances"), heart failure.[20]	8	4	4	16

[18] Two FC points added for posthumously inspiring Neil Young's album *Tonight's the Night*.

[19] According to widespread rumors, Terrell's death originated in brain damage caused by a beating inflicted by one of any number of well-known entertainment figures. Deduct six M points for disbelief in this explanation.

[20] Four PC points and two FC points added for conceptual grandeur in song titling.

Sal Mineo, 37, 1976, singer ("Start Movin' "), actor ("Plato" in *Rebel Without a Cause*), stabbed.[21]	8	0	8	16
Cassie Gaines, 29, 1977, Lynyrd Skynyrd backing vocalist (*"Street Survivors"*), plane crash.	3	5	8	16
Phil Ochs, 35, 1976, singer-songwriter ("There But for Fortune"), suicide by hanging.	5	3	8	16
Keith Relf, 33, 1976, former Yardbirds vocalist ("You're a Better Man Than I"), electrocuted by guitar at home.	7	0	9	16
Sid Vicious (John Ritchie), 21, 1979, Sex Pistols bassist ("Belsen Was a Gas"), heroin overdose.[22]	5	1	1/10	7/16
Arlester Christian, late 20s, 1971, leader Dyke & the Blazers ("Funky Broadway"), shot during performance.	4	3	10	17
Jim Morrison, 27, 1971, Doors singer ("Light My Fire"), "heart attack in bathtub in Paris."[23]	8	3	6	17

[21] Though "Start Movin' " was actually a Top Ten hit (in 1957) Mineo has received five added PC points for mythic aura: as Plato, he no less than James Dean summed up the persona of the rock *fan*.

[22] Vicious's death is rumored to have resulted from a "hot shot," i.e., murder. Deduct nine M points for disbelief in this explanation.

[23] Should it ever be established that, as has long been rumored, Morrison is still alive, he would either gain four or lose six M points. Since it has been impossible to determine which change in score would be appropriate, this factor has not been taken into account.

Clyde McPhatter, 38, 1972, former
   lead singer of Dominoes ("Close
   the Door"), Drifters ("Money
   Honey," "Adorable," "White
   Christmas"), and solo performer
   ("A Lover's Question"), liver,
   kidney, and heart disease from
   alcoholism.

	10	2	5	17

Keith Moon, 31, 1978, Who drummer
   ("A Quick One While He's
   Away"), accidental overdose of
   sedatives.

	10	3	4	17

Janis Joplin, 27, 1970, Big Brother
   & the Holding Company singer
   ("Ball and Chain"), solo
   performer, heroin.

	10	7	1	18

King Curtis, 37, 1971, saxophonist
   (Coasters, "Charlie Brown"),
   stabbed to death in front of own
   house.

	6	4	8	18

Mary Ann Ganser, about 23, 1971,
   Shangri-las singer ("I Can Never
   Go Home Anymore"), encephalitis.

	8	5	5	18

Gene Vincent, 36, 1971, rockabilly
   singer ("Race with the Devil"),
   bleeding ulcers and alcoholism
   aggravated by leg injury
   worsened in 1960 car crash which
   killed Eddie Cochran.

	8	3	7	18

"Scarface" John Williams, age
   unknown, 1972, original vocalist
   for Huey "Piano" Smith & the
   Clowns ("Don't You Just Know

It"), Mardi Gras Indian, eulogized in Wild Tchoupitoulas's "Brother John," murdered.[24]	6	3	9	18
Howlin' Wolf (Chester Burnett), 65, 1976, bluesman ("How Many More Years," "Coon on the Moon"), heart failure.	10	4	4	18
Lowman Pauling, early 50s, 1973, with "5" Royales R&B vocal group both composer ("Dedicated to the One I Love") and perhaps first great rock guitarist ("Slummer the Slum," "Think"), natural causes.	10	4	4	18
Steve Gaines, 28, 1977, Lynyrd Skynyrd guitarist (*"Street Survivors"*), plane crash.	4	6	8	18
Nolan Strong, 43, 1977, lead singer of ethereal doo-wop group Diablos ("The Wind") and solo performer ("Since I Fell for You"), heart failure.	8	6	4	18
James Sheppard, age unknown, 1970, leader of Heartbeats ("A Thousand Miles Away") and Shep & the Limelights ("Daddy's Home"), mob execution.[25]	7	2	10	19

[24] Two M points added for mythic conformity: Williams was killed on Ramparts Street in New Orleans just after the end of Mardi Gras.

[25] After losing a suit by the publisher of his 1960 hit "A Thousand Miles Away," in which he was accused of plagiarizing himself with the 1961 hit

Sandy Denny, 31, 1978, former Fairport Convention ("A Sailor's Life") and Fotheringay vocalist, cerebral hemorrhage after fall down stairs.	10	5	6	21
Al Jackson, 39, 1975, Booker T & the MGs drummer ("Hang 'Em High"), shot in own home.	8	5	8	21
Gram Parsons, 27, 1974, country-rock avatar (International Submarine Band, Byrds, Flying Burrito Brothers), drugs.[26]	7	7	7	21
Paul Williams, 34, 1973, former Temptations vocalist ("I Wish It Would Rain"), gunshot, suicide verdict.[27]	8	3	8/10	19/21
Leslie Kong, 38, 1971, rock steady and reggae producer (Desmond Dekker & the Aces, "Israelites," Melodians, "By the Rivers of Babylon"), heart failure.	10	8	4	22
Elvis Presley, 42, 1977, singer ("Rock-a-Hula Baby"), multiple drug overdose after lifetime of professed clean living.[28]	10	7	5	22

"Daddy's Home," Sheppard fell into penury, and was forced to seek assistance from loan sharks.

[26] Body stolen and burned in desert. Six M points added for melodrama.

[27] Deduct two M points for disbelief in mob involvement.

[28] Four M points added for shock value.

Duane Allman, 24, 1971, Allman Brothers ("Statesboro Blues") and session guitarist (Boz Scaggs, "Loan Me a Dime"), motorcycle crash.	9	8	6	23
Jimi Hendrix, 27, 1970, singer and guitarist ("Voodoo Child"), inhalation of vomit after use of sedatives, complicated by poor medical treatment.	10	10	5	25
Ronnie Van Zant, 28, 1977, Lynyrd Skynyrd lead vocalist (*"Street Survivors"*), plane crash.	8	9	8	25

Thus rock death in the seventies. If no one matched the all-time scores of Buddy Holly (10-8-8) or Sam Cooke (10-9-8), there was at least no dearth of attempts. Rock death made the decade what it was: without plenty of nonsurvivors as a yardstick, survivors and their chroniclers (for, after all, when one praises another as "a survivor," the praise rebounds upon oneself) would have had no standard against which to measure themselves. It shows no disrespect to those who are gone, then, to give ourselves a little pat on the back for having outlasted them; by so doing, we help keep them dead.

—*Village Voice*,
17 December 1979

1980

Fear in the Marketplace:
Real Life Rock Top Ten
1979

There is no stronger proof of the growing conservatism of the rock 'n' roll mainstream—by which I mean the audience that puts records on the charts, and the radio stations that play them—than the reception received by Fleetwood Mac's double lp, *Tusk*.

The appearance of this album should have been an event, and not just because Mayor Tom Bradley declared October 10 Fleetwood Mac Day in Los Angeles to celebrate its release. The band's previous two lps, *Fleetwood Mac* and *Rumours*, had sold close to twenty million copies worldwide, and were still on the air: huge numbers of people were eager to find out what the group would come up with. Coming off a very bad year, large numbers of music-business people were eager to find out if the release of a certified blockbuster would stimulate across-the-board sales, remind everyone that records make good Christmas presents, and thus save a lot of worry about the immediate future. For that matter, the financial prospects of *Tusk* were probably not without interest to Fleetwood Mac's fans. In the past decade, even as a noisy but small minority has pledged allegiance to the willful outcasts and obscurities of popular culture, the vast majority has taken extreme pleasure in consciously associating with success—or, as it is now called, money.

People bought *Tusk* straight off, before they heard it. The album ran up the charts, only to bump into new product by Led Zeppelin and the Eagles. But as far as the radio went, the al-

bum might well not have been released at all. Given Fleetwood
Mac's commercial status, airplay on *Tusk* has amounted to a
near blackout, which makes me wonder whether all those copies of *Tusk* that have passed over America's counters are really
being listened to.

For if Fleetwood Mac is mainstream in its place in the music
world, *Tusk* is radical in its refusal of the mainstream's limits,
and the band is paying the price. The band tipped its hand early
on, issuing the lp's title track as a 45. More a set of fragments
than a song, "Tusk" was as unlikely a prospective hit single as a
major group has offered in years—a Bronx cheer to radio programmers—and it died a quick death. The album itself seemed
more palatable—Stevie Nicks stuck close to form, Christine
McVie remained rock's answer to Lorelei—but only at first, or
only if you sat down and played the two discs all the way
through. Jarring, disorienting accents emerged from the sound
and then took it over; the vocals, especially Lindsey Buckingham's, retreated, came shouting back, and then faded again.
The fragmentation evident on the single defined the album: the
most striking tracks were not quite songs, and they didn't
make their claims as tracks. Programmers looked for The Cut,
the one tune that hooks an album onto the air, the single number that will make programming rational, and programmers
couldn't find it, because Fleetwood Mac had left it off. Instead,
programmers just kept on playing *Rumours*. One can assume
many listeners were, more than anything, relieved.

I think the stand Fleetwood Mac has taken with *Tusk* is as
brave as that Bob Dylan took with *John Wesley Harding*—
braver, maybe, because Fleetwood Mac cannot rely on Dylan's
kind of charisma, or on the kind of loyalty he commands. The
members of the band have never made themselves felt as personalities; they rely strictly on their music, which is strong on
intelligence and invention and weak on drama. With its insistence on perceptions snatched out of a blur, drawing on (but
never imitating) Jamaican dub and ancient Appalachian ballads,

Fleetwood Mac is subverting the music from the inside out, very much like one of John le Carré's moles—who, planted in the heart of the establishment, does not begin his secret campaign of sabotage and betrayal until everyone has gotten used to him, and takes him for granted. *Tusk* is, in its lyrics, about romance out of reach; its music is also out of reach, which means that you have to make a certain effort to get hold of it. That people seem less than delighted with the prospect is no doubt just the right note on which to enter a year dominated by the Knack, Journey, the Doobie Brothers, and the Blues Brothers: retreads all, flushed from encores for a performance that never took place.

As for the rest of the year, what follows is the Real Life Rock Top Ten for 1979—with a few opposite numbers.

1. *Rust Never Sleeps*, Neil Young. Divided equally between graceful acoustic reveries and viciously hard rock, this was a sneak attack on entropy, its explicit subject. Up against the most reliable and unpredictable rock 'n' roller of the decade, entropy never had a chance—at least while this album was playing.

2. *Into the Music*, Van Morrison. As with his *Astral Weeks*, the best of it will never wear out. Toni Marcus takes the Most Valuable Player award for her violin work. Signs of life: Iron City Houserockers' *Love's So Tough*, a blazing, soulful, altogether ignored debut lp, and Tonio K's *Life in the Foodchain*, on which an Armenian-American from the Central Valley declaimed with great good humor about the general unmanageability of all things under the sun. Worst album, in heavy traffic: *Evolution*, by Journey.

3. "Hot Stuff," Donna Summer. In a poor year for singles, nothing came close. The difference was the beat, Jeff Baxter's shredded guitar solo, and, you know, sex. The race for worst single was much tighter, and when the Knack's smutty little Beatles imitation, "Good Girls Don't," broke out of the pack (the pack being the Doobie Brothers' "What a Fool Be-

lieves" and Journey's "Just the Same Way" and "Lovin',
Touchin', Squeezin'"), it seemed to be all over. Then, out of
nowhere, Rupert Holmes roared by on the outside with
"Escape (The Piña Colada Song)" and, confounding tip-
sters everywhere, made off with the prize. The prize is eternal
obloquy.

4. Graham Parker and the Rumour, in Berkeley, June 27.
Guitarist Martin Belmont kicked off one last tune, a harsh version of "Pourin' It All Out," which defines what Parker's music
is about and what it's for; Parker absorbed that harshness and
somehow turned it into an embrace. Then, along with his band,
he did pour it all out, and if there was anything left in the six of
them by the time the song was done it would have taken surgery to remove it.

5. *In the Skies*, Peter Green. Fleetwood Mac's original lead
guitarist returned from the wilderness to close the seventies
with an album of the quietest slow blues—every note chosen
with reason, every inflection put down with authority. Runner-
up in the Comeback Sweepstakes: Marianne Faithfull, who
leaped out of the oblivion of heroin addiction with an lp called
Broken English, and scared everyone who noticed half to
death.

6. Gang of Four, in San Francisco, September 11. So strong
I didn't even stick around to see the starring act, the
Buzzcocks, which I'd wanted to hear for years; I didn't want
anything to interfere with what had just happened. Not quite
what Jiang Qing meant by People's Opera, but if this is the
future of rock, I can't wait.

7. Candi Chamberlain's "Golden Gate Greats," KYA-AM and
FM, San Francisco, 6 to 10 P.M., Saturdays. I've been listening
to rock 'n' roll a lot longer than Ms. Chamberlain, and each time
I tune in her show I catch something wonderful I've never
heard before—a stray Miracles cut, "Let's Go Together" by the
Raindrops, "True Love Affair" by the Elegants. As she put it
one night, introducing the Edsels' "Rama Lama Ding Dong":

"Now, I don't know what this means—well, I know exactly what it means. But I'm not telling."

8. *Jimi Hendrix: Voodoo Child of the Aquarian Age,* by David Henderson. An Afro-American poet from Berkeley reclaimed a legacy for black America, and in the process set the standard for rock biography.

9. *Heroes of Rock 'n' Roll,* produced by Malcolm Leo and Andrew Solt, February 9, ABC TV. What you never saw before—what you never even hoped to see. When's the rerun? And, in a fallow year for rock 'n' roll movies, a quickened heartbeat for Francis Coppola's use of the Doors' "The End" in *Apocalypse Now.*

10. "Money Changes Everything," the Brains. Singer Tom Gray told his story in a strangled voice, as if he were trying to explain, but instead he laid a curse. This damned single ranks higher than I've placed it, but if it were anywhere else I couldn't end with it, and there's no other way the decade could end.

> She said, I'm sorry, baby
> I'm leaving you tonight
> I've found someone new
> He's waiting in the car outside
> Oh honey, how can you do it
> We swore each other everlasting love
> She said, Yeah, well, I know
> But when we did
> There was one thing
> We weren't really
> Thinking of
> And that's money
> Money changes everything
> Money
> Money changes everything
> We think we know what we're doing

We don't pull the strings
It's all in the past now
Money changes everything

—New West,
14 January 1980

Hi, this is America. We're not home right now, but if you leave a message after the beep, we'll get back to you as soon as we can.

London Calling is a two-record Clash album with nineteen songs and an in-store price of about eight bucks. Pointed toward the future, it's also full of history—but the sleeve design, lifted from the first Elvis Presley lp, is almost a false clue. History here includes the history of times barely left behind: a history left unmade.

Always classicists—the 101'ers, the band singer Joe Strummer left in 1976 to join the Clash, just after seeing the Sex Pistols for the first time, was something of a rock 'n' roll revival outfit—the Clash meant to occupy the gap the Sex Pistols had suddenly opened in the rock tradition. For a moment, anything seemed possible: that the strangest noises could sweep the world, or that Western society was so corrupt its own fear and guilt might send it spinning off its axis. None of that happened. The moment passed, the punk no quieted, but for those who'd been part of it, things were not the same. After Johnny Rotten's negations, some could not go back to the false pop promise of—to use a phrase by Norman Mailer—an unearned freedom from dread.

The Clash's promise has been that a sense of dread, far from something to get free of, is a purchase on reality that must be sought out, constantly tested and renewed: the Sex Pistols' no has always been the Clash's yes. Dread puts the edge on. It shapes fear, gives a laugh weight, strips away mystification, and reveals paradox; song by song, *London Calling* does the same. History—pop history, political history—has closed around the Clash; they seem to have found a place in it. They play with a new confidence, with joy, a swagger, a casual look, as if with so many songs a half dozen you don't like could matter less *(My hair may not move you, but what about my clothes?)*, with the time to tell every side of any story.

The title song, a doomsday scenario stoically chanted to a clattering martial beat, opens the set: there's been a "nuclear error," the result is a new Ice Age, the river is rising (with an Ice Age, it would fall, but a smashup of all disasters is the point), there's panic in the streets. It's silly at first, but after a verse the fantasy gathers its charm. As music, the prospect is too exciting to resist, the tale-teller too human. As the only one left with the presence of mind to warn the rest of the world, Strummer is back in 1938, in Orson Welles's *War of the Worlds* broadcast, and crying out from 1956, in Hungary, the last revolutionary at the last open microphone, refusing to believe the rest of the world won't ride in like the cavalry she's seen in too many John Ford movies. The song ends in suspension, everything in doubt; without a pause we're into "Brand New Cadillac," a borrowed swath of rockabilly so modern in its sound and so Presleyish in its lyrics ("Baby, baby," Strummer sings with naked glee, "won't you hear my plea?") that the tune stands both as an affirmation of the timelessness of a beloved style and as a celebration of female nerve: when you get down to it, the singer knows he simply doesn't measure up. Punk once went from the smallest provocation to the biggest demand; now the road can run the other way, too. The band moves to the smoky gin-joint blues of "Jimmy Jazz," where Strummer, drunk but suddenly alert, draws out an encounter with a cop into a coolly staged one-act play that moves from running sweat to an evasive shuffle to relief. The politics in each number are inescapable but natural—they're the politics of ordinary life, heightened by that sense of dread, that sense of history. *Baby, baby, can't you hear my plea*, says the Hungarian revolutionary as her mike goes dead; Soviet troops arrive; *Hey, I just work here*, she says; they let her go.

Strummer is the key. From track to track (or within a track) he can be pleasantly conversational, horror-struck, crafty, damned, burning with lucid outrage or quite lucidly soused. He uses four, maybe five different voices in "The Right Profile," a hilarious account of the last days of Montgomery Clift. The listener is jerked from one view to another (after his 1957 auto accident, Clift, scarred on the left side of his face, permitted photos only of the right), now thinking of a star's betrayal of his talent, now of the indelible image of a character whose toughness came from his lack of hope. Clift swallows a roll of Nembutals; Strummer throws up all over the song. Without missing a beat he pulls himself together for the chorus:

> And everybody say
> "What's he like?"
> And everybody say
> "Is he all right?"
> Everybody say, "He sure look funny"
> "That's . . . Montgomery *Clift*, honey!"

Which means, who cares what he looks like? We *saw* him!

On *London Calling*, images of pop culture—of stardom—and images of political culture—in the Clash's spectacle, of anonymity—are not at war with each other. The album finds its idea in simultaneity and multiplicities. You're reminded of the horn riffs from "Sea Cruise," then of the hands of Robert Mitchum's mad preacher in *The Night of the Hunter*, then of

Spanish freedom fighters emerging from four decades of oblivion. Men and women of different classes, races, nations, and
times appear and move on.

What I hear most of all is the conviction that the job of the
band is to present life in all of its parts, that conviction always
playing against the fear that no action matters at all. The result
is a faith that more is at stake in any choice (*Do I dare speak
into this microphone? How are my clothes?*) than is ever apparent—and you can hear this best in "Death Or Glory," the most
obviously important song on *London Calling*, and in "Revolution Rock," seemingly its most trivial.

"Death Or Glory" follows a reggae version of "Stagger
Lee," here carrying a Jamaican title, "Wrong 'em Boyo." The
easy, happy beat, for a song about murder, cuts into "Death Or
Glory" 's scattered, then building fanfare, music of such passion
and force the sound seems to close around you. The band locks
into the tune, and Strummer lashes out with the first verse.
"Every cheap hood," he says, as if he's thought about this for a
long time, "strikes a bargain with the world."

> And ends up making payments on a sofa or a girl
> Love 'n' hate tattooed across the knuckles of his hands
> The hands that slap his kinds around 'cause they don't
>   understand
> How death and glory
> Becomes just another story
> Death or glory
> Just another story

So Stagger Lee, the embodiment of black rage who lives in
a world so fettered he can take out his hate only on his own
kind, reemerges as a white man, the punk rebel of any era: the
poor-white Elvis, selling his blood for fancy black pimps'
clothes at Lansky's in Memphis; the London Edwardians of the
1940s and their 1950s Teddy Boy progeny (never vanished, still

present in the Clash's London, ready to fight over the wrong suspenders, the wrong shoes); the early-seventies London skinheads, moving out on a summer night to beat Pakistanis, who, unlike the Jamaicans whose ska sounds the skinheads loved, were the wrong shade of black. But this is a Stagger Lee one has never met before: Stagger Lee grown up, middle-aged, fat, balding, Stagger Lee denied his flaming death and made domestic, afraid to leave home, beating his wife to the floor, then looking at his children as they cower, quiet, as they've learned to be quiet when this happens—and then Mick Jones steps out to take the vocal from Strummer, to run the squalid reality off to the fantasy behind it, to celebrate—Death Or Glory! Alright! The stupid, risky promises of the rebel's youth can make you sick or break your heart. The dead Hungarian revolutionary (the Soviets were fooled only for a minute) is replaced by the Light Brigade; the no is turned again into a yes, and it's up to you to weigh the one against the other.

"Revolution Rock" wraps up the album; another reggae number, and, like "Wrong 'em Boyo," picked up from an obscure 45, an old skinhead favorite. Nearly sobbing with delight, Strummer rings the eternal changes of the lines:

Everybody smash up your seat and rock to this brand new beat
This here music mash up the nation
This here music cause a sensation!
Tell your ma, tell your pa, everything gonna be all right. . . .

"Revolution rock"—that was what the Clash started with, and "revolution" was more than a joke then, so long ago, three or four years ago. Here, a joke is all it is: Strummer sounds as if he's waited all his life to sing something so dumb.

The song, though, hangs in the air. Coming out of the fear and self-loathing the rest of the album has played through— half of it about the heroism of youth, half of it about the perversion that follows—the trashy, irresistible song says that while revolution made by music is a joke, rebellion sustained by music might not be, though it has room for plenty of jokes: what is a revolution, especially one that's failed, without humor? Up on the bandstand, crooning "Revolution Rock"—you can hear him promise he'll sing anywhere, weddings, Bar Mitzvahs, and the way he sounds he should—Strummer is having the time of his life.

—*New West,*
11 February 1980

War in the Catamaran

"Military intelligence isn't what it used to be," chanted John Cale in the nightclub of San Diego's Catamaran Motor Hotel, somewhere around midnight. "But—so what? *Human* intelligence isn't what it used to be, either!"

I was primed to respond to lines like that. A couple of hours before, up in my tenth-floor room in the Catamaran, I'd watched *Bill Moyers' Journal*, which documented the transformation of Philip Caputo's Vietnam memoir, *A Rumor of War*, into an upcoming TV movie. The book ends with a mini–My Lai, as Caputo and some of his troops commit a certified atrocity—Caputo faced charges for the murder of innocent civilians—and that was the focus of the program: after all, the atrocity was the hook. The question of the film about the film was, in essence, "How could good, normal American boys do such a thing?," and Caputo had lots of answers.

He was very serious on camera—very much the soldier/ writer, which is to say, the witness. ("I described that in my book," he kept answering to Moyers's general questions, as if his book were not merely the text of his version of his own story but of the war itself.) He was quotable, epigrammatic. "It was one of the paradoxes of the war," he said. "You had to burn your way through it." "It was an emotional necessity." The same "momentum" that led to "it" produced "the victories of D-Day."

"It," as you may have gathered, referred to the atrocity mentioned above—though no such word was ever spoken, not even when we saw the incident being filmed, and flinched at the sight of Asian women screaming for mercy. But Caputo's language wasn't just sanitized. It was seductive, with appeals to ambiguity (his description of an atrocity as a "paradox" is a postmodernist masterstroke), to the primacy of feeling (we all know what happens when emotions are repressed), and even to our fears for the survival of Western civilization (the casual parallel drawn between D-Day and a Vietnam atrocity). "All that stuff," he said to Moyers, "—the heat, the insects, the pressure—made me *snap.*"

As Caputo grew even more serious-looking, the weight of what he had to say shifted. Caputo was no longer speaking as a witness—and it is remarkable enough to be a witness to one's own actions—but as a victim. He communicated the conviction that it was he who had suffered most from the incident the film crew was reconstructing, and as that obscene idea made its way from the TV set into my room, the Vietnamese scurrying in the background became less than real, as was surely true at the time of the atrocity itself. It was as if they had been created by God simply to serve as the means by which certain Americans could, in their agony, purge themselves of all sorts of bad feelings, from irritation to man's-innate-urge-to-murder. That was probably not what Norman Mailer was talking about when he said, on his release from jail after the march on the Pentagon in 1967, "We are burning the body and the blood of Christ in Vietnam."

Punk avatar John Cale has used murder and war—or, perhaps more specifically, the burning of the body and blood of Christ—as song material for years, but I hadn't expected to be able to follow Philip Caputo with a doom-laden rock 'n' roll show in the Catamaran's equivalent of any overbuilt tourist hotel's Mongo Bongo Room. I was at the Catamaran visiting family, and when I saw JOHN CALE on the big outdoor sign normally used to announce conventions and lounge acts, I assumed it referred to somebody else. But the Catamaran is now a regular rock venue in San Diego, part of the California club circuit—

and at any rate, John Cale has never had much use for cultural barriers, no matter how degraded.

Now thirty-nine, Cale left his native Wales in 1963 and came to New York on a Leonard Bernstein fellowship to study avant-garde music with John Cage and La Monte Young. There he met Lou Reed, then contriving one-take biker and hot-rod rock for the trend-jumping Pickwick label. In 1965, after time as the Primitives, the Warlocks, and the Falling Spikes, they founded the Velvet Underground, and came under the aegis of Andy Warhol. Cale's furious electric viola playing was a good part of the horrific beauty of "Heroin" and other indelible numbers; when he was forced out of the band in 1968, he was part of a legend.

Cale followed his tenure with the Velvets with *Vintage Violence*, an exquisite, unheard solo album that was in some ways comparable to Van Morrison's *Astral Weeks*: the personal vision was that intense, the execution almost as graceful. Though Cale continued to make his own records, he held on to cult status mainly as a producer, signing his name to the prophetic and now revered first albums by the Stooges, Jonathan Richman and the Modern Lovers, and Patti Smith—though interestingly he was not asked to produce anybody's *second* album, and his best production was probably no early punk classic but the forgotten *Desertshore* by Nico, the Velvets' original chanteuse. As a recording artist, Cale drifted from CBS to Warner Bros. to Island; by the time he arrived at the Catamaran he was down to a second-class live album, *Sabotage*, on New York's tiny Spy label. Naturally, then, he played as though he had a world to win.

From the way Cale took and held the stage, you would have thought war had been declared and the purpose of his concert to choose sides and get down to basic emotional and philosophical training. A big, heavy-set man dressed in a marine camouflage suit, he made his opener, Rufus Thomas's "Walkin' the Dog," sound like a dangerous mission (an impression not heightened, however, when he jabbed his left arm on the "She broke a needle and she can't sew" line—*needle*, get it?). With a good-sized band behind him, Cale moved from violin to piano to guitar, dwarfing everyone else on the stage, building from stoic, heavily ironic talk-singing to screams that had nothing to do with any kind of irony. Both "Mercenaries" and "Sabotage" sounded hokey and smug in their first moments; by the time they ended, with martial choruses thudding off the walls, the mood was sordid and raw. The mood was so strong that it wasn't lost—not for long, anyway—even when Deerfrance, Cale's wispy female backup singer, stepped forth to do a grue-some Jane Birkin imitation. (What? You've forgotten "Je t'Aime"?) Cale used Chuck Berry's hallowed "Memphis" as a blank canvas. Because the words and the tune were absorbed so long ago into the rock 'n' roll collective unconscious, one can no longer quite hear them or listen to them. You hear instead the performer's voice, hear it straight, as if he or she weren't singing words at all. What Cale brought to the song was sup-pressed rage, a memory he had killed and was trying to revive, something elemental and ugly, and when you remembered what all that loathing was wrapped around—"Marie is only six years old, Information, please . . ."—you got the shock Cale meant to deliver.

What did all this have to do with Philip Caputo's version of Vietnam? Well, that was a lie, a lie compounded by its artful-ness, and Cale's performance was real, and satisfying partly because one could not help seeing how contrived, how thought up, the performance was. Cale began with dumb ideas (look at me, I'm a mercenary) and scared you with them; he began dia-lectically (I'll test the paranoia I share with the audience against real events, terrorist bombings and the wars in south-ern Africa, and then explore the fantasies that result when the paranoia comes together with the events) and produced both humor and dread. His performance erased the moral squalor of the lie I had brought to it—and mine was not the only such lie one might have brought.

In the middle of the show—though I can hardly think of it as anything but the finale—Cale took it all back, or rather looked the dread he had raised in the face and forced it to retreat. This was "Chorale" (which does at least end the *Sabotage* lp), a church in the wasteland, a song you can imagine John Ford using for a late-night pub scene in one of his Irish movies. It was that corny and that passionate. It was a pledge of fealty, a pledge of faith, riding a slow tempo, the instruments playing dimly and the strain of Cale's thick, raspy voice suddenly gone, his voice made whole somehow by the old, unspeakably lovely melody. Cale was laying a blessing; the instruments dropped out altogether, and he sang a cappella with all his heart, a few of the band members coming in quietly behind him. There was perfect peace of mind in this song, and the promise that the moment it ended, peace of mind would be out of reach, just another casualty.

As the song did end, the beat turned subtly military. The drummer tapped as if on duty at a funeral. That made the piece a requiem, and it also reminded a listener of everything Cale was forcing to surround it. It was the kind of song you might have to sing before going to war, and the kind of song you might have to sing when you came home, with memories too bitter to put to rest. God knows, it is a song John Cale can sing all his life—no matter how his music changes, no matter what new themes he takes up, he can always find a place for it, because the world will always make one.

—*New West,*
5 May 1980

Plague Disco

"Warner Bros. wasn't interested in a cannister," John Lydon said to Wayne Robins of *Newsday*. "It's something I complained about extremely bitterly." Lydon—once known to all as Johnny Rotten, a.k.a. the Antichrist, and now, as it were, un-born again under the name given him when he was christened in the Catholic church—was speaking of the refusal of the parent company of his new American label, Island, to release the second album from his band, Public Image Ltd., or PiL, in its original U.K. format: three twelve-inch 45s packed in a film can and titled *Metal Box*. "All our wonderful ideas," Lydon said. "Shattered."

As one who shelled out the import price of twenty-five bucks for *Metal Box*, I liked to think Lydon was being at least somewhat ironic. Taken simply as a usable object, *Metal Box*— recently replaced in the U.K. as in the U.S. by a standard-form double lp retitled *Second Edition*—was an exercise in abject perversity. The discs were fitted into the cannister so tightly that the only way to get them out was to turn the can upside down and shake it. Since the records were not in sleeves, but merely separated by loose sheets of paper, they were more than likely to drop directly on top of one another, producing myriad nicks and scratches. So much for the marginally superior aural presence of 45s. Played often, the thing threatened to self-destruct.

Nor was the music—on first listening, little more than Lydon's denunciations, bad dreams, and Bela Lugosi imitations set against Jah Wobble's pompous bass and Keith Levene's endless guitar and synthesizer noodling—short on perversity, and the fact that you had to get up and change sides every ten minutes or so didn't make the music any more inviting. Or was that the idea? And if so, who cared? If, as Lydon has been announcing since 1978, lately with increasing vehemence, the Sex Pistols "finished rock 'n' roll," what point was there to his sticking around if all he had to offer was an expensive practical joke?

PiL's music is no joke. It is, as Lydon claims, "anti-rock 'n' roll"—territory staked out in opposition to what we now accept as rock 'n' roll—but it is also a version. Like disco, or especially the bass-led, out-of-reach rhythms of dub, PiL's sound is at once the rejection of a form and an attempt to follow certain implications hidden within that form to their necessary conclusions. PiL's music may contradict rock 'n' roll as it is generally understood, but without rock 'n' roll it would make no sense whatsoever, and it makes a great deal of sense. For that matter, it makes sense of other records: after hearing it, all sorts of stuff, from *The Trojan Story* to U.K. avant-garde obscurities to Linton Kwesi Johnson's dub poetics, kicks in as easily as a new Blondie single.

On casually playable lps, the twelve numbers from *Metal Box* initially shape *Second Edition* into an abstract, oppressive presentation of dispassionate morbidity: the hot new sound of a first-class dance band taking up residence in the only disco to remain open in the wake of the plague. Then the compositions begin to work off of each other, and tracks that at first seemed dully similar (how do you Do the Plague?) are thrown into relief. What you hear is a sometimes scattered and sometimes momentous beat, provided by bassist Wobble and session drummers; textures, or perhaps less textures than the shifts between them; for any given song, less a vocal than the idea behind it; less passion or dispassion than the component emotions of either; less a rhythm than a rhythm in the process of constituting itself. You begin to hear the music being made. Like a piece of modern architecture that puts the inner workings of a building—heating pipes, electrical systems, support structures —in plain sight, you hear PiL's music inside out.

When at a recent press conference I heard John Lydon announce yet again that "rock 'n' roll is finished," I had two reactions: first, that he probably hadn't heard Robin Lane and the Chartbusters' debut album yet, and, second, that he was in some ways all too correct. As critic Ed Ward recently noted, rock 'n' roll, which used to be about breaking rules, now seems to be about learning them—and many of the rules are patently those of pre-rock show business. A group like the Doobie Brothers has nothing to do with rock 'n' roll—rock 'n' roll as an affront to entropy and a refusal of stasis—but for millions the Doobie Brothers are the thing itself. As mainstream music, rock 'n' roll in the U.S.A. now means any number of already marked-off pieces of ground, and the goal of most bands, from the Grateful Dead to Pearl Harbor and the Explosions to Styx, is to find the right plot and occupy it—ideally, forever. The true story of present-day rock has less to do with how many albums Bruce Springsteen has sold, or even with the Clash's narrow but deep American breakthrough, than with the fact that many of the most adventurous groups of the time—Essential Logic, Young Marble Giants, the Feelies, X-ray Spex, the Adverts, or the Raincoats (at the press conference I attended, the only band Lydon would admit to liking)—have not even had their records released in this country.

PiL rightly want distance from such a scene—as, quite consciously, do most of the groups just mentioned—but what sort of distance? On *Second Edition*, Lydon, Levene, and Wobble are insisting on the kind of outsider status that a dub composer like Augustus Pablo, or even a weird soul singer like Al Green, takes as a given—at least as far as any broad-based popular audience is concerned. This isn't to say PiL want to be ignored; rather, they want the freedom of the pathfinding black popular musician to be insulated from the mass audience, and to be discovered by that audience, or simply used, when the time is right. They want to be discovered, to be used, and to remain too resistant to be absorbed, to be pinned down in anyone's mind—for it's when an audience thinks it knows exactly what an artist is about that the artist faces the greatest temptation: the temptation not to confuse anybody.

Second Edition, then, is an attempt to present a band that cannot be fitted into the scheme of things. It begins by driving the listener away, offering murk, self-pity, dopey horror-movie sound effects, unexamined images of bad news—and yet it is self-evidently not a *mess*, as was PiL's debut album, the 1978 *Public Image/First Issue*, which has never been released in the United States. The murk is artful, even arty, the self-pity only a first face, the unexamined images often an entry into trance music.

In "Albatross," the long opening cut, Lydon's weary, bored chant—"Getting rid of the albatross, getting rid of the albatross"—digs in. As with PiL's debut single, "Public Image," he seems to be referring, again, to his old identity as Johnny Rotten, which is not very interesting. As the music thuds along and Lydon begins to sound as if he's trying most of all to support its weight, it seems possible he is referring to something much harder to slip: his whole life, perhaps, and that is not uninteresting at all. Word by word, you can hear him trying to decide how to sing the song, testing emotions, rejecting them. Wobble's bass thumps the albatross against Lydon's chest.

With "Memories," the music begins to gather up momentum, demanding volume. "Swan Lake," released as "Death Disco" in an earlier, single form, justifies both titles: the beat is absolute, some uncanny synthesis of reggae and disco, with Lydon offering full-blown shrieks. The taste of Tchaikovsky's "Swan Lake" that long ago became name-that-tune shlock is quoted at every turn, until Lydon's cry rises in one great swoop and the production is cut off at its height. Then "Poptones," close to a regular song, driven by an anguished, quiet, bitter, all-accepting rant. Lydon has said it's about male rape, but you wouldn't know it from what's on the record, and some people have heard it as a murder mystery, sung by the corpse. And then "Careering," punctuated with gunshot percussion, ending in a barrage.

Much of the third and fourth sides pales in comparison— "No Birds," "Graveyard," "Bad Baby," and most notably "The Suit," a one-dimensional sneer and a true room-clearer—and a lot of what you might hear on first listening remains weeks later: a certain smugness, a sense of random choices artily disguised as a challenge to your own smugness. And yet even on the weakest numbers, the blank suggestiveness of the music is working. Lydon's casual negations, his awesome self-pity, give up a hint of guilt—the guilt he faces for having allowed himself to be turned into what he set out to destroy, which is how he says he now understands his experience with the Sex Pistols; or, as he implied in a recent interview, the guilt he is prey to for having damned the church and the society from which he has come. *This* sound is implacable: pressure builds in Plague Disco, and there's no exit.

The record bears down hardest as it ends, with the syncopated funk rhythms of "Socialist," "Chant," and the utterly anomalous "Radio Four." This piece, sometimes used by PiL to both open and close concerts, is little more than Keith Levene's synthesizer—there is no vocal—and it's a shock. In almost every other tune, the textures seem enormous, the whole of the music intentionally misshapen and yet flatly too big to get around; here every element is perfectly balanced. Elsewhere you have to go to the music; here it comes to you. Behind a confident, almost blasé bass lead, Levene takes the sound through one harmonic shift after another, and what he's after is not a specter of disorder or vileness or termination, but peace of mind. The piece embraces beauty, as concept and act; it is simple, direct, unburdened by the dread of the nearly sixty minutes of music that has preceded it. It contradicts everything that's come before—it's the exit the rest of the record has so forcefully and elegantly closed off. And yet it takes nothing back; it merely suggests that there is more to life than PiL are willing to talk about at length, right now.

In 1967, Jean-Luc Godard closed his masterpiece, *Weekend*, with these words on the screen: "End—End of Cinema." Godard announced the death of the movies, and, dismissing everyone else's films as exercises in solipsism, narcissism, or petty reactionary blindness, immediately proceeded to make more movies, turning them out at a pace astonishing even for him. He slashed his budgets and began to work as part of a collective, intent on "smashing the dictatorship of the director." One of his first postmovie movies was *British Sounds*, which opened with a ten-minute tracking shot of an assembly line in a U.K. automobile factory. To watch the shot was torture, but after six or seven minutes those who had not fled to the lobby for a drink of water—or a provocative, sustaining talk about the weather—actually began to move to the rhythms Godard was picking up. The shot was, of course, "a metaphor," but it was also a violent act of pedagogy: a way of teaching the viewers that they were capable of seeing in a way they had not seen before. Such a stance cost Godard most of the audience he had built over the previous ten years; it also allowed him to put things on the screen he would never have thought would fit it, and to imagine new audiences.

PiL are still some distance from that ten-minute shot, but they already share the ambitions behind it. From the way Lydon is talking, he wants very badly for *Metal Box/Second Edition* to be hailed as a historic breakthrough or written off as a fraud, and it is neither: one of the reasons you can hear Lydon trying to decide how he wants to phrase a line is that he doesn't know quite what he wants to say. He claims that PiL have no competition and no comrades, and that is not true either: there are a lot of groups, almost all of them British, standing outside the boundaries of rock 'n' roll and aiming their sounds inside. What PiL have established is that the limits on what they have to say are not at all apparent. The same cannot be said of many bands in the spring of 1980.

—Rolling Stone,
29 May 1980

Ripped to Shreds

Once the world was a simpler place: Calvin Coolidge was president, Bob Dylan was a Jew, and the illustrated fan-bio could be dismissed. Then Dave Marsh appeared with *Born to Run: The Bruce Springsteen Story* and, despite the obligatory inclusion of countless random photos, produced a serious book. Now my old friend Lester Bangs has broken the last rule of the genre. His *Blondie* is not even very nice to its subject.

Given that Bangs was merely a hired hand on a project cooked up by a book packager, it's amazing what he was able to get away with. He isn't unfriendly; he doesn't take cheap shots. With his usual multileveled alacrity, Bangs traces the prehistory and history of the band, pretty much telling you all you want to know. He profiles DEBORAH HARRY FOR MURJANI™, the other members of BLONDIE IS A GROUP and also *Parallel Lines* producer "Commander" Mike Chapman. (Chapman: "Punk-rock doesn't exist or it does in England but they're so far behind the rest of the world that it really doesn't matter." Bangs: "Guess that takes care of that.") He covers each album and recounts a lot of good stories. He makes one horrible mistake ("My Boyfriend's Back" was by the Angels, not the Crystals) and ends, the publisher no doubt holding a gun to his head, with a notably pusillanimous future-looks-bright last page. But Bangs also looks for the reasons behind Blondie's enormous success, and finds them in the group's obliteration of emotion.

The thing that makes *Parallel Lines* so assuredly avant-garde is precisely that it's so airtight and multiple-varnished, such a pris-

tinely slick piece of product, it's not even vapid like Barry Manilow, who can at least embarrass/make you throw up once in a while
with an "At the Copa." . . . Each song is a perfectly constructed
concave system in which every single piece of information offered
up in the lyrics cancels out another corresponding piece of information, kinda like a jigsaw puzzle except at the end instead of a picture you get a perfect blank. And that blank of course is nothing
less than Deborah Harry's face.

I used to think a lot of Blondie's more recent songs were about
emotional ambivalence—now I know that's investing them with far
too much tragic weight. They'd collapse under the strain.

What, one might ask, does this have to do with the future of
the human race? In a chapter titled (this is a fan-bio, remember) "On the Merits of Sexual Repression," Bangs continues the
argument:

. . . the music seems to have no really strong emotions in it, and
what emotions do surface occasionally, what obsessions and lusts,
are invariably almost immediately gutted by fusillades of irony,
sarcasm, camp, what have you, ending up buried.

IF THE MAIN REASON WE LISTEN TO MUSIC IN THE FIRST PLACE
IS TO HEAR PASSION EXPRESSED—as I've believed all my life—
THEN WHAT GOOD IS THIS MUSIC GOING TO PROVE TO BE? What
does it say about us? What are we confirming in ourselves by doting on art that is emotionally neutral? And, simultaneously, what in
ourselves might we be destroying or at least keeping down?

Irony, Bangs understands, has become the card up the
sleeve of contemporary art—or the mickey art drops in the audience's drink. Irony is used to support not only Blondie's music but the group's exploitation of Debbie Harry as international sex symbol, and Bangs takes up that topic once he's
finished turning the fan-bio into an antipostmodernist manifesto. Bangs resurrects an old Blondie ad—a picture of Harry
graced by the slogan WOULDN'T YOU LIKE TO RIP HER TO

SHREDS?—and then cuts through to the heart of the problem: irony is dissolved by its use as public discourse. On a cult lp, Nick Lowe's "Cruel to Be Kind" might have been a nice ironic satire of the sappy pop love song; as a Top 40 hit, it was a sappy pop love song and nothing more, even if you'd already gotten the joke. Making Deborah Harry into a mass sexual fantasy may have been an in-joke for the group, a satire of marketing as well as marketing at its most effective: the joke now justifies the group. The group may not get the joke, or think much about those for whom the joke is no joke at all—and if you don't think such diddling with popular culture has brutal consequences, listen to the song "Blondie" on the Iron City House-rockers' *Have a Good Time (But Get Out Alive)*, where marketing takes away one man's subjective fantasy and sells it back to him as an objective fact, and at a price—no spiritual metaphors, just dollars and cents—he can't afford. Bangs, writing about the *TV Guide* ads that peddle posters of Cheryl, Suzanne, Farrah, and "Blondie":

If [the ad] said "Deborah Harry," chances are almost nobody would send in the $2.50, because they don't know who Deborah Harry is. They just don't want to know anything about any of those women. . . . I think that if most guys in America could somehow get their fave-rave poster girl in bed and have total license to do whatever they wanted with this legendary body for one afternoon, at least 75% of the guys in the country would elect to beat her up. She may be up there all high and mighty on TV, but everybody knows that underneath all that fashion plating she's just a piece of meat like all the rest of them.

And that's what all this has to do with the future of the human race. That's one result of Blondie's coldness, their arty smugness, the group's distance not only from their audience but from their own music. It is, Bangs stops just short of saying, all of a piece.

What Lester Bangs has done with his quickie book is altogether remarkable. He hasn't stopped me from being a Blondie fan, or from turning up the volume every time "Call Me" comes on the radio—I doubt that was his intention. Rather, he has broken down the self-exculpatory strategies Blondie uses to deny the regressive and conventional meanings of their music. By so doing, he's made the group count—and made it clear just why listening to a simple song is not a simple matter.

—Rolling Stone,
24 July 1980

It's Fab, It's Passionate, It's Wild, It's Intelligent! It's the Hot New Sound of England Today!

"**D**on't romanticize it," Geoff Travis said to me. Travis is the founder of Rough Trade, the U.K.'s most important and adventurous independent record company. He was talking about Britain's postpunk pop avant-garde, of which Rough Trade is a vital center—or perhaps the only center.

If, that is, the term "postpunk pop avant-garde" means anything at all. That was a line I'd thought up in California, after listening to the new music coming out of England: some of it willfully obscurantist and contrived, and some of it—most notably the late-1979 debut albums by Essential Logic, the Raincoats (both Rough Trade bands), and the Gang of Four (a leftist group signed to the EMI and Warner Bros. multinationals)— sparked by a tension, humor, and sense of paradox plainly unique in present-day pop music. These records—Essential Logic's *Beat Rhythm News*, *The Raincoats*, and the Gang of Four's *Entertainment!*—were energized by the desire to communicate versions of shared social facts, and they were bent on testing a form called "rock 'n' roll"—as music, culture, and commerce—while still maintaining a certain wary distance from it. This music wasn't aimed at a mass audience, and it didn't seem likely to reach one. It did speak with a disoriented passion and an undisguised critical intelligence strong enough to lead new audiences to identify themselves with it: ideally, audiences suf-

ficiently passionate and critical to keep the musicians questioning their work.

A few days after receiving Geoff Travis's warning, though, I
would get another, from Gang of Four lead singer Jon King:
"The avant-garde is ideologically unsound." He was, by his
choice of words, parodying the neo-Marxist reputation the band
has picked up (given that the Gang of Four often works from
reconstructed James Brown rhythms, "neo-Marxist funk," or
King's own "perverted disco," might do as well). But King also
meant what he said, and knew what he was talking about.

Like guitarist Andy Gill, King is a fine-arts graduate of the
University of Leeds; the two ran the campus film society.
Drummer Hugo Burnham graduated from Leeds in drama; he
turned to music when, after setting up an agitprop theater
group, he grew tired of "preaching to the converted." Dave Allen—like the rest, in his mid-twenties, unlike them from a
working-class background—was a small-town journeyman musician until he came to Leeds looking to get into a punk band.
He first caught sight of King going down under a policeman's
club at an anti–National Front demonstration, and joined the
group in response to an ad soliciting a bass player for a "fast
R&B band." A never-ending four-way argument about art and
politics began as the band formed and has kept it going; I found
myself sucked right in. It was the best talk I'd heard in years.

When, only a few hours into my visit to England, Geoff
Travis told me not to romanticize what I'd come to write about,
he wasn't hinting at betrayal or sellout. Travis was simply
working from the basic premise of rock 'n' roll as it is being
reinvented in the U.K. today, which is to take nothing for
granted, to think, to hold off on visions of a new pop vanguard
even as one takes part in it.

I would find that attitude everywhere over the next week,
as I spent time with the Gang of Four, the feminist Raincoats,
the men and women at Rough Trade, and with Lora Logic, the
nineteen-year-old leader of Essential Logic. Never have I met

rock 'n' roll people who so insistently interrogated pop music. What, someone would ask, did it mean for millionaires like Pink Floyd to have a bunch of school kids singing "We don't need no education" on the radio every hour? How could the Pop Group be made to understand that a collage of a dead fetus and an H-bomb on the sleeve of their next 45 would be taken as anti-abortion propaganda? Because the activists who started Rock Against Sexism gave themselves a name whose inevitable acronym, RAS, suggested Rastafarians, notorious for their suppression of women, did that mean those activists were fakes, or just stupid? Why, Hugo Burnham wondered, did he say "Cunt!" so much?

Such talk was part of any day's business: the business of those who thought pop culture had consequences. The governing reality principle, it was soon clear, was a consciousness of sexism, understood as a challenge to one's conditioning, which naturally still made itself felt every day. In the context of Margaret Thatcher's right-wing clampdown, increasing racial enmity and skinhead-fascist violence, and a pop scene in which the rage was no kind of avant-garde, but the anti-avant-garde of the 2-Tone ska revival, such a struggle—no better word for it—made real sense. It did more than that: it made life interesting, and rescued life from the triviality of a day-to-day existence in which everything is merely personal and nothing connects. As Essential Logic put it in "Wake Up": "Basically we're alone/ But you better pay attention to detail/ Life ain't gonna show at a retail/ Pri-eee-yii-eee-yice."

I met the Gang of Four in early February, in Portsmouth, a shipyard town about seventy-five miles southwest of London, as they were halfway through a two-week swing across England. The shows on this tour had two things in common: the first act was a kindred band from Leeds (or Birmingham) or Rough Trade or both (Scritti Politti, the Mekons, Delta 5, Au

Pairs, Red Crayola—save for the all-male Scritti, each had male
and female members), and the venues were tiny. The four hundred or so people packed into the Portsmouth Polytechnic
Union House were filling a space not much bigger than my living room. A poster gave the week's schedule:

> THURS—'SOCIOLOGY DISCO'
> FRI—'DISCO'
> SAT—'CHILE SOLIDARITY DISCO'
> SUN—FILM: 'WILD ANGELS'
> MON—OPEN
> TUES—'GANG OF 4'
> WED—FILM ON N. IRELAND: 'THE PATRIOT GAME'

Among the many mysteries of British popular culture I know I
will never solve is the meaning of "Chile Solidarity Disco."

This night, the Raincoats opened the show: Vicky Aspinall,
twenty-four, violin and guitar; Gina Birch, twenty-four, bass;
Ana da Silva, thirty-one, guitar; and Ingrid Weiss, nineteen,
drums. It was their first gig since their first drummer,
Palmolive—once of the Slits, the first all-female punk band—
had decamped to seek enlightenment in India.

They leaped into their first number, Aspinall getting a hard,
abrasive sound out of her violin, the beat stuttering, three high
voices harmonizing with an off-stage realism across the sharp
edges of the melody, and within a minute or so the Raincoats
seemed to have trashed every female stereotype in rock 'n' roll.
It was a matter of demeanor, backed up by a new sound: without gestures, without a trace of rhetoric, the Raincoats got it
across that they had no interest in whatever images of the-
woman-in-rock one might have brought to their show, and no
interest in providing any.

Women in rock have never had access to the levels of prosaic reality available to men, whose presence on a stage is not,
before it is anything else, a novelty. Women have had to ac-

knowledge this contradiction with a ready-made sexual persona: tough chick, sufferer, dirty mama, etc. The highly touted new—that is, recent—American female singers—Carolyne Mas, Pat Benatar, Pearl E. Gates, and Ellen Foley—could not be more reactionary. Their music exists to support images presold years ago.

Poly Styrene, the great vocalist for the seminal punk band X-ray Spex, may have escaped this trap; Carole King could have; Robin Lane and Chrissie Hynde may; Lora Logic and the Raincoats definitely have.

"The basic theme in rock 'n' roll is what goes on between men and women," said the Raincoats, each one chipping into the conversation. "Rock 'n' roll is based on black music. And it's based *in* the exclusion of women and the ghettoization of blacks. Which is why we want to put a bit of distance between what we do and the rock 'n' roll tradition." But as the Raincoats stand back from the tradition they also open it up. There's something wonderfully anonymous about these women and their music: as four women appearing as nothing but themselves, they demystify each other. The very idea of roles is done away with. The Raincoats would not, it's suggested, relate to each other or to other people much differently if they were four carpenters. But because they are onstage, in front of an audience, they are moved to give full play to all the wit, brains, anger, and affection they have in them. They seize the prosaic and fling it back with the intensity of a terrible quarrel, with the satisfaction of a moment in which nothing needs to be said. I was amazed.

The members of the Gang of Four also seem anonymous, if in a very different way: as extras from one of those British end-of-the-world movies suddenly forced to carry the film. The band took the stage and threw out an instantaneous, doomstruck, forbidding tension. The high volume and the syncopated metallic grate of the sound produced a direct attack, but behind that attack was its contradiction, and before long one heard the contradiction as the attack. Rhythms shifted, stopped, re-formed; violent pauses broke the songs into pieces. Andy Gill's guitar and Hugo Burnham's drums might drop out as Dave Allen, on bass, played on, seemingly not noticing that he was alone, and then not noticing when the guitar returned and *he* stopped playing. Jon King, shaking his fists in front of his chest and pumping his legs in place as if victim of the devil's treadmill, did most of the singing, but anyone might take a mike for lyrics that sometimes fought each other like images in a cubist painting. "Damaged Goods" is one enormous, self-destructing pun built around the title phrase as a metaphor for shopping and sex, organized by the supermarket slogan THE CHANGE WILL DO YOU GOOD, which here means both the end of an affair and a few pennies saved. "Damaged goods, take them back," runs a lament, then a shouted "YOU SAID YOU'RE CHEAP BUT YOU'RE TOO MUCH!," the singer jammed in at the checkout counter, and what might have begun as a ditty about the commodification of love is now unstable, the pain of a breakup transferred to an unsatisfactory purchase, shopper's lust now a lover's question. The Gang of Four too would be insistent about a need for "distance" from rock 'n' roll, from music and mannerisms perfectly congruent with the expectations one brings to a record or a concert, because expectations, if catered to, always absorb novelty. As Gill aimed clipped notes against the groove and the rhythm seemed to retreat under his assault, the band made that distance almost physical, and without ever losing the backbeat.

If the band had a center, it was Allen's bass: rough and taut in tone, each note standing out, it hung over the music like some final synthesis of Motown finesse and reggae weight. Weight, not John Entwistle steadiness: Allen too was part of the context of speed, of rushed tempos coming to a halt like a dog snapped back at the end of a rope, a near crackup. One listened with two minds, excited by the music, and wondering why it did what it did. Even if one was familiar with the songs, and almost everyone at Portsmouth was, it was impossible not to be surprised by each seemingly blind change. And yet the music was maniacally danceable. The crowd, jammed into the hot little room, shook like a centipede on its back.

The band's dynamics had a pointed political purpose: they kept one's attention from settling on a single performer. But the continual reconstruction of rhythms also freed the rhythms from clichés; more vitally, the shape of the music provided a metaphor for the sense of contradiction that shaped the band's lyrics ("At home he feels like a tourist," "Is this so private/ Our struggle in the bedroom"), just as the disjointed antinarrative of the lyrics worked as a metaphor for the band's sound.

It's a sound you might trace easily to the Maytals' "Funky Kingston," the dub pressure drop of Big Youth's *Screaming Target*, Wilson Pickett's "In the Midnight Hour," Jimi Hendrix's "All Along the Watchtower"—if you omitted half the pieces and kept shuffling the rest. You might liken it to the sound of Talking Heads' "Life During Wartime"—except that Talking Heads have one point of direction, and the Gang of Four have four.

Jon King: You've got a description of events, not necessarily an emotional identification with those events, but a description, or, given the received ideas people bring to events, a redescription

—of, say, consumer melancholy; torture in Ireland erased by the discovery of North Sea oil ("It's at the end of the rainbow," King sings; "White noise in," answers Gill); a newspaper article about housewives, "The Unsung Heroines of Britain"; a man obsessed with order; a couple in bed—

and the music that goes with it attempts to recreate, to reinvent a form to accompany that redescription of the world. It's not standard form, it's trying to reinvent a form in a way that suits the redescription of things—that's why the music does what it does.

That's why it's in the middle, between "realism" and "the avant-garde." It's not "normal." But it's normal enough to make a certain kind of sense.

Hugo Burnham: It's very consciously like the split screens Godard used in *Numero Deux.* The main shot shows life proceeding in what one thinks of as normal fashion, but there are other images used simultaneously, which may support the first shot and may not. The first image may show a woman preparing breakfast for her family and the next might show her jerking off her husband. It's the idea of counterpoint, undercutting a theme, throwing each bit into relief.

King: We mean not to state things baldly, because—

Andy Gill: —because it's the stating of things baldly that tends to be the problem. It's a lack of subtlety and *thinking*—which leads to clumsy theory, and bad practice. If you're not aware of the processes and thoughts by which you arrive at a statement about a situation, if you're not aware of that, then you probably can't sufficiently analyze the situation.

The off-stage personalities of the band members disappear into those processes and come out altogether changed. Head down, Gill rushes across the boards in jerky, pigeon-toed movements, taking evasive action against some unseen enemy, carrying himself with a physical presence so stoic and dissonant one doesn't even connect him with the sounds coming out of his guitar. Allen throws up cautionary barriers to Gill's jittery march—until he too starts blowing fuses.

Burnham marches out from behind his kit to sing "It's Her Factory," the song about housewives, while Gill takes the drums and lays down a beat that could come from Richard Manuel, if "Rag Mama Rag" were done at half-time. Burnham's BBC accent smears the image of his stereotypically working-class looks: with his half-inch hair, heavy boots, and block-of-rock body (five feet five inches and 156 pounds), a foreigner like me would take Burnham for a skinhead; an English person would recognize him as a serious football fan. Swaying to the beat, hands clasped genteelly behind his back, he delivers a point-by-point dissection of media sexism, all framed with lines from James Brown's "It's a Man's Man's Man's World."

King abruptly becomes a man transformed by the chance to unburden himself of everything he's ever wanted to say. As he begins to shout, each statement, each insight, miraculously produces another. He seems gaga with angst, and it's a joke, for half a song. Then it's no joke at all. Just as suddenly as the ability to speak appears, the ability to say what one means slips away, and the confusion and passion shaking King like a marionette overwhelm his absurdity.

Gill is still wary and alert, searching for the sniper. The instruments vanish behind him and he goes blank—and keeps playing, as if he can't afford to think. King, bent over his melodica, a reggae plastic horn, puts his whole body into the few skimpy notes the toy can produce (imagine Carlos Santana going through his the-pain-of-the-universe-is-in-my-guitar routine, with a ukulele). Gill, staring over his shoulder, crashes into King. King spins to the opposite side of the stage, sights past Allen's moving screen, and takes his mike back on the run. What it looked like was straightforward enough: the Odessa Steps montage in Eisenstein's *Potemkin.*

Like the music, the band's words are full of gaps: they offer cut-up, fleetingly detailed accounts of the paradoxes of leisure as work, home as factory, resident as tourist, history as ruling-class private joke. On the hook of a familiar catchphrase hangs not so much any plain message as that sense of paradox itself. What you hear in the nervous soap opera of "Damaged Goods" is someone struggling against chaos, trying to see through to its source, gaining a moment of clarity, and then falling back, accepting self-serving lies as orderly life—as the way things were meant to be. Layers of false consciousness are stripped off, only to re-form, and take back the subjects of the songs.

The Gang of Four's politics, as politics are usually understood—their ideas about class, race, sexism, etc.—are evident in the way they deal with their record company; how they re-late to their coworkers, fans, other bands; how they set up gigs; why they work with Rock Against Racism and Rock Against Sexism; positions they stake out in interviews. But those poli-tics don't exactly shape the band's music. They motivate the music—but to borrow critic Dick Hebdige's words on the Ras-tafarians' transformation of reggae from protest to ontology, the Gang of Four's songs move beyond the obvious arena of contesting what is right and what is wrong "to the level of contesting the obvious itself." When Hebdige writes that "ide-ology saturates everyday discourse" in the form of a false "com-mon sense," that "social relations and processes are shrouded in a 'common sense' that simultaneously validates and mystifies them," he could not be closer to identifying what the Gang of Four mean to confront, or how the politics of their music are meant to work.

Jon King: The attitudes and beliefs that people take as natural and given have been inherited through the social structure they're brought up in. An example is the man who believes that women are by definition more suited to working in the home than to mak-ing decisions. If you believe these attitudes are natural, the belief in the natural puts all this outside the realm of debate—and unless you have an awareness of your views as political manifestations, you won't believe you can change them.

Such a point of view is hardly new. What is radically new is to see it acted out as process, to see the process break down as it turns into first-rank rock 'n' roll: as guitar and drums drop out and force a listener to question the nature of a band along with the process, as a singer glimpses the politics of the phrase "damaged goods" and the band rips the music away from him before he can be sure of what he's seen, as one musician careens into another and the emotions shaken loose by the breakdown of the process turn violent.

Onstage, where all of this was happening, the Gang of Four headed into the end of their set. "I found that essence rare," King cried, copping an image of fulfillment off a perfume bottle. "I knew I'd get what I asked for." He might have been fending off the images of corruption and deception he'd rail out in the next seconds. The fury of the show, building for close to an hour, hit its peak. Driven by the force of bass and drums pulling away from Gill's viciously curling blues runs, the song was taken so fast one could no longer quite catch the rhythms; the music went down to pure momentum, a train picking up speed as it headed into a bad curve. In the heat and the noise of the jumping room, it seemed as if you could actually feel the room tilt.

After that, the final encores—the Mekons' "Rosanne" and the Rezillos' ridiculous "I Can't Stand My Baby"—were relief; "distance" between the Gang of Four and rock 'n' roll was purposely collapsed. Halfway through the Rezillos song, a fan climbed onto the stage. Roadie Jol Burnham, a much bigger version of his brother Hugo, wrestled the kid to the back; the fan put up a terrific struggle, and Jon King signaled him loose, whereupon he took a mike, grabbed lines from the song, and danced through the breaks. He was very good; in the end the band gave him the number and he closed the show.

When I heard Rough Trade was planning a U.S. operation not only for the release but for the manufacture of its records, I realized the company was serious. The usual procedure is somewhat different.

The independent label—let's say with one hot artist and lots of good press—contracts with a major for "manufacture and distribution": nuts and bolts, street-cleaning, nothing more. The indie announces that it has retained "complete artistic control," signs up all sorts of interesting performers, and releases a great many records in a very short time. Since the actual capitalization of the indie (now ensconced in new offices with eye-catching stationery and a logo by Hipgnosis) may consist of little more than the reputation of its one hot artist, the major encourages the indie to solve its cash-flow problems by accepting the advance of large amounts of money.

Everyone is happy, until the indie discovers that it is monumentally in debt and that monthly receipts do not even cover the interest. The major calls in its loans, dissolves the indie or reduces it to a vanity label, and takes over rights to the one hot artist the indie started with.

The contradiction here is in the notion that artistic control exists independently of the means of production—or that the means of production have no aesthetic meaning. The defeat of that contradiction is the idea behind Rough Trade—and it is why, down at the Rough Trade offices, you can find Lora Logic doing her own books.

Rough Trade is a storefront at the seedy end of Kensington Park Road, one block over from the Portobello boutiques. Now a collective, it opened in the spring of 1976 as a record shop, and was soon caught up distributing the homemade singles and fanzines that sprouted like mushrooms in the wake of the Sex Pistols. Behind the shop, a hangout for punks, Jamaicans, students, and occasional skins, is a rickety three-storey building with a few offices, all in a mild hubbub of typing, talking, mailing, and phone-answering. Upstairs, Chris Williams, Shirley O'Laughlin, and Scott Piering, Rough Trade's token American, handle publicity and concerts; downstairs, Geoff Travis and Richard Scott oversee pressing and distribution, which cover not only Rough Trade discs but dozens of independent singles, lps, and cassettes from all over Britain, Europe, and the United States. The place resembles nothing so much as a sixties underground press office—except that the Rough Trade hot plate produces the best coffee in London.

"Changing things from the inside is nonsense," said Geoff Travis—twenty-eight, a former actor and drama teacher. "So is the ghettoization of a hip paradise. It doesn't matter how much 'creative control' a band is given—you're still indentured. Long-term contracts"—Rough Trade works on a record-to-record basis—"will put a band in debt from recording and touring costs. Then you have to produce when you're not ready. You have to write songs when you have nothing to say."

I asked why the Feelies, a nouveau surf band from New Jersey whose first single had come out on Rough Trade, had gone to the Stiff label for their album. "Because," Travis said, "I knew we couldn't handle them when I saw how they used the studio: the album would have cost us £30,000. It would have taken money from every other project, and it could have ruined the company. Those economics are just what we're trying to stay away from." The point was not, Travis was saying, to tie Rough Trade's future to a band with the commercial potential to support other bands or good ideas. It was to link Rough Trade's freedom of action to the continuing appearance of new groups that deserved to be put before the public.

"I don't see Rough Trade as 'the record business,' " Travis said. "And I hate the idea of 'artists.' Rough Trade is a place where people are simply doing their work. It's a place where people can get support, meet other people, get ideas, listen to each other." And, I asked, make a living? "And make a living. We're just beginning to solve *that* problem." The problem is most crucial for musicians, who work without the debt financing of a conventional label. The twenty or so people who work at Rough Trade are paid equally for time put in, there is profit sharing after a year, and the company is in the black, but as yet no one has figured out how to put musicians on that sort of payroll—something that had to be done soon, the Raincoats said with no little vehemence. And there are a growing number of bands, all operating more or less hand-to-mouth: playing on each other's records, sharing gigs or equipment, two groups sometimes piggybacking on the same 45.

No matter what Travis was talking about—skinhead violence in the record shop, which has ranged from unpleasant to life-threatening; what he saw as the reactionary pull of the ska revival (though Rough Trade distributed the first neo-ska disc, the Specials' 2-Tone 45 "Gangster"); the shift in sexual politics implied by the surge of all-female bands and, even more encouragingly, by the emergence of one good band after another made up of both men and women—you couldn't miss his delight and worry at the possibilities and obstacles pop music was offering. Rough Trade's main risk is clear: artiness, solipsism, moral superiority, snobbery—the typical dead end of an avant-garde too comfortable with the concept. Looking for a new bass player, Lora Logic thought that if she put up a notice at Rough Trade she'd get only "very elitist people—cultists"; as Jon King put it, "There came a point when modernism went up its own ass," and you can hear that event in some Rough Trade records. But most seem to point to events that have yet to take place.

"No matter what our politics, no matter how the music works, we still get an overwhelmingly male audience," Hugo Burnham said.

"I can't see any tactic to change that," said Jon King. "Women get hassled at gigs if they're not with a bloke. And so a lot of women stay away."

Burnham: "Last time we played London a friend of mine was down front, and she was manhandled *five times*, by five different blokes, in the course of the hour we were onstage."

"It's very odd," I said, "since the Gang of Four were led by a woman."

"Do you mean," Andy Gill asked, " 'If we were led by a woman'?"

"No," I said, wondering what I possibly could have meant, "I mean—"

Burnham: "Actually, that's something that's occasionally been said: 'Why haven't you got a woman in your band?' "

Gill: "That would be quite—I mean, imagine . . . if we were women. Is our music male music?"

Burnham: "That's an example of the kind of question we're asked?"

Gill: "No—I'm asking you."

Burnham: "You're asking *me*, is our music male music?"

Gill: "Right."

Burnham: "What do you mean by 'male music'?"

Gill: "Would women play what we do? Could we be women? I doubt it."

Burnham: "I don't know. It's a ridiculous question."

King: "It's not ridiculous."

Burnham: "I suppose we *wouldn't* be playing the same music. I *suppose*. But is the Raincoats' music 'female music'?"

Gill: "Quite."

Burnham: "*Why* is it?"

Gill: "No—that's the question. I'm not sure. Having said what I've said—it strikes me as dangerous to equate certain types of music with men or women, with sexuality."

Inspired by this colloquy, I asked an absurdly pretentious question about how, for the Gang of Four, a consciousness of sexism fit into their everyday lives—for some reason unaware that it had just been answered. There was a long pause.

"Well," said Jon King finally, "when we go into a pub, we don't go up to the barmaid and say [in a beery voice], 'GIVE US A PINT, DARLING!' We say [politely]: 'Hello, comrade.' "

" 'Brotherette,' " said Dave Allen.

When a review of Essential Logic's *Beat Rhythm News* compared it to Frank Zappa, Lora Logic got hold of a Zappa lp, but failed to see the connection. When another notice insisted on an unmistakable Captain Beefheart influence, she picked up a copy of *Trout Mask Replica*, and found a kindred spirit. When a third writer, desperate for a handle on a singer who phrases scattershot lyrics off the madly jerked riffs of her saxophone, declared Essential Logic the harbinger of a beatnik revival ("*beat* rhythm news," you see), Lora dutifully bought herself a Jack Kerouac novel, which she was unable to finish.

Lately, Lora Logic has been listening to Kurt Weill, though not because anyone has yet compared her to him. Her father, resigned to his daughter's career, told Lora—née Susan Whitby, not long ago a pink-uniformed student at the City of London School for Girls, and in the halcyon days of '77 the six-teen-year-old saxophonist for X-ray Spex—that Kurt Weill was her distant cousin. True to form, she had never heard of him.

Lora Logic is one of the most self-composed people I've ever met: terribly soft-spoken, a small laugh in every sentence, and if she were telling you her deepest secrets you'd probably still sense a certain reserve. She's a nineteen-year-old girl full of confidence and doubt; a woman of seventy mulling over her mistakes and proud of her past. At once a punk founder and inheritor, Lora Logic still has her feel for harmonious insurrection; now in careful pursuit of sounds no one else would think to make, she conveys an almost frightening commitment to self-reliance.

Out of these impressions I tried to trace the skewed intensity of the music Essential Logic is making: imagine Alice forced to get a band together and play for the Red Queen, hiding none of her fear but still putting a few over on the old girl—it's not worth saving her life if she can't raise an eyebrow now and again. All across *Beat Rhythm News* you can hear someone in a trap, hear her register surprise and pleasure as she draws on resources of intelligence and passion she didn't know she had, follow her as she sets herself to break loose and goes about making a home for herself in the meantime. You understand that the real task, or the only task the trap allows, is to pay attention to detail, and you do.

Lora seems to drift with her saxophone, but pushing from the edges of the music into its center, then spinning back to its borders. Her voice twists words so far out of shape you can't help but question their meaning—or the way, back in the world, words are so easily used to mean nothing. Lines of melody fragment; dub rhythms double back. Sarcasm explodes into a plea—Lora's wail heads into a tunnel as a shriek and comes out a trill. Her band (Philip Legg, guitar; Dave Wright, second sax; Rich Tea, drums) isn't so much led as subliminally organized by Lora's soprano sax; they clatter away into a noise that, once you get to know their music, sounds quite elegant: a modest, perfectly intentional demolition of the ability to take anything at face value.

Lora Logic: X-ray Spex was my first band. I answered an advert in *Melody Maker.* And with my first advert, I happened to be accepted, it happened to work, I happened to get famous very quickly. I'd been playing saxophone for about three years—in a closet in my room. I thought, I'd better *do* something.

I ran away. I *did* it. And I got dragged back. My parents came to fetch me—they came to *save me!*

It was all suppressed, in the beginning. I wanted to act, and that was suppressed. So I thought, I'll try something a bit closer to home. I'll try music. Saxophone was always my favorite instrument; I doubled on violin and piano, classical things at school.

The punk scene was totally new to me. I'd only been to a few gigs: people like David Bowie, real *idols.* I didn't know much about rock 'n' roll. The only reason I was taken into X-ray Spex was that I was a young girl playing saxophone: great gimmick!

I was in X-ray Spex about ten months: X-ray Spex only played about thirty gigs in its whole life and I played twenty-four of them. It was supposed to be Poly and her backup band; I started getting too much attention, so . . . I went. I was kicked out. It was everything I'd ever wanted—just being in a band.

Those are vague, hazy days—a lot of violence. Anybody got onstage, anybody played; and nobody could play and nobody could sing. Sometimes, looking back, it shocks me. It was all manipulation: the bands didn't realize how they were used. Most of the people who were around then have disappeared—the people in the audience. You used to recognize everyone, know everyone. I look

at gigs now, and there're none of them there. I don't know where
they've gone to—a lot of casualties.

In a way, it created worse barriers than there were before. You
know: "Oh, what are you?" "We're punk." "We're mod." I don't
know what *those* sort of people would categorize *us* as.

Still in school after X-ray Spex, Lora made some money
playing on a Stranglers lp, and formed an early version of Essential Logic. She brought a tape to Geoff Travis, who turned it
down, changed his mind, and released "Aerosol Burns" in the
summer of 1978. Out of school and living on her own, Lora
formed a new band, and began moonlighting with Red Crayola;
along with Gina Birch of the Raincoats (Lora kicked in a little
saxophone to their album), she remains part of the group. Essential Logic then made a superb EP for Virgin, and lost it to
the law: wandering through the Leicester Square cinema dis-
trict, Lora saw a man in a rabbit suit, took a picture, and used
it on the sleeve. It turned out to be the March Hare, shilling for
a Disney theater; Disney complained, and Virgin quickly de-
leted the record. Soon after, Lora drew out her savings, took
her band to a friendly studio in Wales, slept on the floor, and
cut her album in a month.

There're a thousand different interpretations of the lyrics I
wrote. They were meant to be vague. They obviously meant one
thing to me at the time—but I like to think that anyone who read
them made up a slightly different version. They were just sparks;
ideas next to each other. They're very naïve; questioning a lot of—
conditioning. I've lived a pretty normal life in England—I see it as
having been a suppressed life, now. What I wanted to get across
was just—the attitude of *inquiry*. And that's as close as you're
gonna get.

In three years, Lora Logic has appeared on six albums, including one by the Finnish punk band Kollakestäa (Lora's
mother was born in Finland, where Lora is now known as "The

Godmother of Punk"), and at least as many singles and EPs. Unlike a lot of Rough Trade musicians, she has no interest in organized politics ("We played a Rock Against Racism gig," she said mordantly. "When we got there, it had turned into Rock Against Radiation"), and she doesn't hang around the office. In a friendly, beguiling way, she keeps her distance. The company isn't an answer for her, simply a tactic, in the meantime.

"We're only just starting," Lora said, as if everything she had behind her would soon be no more than a footnote. "As a working unit, we're only just getting to know one another. And we've got to find a new bass player! Sometimes it's gotten to be too much, doing everything: having to organize the gigs, having to find a cheap roadie and pack all the gear, having to make sure everyone's quite sober when they go onstage—I suppose if you're Rachel Sweet you just ride with the record company. But I like driving people to the gigs and I like writing the songs. It's very satisfying, doing everything. So I do it."

I asked if she thought she'd still be going in five years.

"Oh, yes," Lora said. "If there's not a third world war."

"Retford's going to be a hole," Jol Burnham said.

"A hole?" I asked.

"Dead rats," he said.

Retford was a hole. A small town in the middle of D. H. Lawrence country—the Midlands coal fields—it had one restaurant, Fred's Chinese Food. The food lived up to the name.

The gig was in a dingy members-only club one flight up from SUPER TRENDY DISCO, NO DENIMS. The young crowd was 1980s punk, which meant a swarm of male and female Sid Vicious clones: a vision of pasty faces, soft bodies, rampant acne, and compulsive smoking, of a general commitment to ill health. Two bullying disc jockeys held the fort for hours, screaming out demands that the audience sing along with Sham 69's moronic youth anthems. In the dressing room, Jon King finished inking in the night's song list and began singing in a shit-eating nightclub voice. "Yes, yes, ladies and gentlemen, I do 'write the songs,' thank you," he crooned. "And now, with your permission, I'd like to tell you how I—found that *essence rare.* . . ." "I just witnessed the most touching sight," said Kevin Harvey, the Gang of Four sound man, coming in from the bar. "Bloke put out his cigarette on his mate's hand."

The show—on a half-stage, the ceiling so low King bumped it in his more frenzied moments, with the club owner, his eye on the bar trade, refusing to let the band on until well after midnight—held nothing back, and neither did the audience. As the crowd shouted lyrics and organized itself into startlingly apt mass movements for crucial changes in the rhythms, I had the queer impression the Gang of Four weren't so much performing their songs as being performed by them.

Instead of playing to the crowd, the band seemed to hold the stage as fragments of the crowd's superego: the superego shattered by political ideas it knew were false but accepted because they gave comfort, by desires it couldn't understand, sexual impulses distorted by the pull of forgotten advertisements, familiar images garbled by a glimpse of the grotesque. The peculiar distance in the Gang of Four's onstage actions—the way the music might seem disassociated from the people who made it—and the distance in the voice of the songs—a voice that had its analogue in the cubist indirection of the band's sound, but was much harder to pin down—was finally clear.

The stance of the group is not that of the cultural politician, of someone denouncing or criticizing, but of an ordinary person struggling to make sense of his or her life by living out a false separation between what is understood to be personal and what is understood to be political. Because the separation is false, when the person is most conscious, he or she is most aware of a sense of paradox. As I'd half understood before, the voice in the Gang of Four's songs—in "Damaged Goods," "Anthrax," "Contract"—is the voice of false consciousness in rebellion against itself, and, almost simultaneously, the voice of resistance to that rebellion, the voice of a yearning for accommodation, no matter how impossible. The voice is not directed outward, and the songs are not quite aimed at the audience. The audience is put in the position of witnessing an event—rather than, as is usual, put in the position of one to whom something is addressed. The voice is not talking to the audience, in the manner of a blues or rock voice that directly celebrates, regrets, demands, imparts knowledge or emotion (think of "Like a Rolling Stone," "Stop! In the Name of Love," "When a Man Loves a Woman"); the voice is talking to itself, because it is too violently struck by uncertainty to talk to anyone else.

It is, when you begin to see the performance this way, a shocking little drama. Discontinuities and dislocations strike the mind: at home you feel like a tourist; sex becomes a contract; history feels like a trick. You try to get a fix on the real world, but the "real world"—consumer society, the class system, the romantic myths one was raised on—is organized to divert you from seeing it for what it is, and you become aware of *this*; thus no events or images remain clear in meaning, and you begin to redescribe them to yourself. The mind begins to free-associate, and discovers that what it turns up are not "real feelings" but mass-produced images of pleasure and pain, rewards and prohibitions. The mind begins to fantasize, and discovers that its private wishes are publicly approved. Every thought now produces its contradiction, and the distance between what you thought you knew and what you know you must know, between what you can say and what you want to say, is palpable—as palpable as a hole in the Gang of Four's sound when the guitar and drums go dead.

You see yourself as a collaborator in the process of mystification, a beneficiary as well as a victim. The result is anger, confusion, irony short-circuited by desperation, mockery, self-parody, and frantic yea-saying in the face of the negations the mind is kicking up.

The voice is most of all disorienting, and it provokes the state of mind it is describing. Though the voice is recognizing the political in the personal, the economic realities of common sense, there is no question of preaching to the converted, because the voice cannot preach. It cannot give a speech, call for right action, or tell people what to think.

The question is not, as it has almost always been with rock 'n' roll, that of what persona is being presented, what role is being played. There is no question of backing up a persona with an impression of personal authenticity. The Gang of Four replace persona with a dramatization of consciousness and false consciousness battling over the possession of a voice. From that battle comes King's performance as a marionette pulling against its strings; Gill's shell-shocked dashes across the stage; rhythms shot against each other and thrown off into silence. It's not a picture of society out of control; it is a picture of a person in the process of discovering that the opposite is true.

One might ask how much of this a member of an audience is likely to perceive; I would answer that all of it can be perceived without any sort of analysis whatsoever. True to the spirit of a band that argues the way other groups rehearse, and whose slogan, if they had one, would be "I quite disagree with that," the Gang of Four could—did—fight for half an afternoon over the question of whether their fans separated words from music, images from the beat, politics from dance. "You're claiming," Burnham said to Gill, "that it's *impossible* for someone to *just* take us on an entertainment level?" "I'm saying," Gill said, with the maddened patience of someone already an hour into an argument that is giving no sign of resolution, "that if someone enjoys, is watching, is absorbing what we're doing, you cannot *split up* what it is they're absorbing. I don't think people can be entertained *without* understanding what is going on, without understanding the ideas that are there." "Now, look," said Jon King. "A lot of people—"

—*Rolling Stone*,
24 July 1980

Love and Death
in the American Novel

No answer. I tried the knob and went in. . . . I noticed his feet first, because although he had on trousers and a shirt, his feet were bare and hung over the end of the bed. They were tied there by a rope around the ankles.

They had been burned raw on the soles. There was a smell of scorched flesh in spite of the open window. Also a smell of scorched wood. An electric iron on the desk was still connected. I went over and turned it off.

—Raymond Chandler, "Goldfish," 1936

X is the band that has defined the Los Angeles punk scene, and there isn't a lot of room for compromise in what they sing about —or much room to breathe. The scene itself may be the most violent of all the local punk subcultures to appear since 1977: not just the roughest, but the most cruel, as if the Southern Californians attracted by the negations of the Sex Pistols had too much Malibu hype on their backs to afford any sort of restraint. Not long ago, a woman was stabbed at an X show, and not in a fight; someone simply came up behind her and put a knife in her back. That may have been the result of an invasion of punk clubs by Huntington Beach teenagers who've just heard the word about no-future and think they have to prove themselves; a lot of people think so. But after listening to X's first album, *Los Angeles*, released by the independent Slash label, such an incident seems less a matter of chickens coming home to roost than of the chickens never bothering to leave.

Unlike most American punk records of the last few years, *Los Angeles* isn't just a collection of borrowed attitudes and received ideas. It has a sensibility and a terrain: Chandler's L.A. without Philip Marlowe, perhaps, and that means more than that the disc proceeds from first cut to last without introducing anyone likely to turn off the iron. It means the songs are written and sung not from Marlowe's point of view but from the point of view of the losers and misfits he inevitably discovers at the fringes of big-money murders—or whose bodies he turns up. The story *Los Angeles* has to tell takes place in a junkie pad off Santa Monica and Western, and who knows what you'll find when you open the door?

Someone eager to tell you all about how "Johny Hit and Run Paulene," maybe, and you can take your choice as to whether it's just a speed freak's rap or really yesterday's news. Johny shot up some stuff that makes him have to fuck someone every hour—like whatever girl's standing on the corner. Too bad if she's not in the mood, you know? When singers Exene and her husband, John Doe, put this song out it doesn't sound contrived. If the tune contains anything primarily designed to shock it's the opening, a little standard-issue punk guitar running through the first notes of "Johnny B. Goode."

> When he was waking up
> Beside the bed
> He found clumps of hair
> The last Paulene wouldn't cooperate
> She wasn't what you'd call living really
> But she was still awake

There's no humor on *Los Angeles*, and no sense of freedom —no conviction that there's anything to do with it. The music has a strong, tense snap, but it's thoughtless, functional; Billy Zoom doesn't so much play his guitar solos as get them over with. What puts X across are Exene and Doe's lyrics, and their singing; the way Exene follows a flat "Your phone's off the hook" with a shout of "But—you're not!" or the way she drags her voice across half a line of Doe's lead (or vice versa), just walking in on some squalid tale but incapable of surprise. The bitter, sometimes passionate and sometimes distracted vocals bleed the melodrama out of "Nausea," "Sugarlight," "Sex and Dying in High Society" or "Los Angeles," and replace it with knowledge that couldn't have come cheap: "Every time you look at him/ You could almost fall asleep."

Exene's voice has the harder edge. You don't know if she's a spikedriver hiding sweet little-girl memories or if she made a point of killing off her childhood first chance she got, and you may not want to get close enough to find out. The first time I heard her I thought of the woman in "Goldfish" who turned on the iron Marlowe turned off.

The two guns came forward almost on the same level, one small—a .32, one a big Smith and Wesson. They couldn't come into the room abreast, so the girl came in first.

"Okey, hot shot," she said dryly. "Ceiling zero. See if you can reach it."

From the burning St. Andrew's cross on its jacket to the finally-got-smart coldness of "She had started to hate/ Every nigger & Jew/ Every Mexican that give her lotta shit" in its title song, *Los Angeles* carries the bravado of those lines of Chandler's—and the ugliness of the lines quoted earlier. The record also shares Chandler's invisible mastery of craft, that essential commitment to the story being told. X's words read too well—and are sung too imaginatively—to bear comparison to the usual punk fear-mongering. What the craft and commitment say is that X is a serious band.

He got 24 hours
To shoot all Paulenes

Between the legs
He'll throw 96 tears thru 24 hours
Sexed once
Every hour

After a time, you may begin to listen for some sign that the story told on *Los Angeles* is just a story, or that the story is basically artful, a sharp use of seedy Hollywood locales and bus-stop drifters. You'll find neither. What there is to be found, behind the parade of small-time horrors implicitly mocked by L.A.'s quick fix of sun and easy money, is an insistence that those horrors have made the people who live them and who sing about them better than those who don't: not just tougher and smarter but morally superior, if only because they've seen through the moralism other people only pretend to believe in anyway. Out of that comes the plain acceptance of racism that's the subliminal hook of "Los Angeles," and out of that comes the readiness for violence that underpins almost every track on the album itself. X's vision isn't fragmented, it's not secondhand, and its ambition is to discredit any vision that suggests there's more to life than X says there is.

—*New West*,
25 August 1980

Elvis Costello's
Bill of Rights

lvis Costello's *Taking Liberties*—a twenty-cut, 1977–80 collection of B-sides, U.K.-only lp tracks, and three cuts prev. unrel.—is interesting mainly for the light it sheds on the trouble Costello is in. Like any such piece of product, the album is a mixed bag of left-field surprises and obscurities best left obscure, but what's disturbing is that all of the best material is at least two years old. The skin-crawling tension that kicks off the otherwise bouncy, be-my-baby love song "Radio Sweetheart" is just terrifying; the replacement of carefully constructed tension by the inertia-in-motion of something like "Crawling to the U.S.A." is just sludge. Ideas fly all around the earlier numbers—the strange reference to "goose-step dancing" in "Radio Sweetheart," the mystery of "Stranger in the House," the controlled repulsion of "Night Rally." Nothing is very mysterious about "Wednesday Week," "Dr. Luther's Assistant," or "Clowntime Is Over," but nothing is very precise, either; you can pick up a sense of desperation and betrayal, but it's bland for its vagueness. The music is convoluted; with "Dr. Luther's Assistant" the rhythm rolls over and dies. "Night Rally" hardly matches "Radio, Radio" (the song it replaced on the U.K. version of *This Year's Model*), but it has a spine, a progression so insistent it suggests "Like a Rolling Stone" with all of the hope bled out of it, and what could be more appropriate for a song about the rise of the National Front? The most compelling thing about the later "Ghost Train" is its title.

When Costello first came to our attention in the summer of 1977—with his notorious, brilliantly careerist comment that the only subjects he felt qualified to speak about were "revenge and guilt"—he seemed like an anomaly: a craftsman in a season of one-chord prophets, a mirror-star of barely legal age who'd already learned as much from Billie Holiday as from Buddy Holly. Still, he fit the season. Johnny Rotten sang rants and Costello sometimes sang ballads, but they were brothers under the hype. The difference was that if Rotten's flame-out was implicit in his own performance, no less implicit in Costello's was that he was a figure to be reckoned with over the long haul. He said it in his music: in his classicism and in his commitment to form. Almost invisibly, Costello worked out of a mastery of doomy rockabilly nuance that could be traced from Carl Perkins's "Dixie Fried" to Bob Dylan's "Absolutely Sweet Marie." His singing and his melodies were often as fluid as Frankie Lymon's. His sense of small-combo dynamics, which came from Al Green, the early Rolling Stones, Augustus Pablo, and the garage, could not have been more sophisticated or less effete. But Costello didn't sound like his sources; his personality was too strong and the stories he had to tell too intricately demanding for that. It could take years to hear Neil Young's "Cowgirl in the Sand" behind "Watching the Detectives."

Costello's craft carried an authority beyond musicianship because it was linked to an obsession he was driven to develop and get across: that obsession with revenge and guilt, certainly, though it can be more specifically named as an obsession with love and fascism. The idea, scattered across *My Aim Is True* and *This Year's Model*, and then set forth with both greater subtlety and violence on *Armed Forces*, was that fascism, far from being defeated in 1945, simply went underground, where it now functions as the political unconscious of the West. Because it is an id, a factory of wishes and fantasies, it can't be confined to politics: fascism shapes what we do with love, which is the illusion that—we think—makes life worth living. Both love and fascism are utopias—fascism the utopia of control, love the utopia of surrender of control (though fascism is also the utopia of surrendering control of oneself to authority, and love the utopia of achieving complete control over another person)— and both are dangerous and corrupting, because they promise absolutes, and because we can no longer tell one from the other. Both love and fascism are false solutions to the problem of revenge and guilt—false solutions, because they are the true sources.

The expression of such a theme demands the finest feel for detail and paradox, not to mention the will to see the theme through. That will powers *Armed Forces*, but already you can hear the feel for detail and paradox begin to fumble: the vocals are often meandering, the rhythms muddy. The mostly claustrophobic sound of the album was right for the theme, but that sound took over on *Get Happy!!* and blurs the later cuts of *Taking Liberties*. Moving in parallel to the 2-Tone craze for sixties black music as found in ska and rock steady, Costello may have gone to Motown and Stax for the basics of *Get Happy!!*, but all that came through was an echo: Motown changes are there, but everything else of Motown, and close to everything of Costello, is suffocated. The singing is impossible to follow; you tune out. Hints buried beneath the surface stay buried. There's no room for emphasis in the sound, no room for the kind of pause that allowed Costello to stop "Watching the Detectives" dead in its tracks, and you in yours. Costello's ability to speak as the man with the bad news dried up; from accuser he turned to complainer, but you couldn't find the object.

You can hear all of this on *Taking Liberties*, along with no indication of what might come next. Costello's great theme is hardly exhausted, though it may, for the time being, have exhausted him, or closed in on him. I think it remains the key to his career: that will to take revenge on the guilty conscience he has received from the past. The question now is whether Costello can find the music, re-create the craft, to keep the key turning. Yes, he's a star, with a year or so of free ride left in his name, but he's never given the slightest evidence he's interested in stardom for its own sake.

—*Village Voice*,
17–23 September 1980

The Roots of Punk,
#783

I *Me Mine*, by George Harrison, is published by Genesis Publications, Guildford, Surrey, England. It is four hundred pages long, illustrated, boxed, and gilt-edged. It costs $354, and comes in a signed, numbered, limited edition of two thousand copies. But what is it? The ultimate negation of the democratic impulses of popular culture? Sure to be worth at least $1,000 at the 1984 Beatle Collectors Convention? Certain to be marked down to $19.95 by Christmas '81? A practical joke by Eric Idle and the Rutles? Or the final solution to Beatlemania?

Putting philosophical considerations aside for the moment, *I Me Mine* can be described thusly: a sixty-odd-page memoir by George, as told to and occasionally interrupted by longtime Beatle retainer Derek Taylor, and decorated with lovely Rockwell Kentish line cuts; a portfolio of photographs ("Plates") from early to late, including a quadruple foldout depicting the entire Liverpool Institute of 1956; and, taking up most of the volume, the words to all of George's songs, from "Don't Bother Me" to "Blown Away," his various comments on same, plus color reproductions of holograph versions on pieces of hotel stationery, wet napkins, and the like. The paper, printing, and design are of extremely high quality, as befits the book's price— though the careful reader, or investor, will find a defective *a* on page 35 and a misplaced *r* on page 39. Since there can be no second printing of a limited edition of this sort, these are errors we, or someone, will have to live with.*

---

* *I Me Mine* was later published in a $12.95 edition by Simon & Schuster. The errors were not corrected.

George's memoir will surprise few in its confluence of exalted sentiments (". . . try to imagine the soul entering the womb of the woman living in 12 Arnold Grove, Wavertree, Liverpool 15," he begins), down-to-earth language ("Well, it was very heavy"), and rampant psychobabble ("Just before he [Brian Epstein] died he was on the verge of possible realisation which might have brought him to another level"). Though one's eyes do tend to glaze over, there are moments of pathos: George's comment on school ("It moulded us into being frightened"), his recollection of the recommendation he received upon graduating from Liverpool Institute (" 'I cannot tell you what his work is like because he has not done any' "), and his thoughts on his time as a Beatle, which he now sees as an essentially trivial experience. And there is one truly astonishing story. The great "My Sweet Lord"/"He's So Fine" plagiarism suit still goes on, it seems: former Beatles manager Allen Klein, having come to the end of his suits against the former mop tops, has now bought "the rights to 'He's So Fine' "—from which, a court determined, George "subconsciously" took the melody of "My Sweet Lord"—"and the right to continue the suit." (Which brings up an interesting question: why didn't *George* buy "He's So Fine," and thus the right to sue himself? Imagine the tax breaks!)

To return to philosophical matters: can the outrageous price of this volume possibly be justified? Of course it can, and in at least three ways. First, when original Beatle artifacts are fetching hundreds and even thousands of dollars on the open market, George can hardly be faulted for producing an expensive artifact of his own. Second, if John Lennon can charge $250,000 for a cow, George can charge $354 for a book. Third, *I Me Mine* continues an honorable (or honourable) tradition. Books of this sort—privately printed, bound in fine leather, so delicate and elegant one feels derelict turning the pages without gloves on—have for generations been the responsibility of rich, harmlessly eccentric English gentlemen. Such books usually take as their

subject the history of the local ruined abbey, a family geneal-
ogy, or the principles of an obscure religious sect, often headed
by the author, the membership of which is generally confined to
friends, relatives, and employees of the author hoping to maintain a place in the author's will. George's testament, covering as
it does both the Great Chain of Being and the assorted wisdom
of many, many swamis and other flame-keepers, cozily inhabits
the latter two categories. Indeed, it may be all to the good that
I Me Mine costs so much—any cheaper and blank-faced young
persons would be hustling it in airports.

—*Rolling Stone,*
18 September 1980

Yes Nukes

Forget what you've read about *No Nukes*. This documentary of the MUSE (Musicians United for Safe Energy) shows staged in New York City in September 1979 doesn't "knock your socks off," and it isn't "the most vibrant concert movie that has been made." As a film, it's second-rate. As music and politics, it's a study in puerility.

No Nukes begins and ends on the unmistakable note of the well-heeled Good Cause: a smugness that defines the movie cinematically, musically, and politically. Unlike *Woodstock*, it makes no attempt to build excitement through imaginative camera work and editing. Remember how stunning the *Woodstock* filmmakers made nine otherwise-unlistenable minutes of Ten Years After's "I'm Going Home"? Here the appeal of the performers is taken for granted. Save for the hopelessly *Hair*-like, all-hands-on-deck finale of the Doobie Brothers' "Takin' It to the Streets," the camera focuses on individuals, not groups: stars sell. You soon realize the filmmakers have one trick—the soulful close shot with a bit of movement at the edges of the frame—and the picture goes stale visually.

Unlike *The Last Waltz*, the movie isn't personalized; that is, we get lots of persona (Carly Simon, in her unzipped jumpsuit, isn't singing to the audience, she's auditioning for *Vogue*) and very little personality. There's a good deal of backstage footage (mostly of Simon, James Taylor, and Graham Nash), but the main impression is that you're privileged to catch the stars in an unguarded moment. Nor is there any effort to fix the peculiar emotional depths of a specific piece of music—which is probably just as well, given that Simon, Taylor, Nash, the

Doobies, Crosby, Stills & Nash, John Hall, Bonnie Raitt, and Jesse Colin Young are not the Band, Van Morrison, Muddy Waters, Ronnie Hawkins, and Bob Dylan. And unlike *Monterey Pop*, *No Nukes* offers almost no sense that the musicians are taking chances: they perform as pop entertainers, dishing out their hits. A possible exception is Jackson Browne, who delivers a searing and dramatic "Running on Empty" as if he's discovering what the song is all about as he sings it.

The MUSE folk, most of them, appear on-screen as if they have nothing to worry about. The backstage head-shaking over the outrages of nuclear (mispronounced throughout as "nuke-ular") power—Graham Nash can hardly *believe* what Ralph Nader is telling him—is stagy. We know that our-friend-the-atom will be more firmly in place next year than it is now; we don't believe the same of the stars on camera. Their indignation seems secondhand, or borrowed for the occasion—or just stupid. That's partly the result of the filmmakers' fascination with James and Carly, and partly the result of ditties like John Hall's "Power." "But please," he sings to a conventional L.A. fake-rock backing, "take all your poison power away." The presence of computer sax riffs, the horrible use of the supplicative voice, and the inevitable use of the paranoid "you" are enough to make a well-informed citizen opt *for* nuclear power. Worse—though admittedly hilarious—is Graham Nash's "Barrel of Pain" (the reference is to the containers of radioactive waste dumped off the Farallon Islands near San Francisco): "I can see the Farallones from my kitchen window . . . I can barely stand it, what you're doing to me, to me!"

Me, me! That's the politics of *No Nukes*. The performers who speak out in *No Nukes* mainly get it across that their peace of mind is threatened—if James Taylor, with all his money and fame, is worried, shouldn't you be? And such solipsism isn't merely individual—it's regional, or, rather, provincial. One of the most striking moments in *No Nukes* comes during some of the off-concert footage, at a New York City street fair. An activist dressed as a clown approaches a middle-aged man—a Californian, as it turns out—and engages him in nuke debate. "People should vote [on the question of nuclear power]," says the earnest clown. "People did vote," says the man, speaking of the 1976 defeat of Proposition 15, the measure meant to effectively end the construction of nuclear plants in California. "Yes," says the clown in horror and triumph, sealing the argument, "but not in New York!" In other words, if it hasn't happened to *me*, it hasn't happened.

Real politics are the opposite of solipsism: they have to do with an understanding of what you share with others like, or unlike, yourself. Real politics are not a matter of "concern"; they are a matter of a confrontation with events and ideas that leave a person irrevocably changed. Real politics involve the realization that life does not separate into categories. There's less than nothing of this in *No Nukes*—nothing of it in the rhetoric, nothing of it in the "let's get together and take it to the streets 'cause the times they are a-changin'" lyrics, and nothing of it in the music itself, unless "Running on Empty" is again the exception. Nuclear power is presented as an issue of monumental importance, but also as an issue that's complete unto itself—politically sanitized, as it were.

What's most offensive about *No Nukes* is not the insistence that the question of nuclear power is politically crucial—quite obviously it is, and in myriad ways that have little to do with the "safe energy" cottage industries that will be funded by *No Nukes* money (bail and legal defense for antinuke protesters will not be funded). What's most offensive is the implicit insistence that no rational person could be more concerned with any other issue—or think that any other issue might be more usefully addressed by rock 'n' roll singers, or be more effectively dealt with through the money rock 'n' roll singers are uniquely able to raise.

One thinks, for example, of the matter of abortion rights—of the Hyde Amendment, which prohibits Medicaid payments for abortions for poor women, and of the so-called right-to-life movement, which may well succeed in prohibiting abortion altogether. When the Corrie Bill, Great Britain's version of the Hyde Amendment, came up for a vote in Parliament earlier this year, rock 'n' roll groups organized, and not just all-women groups; why has nothing similar happened in the United States? Is it possible that Bonnie Raitt and Carly Simon have never had abortions, or that James Taylor, Graham Nash, and Jackson Browne were never happy their girlfriends or wives could get them?

It's possible, but it isn't likely. Safe energy is a safe issue— controversial but marketable, and marketable partly because it's safely controversial: *The China Syndrome* was there first, after all. That's one reason we're offered *No Nukes* and not, say, *Freedom of Choice*. The deeper reason remains solipsism. Nuclear power does indeed threaten the rich along with the poor (though it's unlikely much radioactive waste will be stored under the beach at Malibu or beneath the Dakota in Manhattan), and it takes little thought to figure this out. The Hyde Amendment does not threaten rock stars, and it takes considerable thought to understand that the right-to-life movement and its New Right allies are bent on a transformation of American society similar to the theocratic transformation of present-day Iran. Raising money for congresswomen, congressmen, and senators targeted by antiabortionists would be a good, useful step in opposition—action that would have a great deal more impact than anything that can be expected to result from the profits of *No Nukes*. But rock stars can afford abortions—and the issue would be more than controversial, it would be divisive. Certain singers, conceivably Bob Dylan no less than Donny and Marie, might organize counter concerts; some theater owners would refuse to show a *Freedom of Choice* film. Some cinemas would be picketed; others might be firebombed. This would lead to real politics, but it would also be trouble.

Which leaves, as far as *No Nukes* is concerned, one overriding question: what about Bruce? It's Springsteen's picture in the ads that's bringing the crowds into the theaters, and it's his performance—or his mere appearance—that has the fans cheering. Well, he's all right. He sings "The River," the title tune from his soon-to-come album; it's a well-meant tale of working-class defeat, but "Up Shit Creek" might better describe both the fate of the song's characters and the song itself. He performs "Thunder Road" messily and closes with a spirited "Quarter to Three," which is sabotaged by atrocious sound. He was far more exciting tossing out a bit of "Rosalita" in last year's TV special *Heroes of Rock 'n' Roll*—but that was a far more exciting film.

The latest word on U.K. neo-revisionist-postpunk-avant-garde: *Born in Flames*, a Rough Trade press release says, is the title of a 1929 Soviet film about the struggle of the Red Army during the civil war of 1918–20. It's also the title of a new single by Red Crayola, a group of moonlighting Londoners that includes recent Pere Ubu recruit Mayo Thompson (who headed the original Red Crayola in Houston during the psychedelic sixties) on guitar, Gina Birch of the Raincoats on bass, Epic Soundtracks of the just disbanded Swell Maps on drums, and Lora Logic of Essential Logic on saxophone. Lora takes the lead, twisting lyrics that depict a fantasy of the-U.S.A.-after-the-revolution into a pattern in which a lust for abstraction battles random images of class war, capitalist iniquity, solidarity, and political heroism. With words by Art & Language, a team of visual artists, the song is insufferably Stalinist and naïve on a lyric sheet; on record it's the most surprising 45 I've heard this summer. There is one haunting couplet: "Of America's mysteries/ None remain."

—*New West*,
22 September 1980

Success and Failure
in the Wilderness

Van Morrison is thirty-five, a Belfast-born mystic raised on the faith of Jehovah's Witnesses and American R&B who lives in a house on a hill in Marin County. Don Van Vliet, a.k.a. Captain Beefheart, is thirty-nine, a son of the San Fernando Valley, raised (by himself, it would seem) on avant-garde art, L.A. doo-wop, and Delta blues, who lives in a trailer in the Mojave Desert. Morrison is a near mainstream performer (his artistic progeny includes Bruce Springsteen and Graham Parker) who has had hit singles and popular albums. Van Vliet is a cult legend (believers include Joe Strummer of the Clash, John Lydon of PiL, and David Thomas of Pere Ubu) whose discography covers everything from seminal masterpieces to failed sellouts, each one a certified commercial flop. Both Morrison and Beefheart are radical individualists whose work is about freedom—how do you get it, what do you do with it, how do you keep it?—and both can be expected to be working on the problem fifteen years from now, just as both were working on it fifteen years ago. Any summing up of Morrison or Beefheart, be it canonization or write-off, is a fraud—which is what makes their failures interesting and their successes incomplete.

Morrison's new failure—his album *Common One*—is interesting mainly because it raises the difficult question of how he's going to get out of it. Given that since the appearance of "Mystic Eyes" in 1965 you could say that as a soul man Van Morrison is a great lyric poet, his more visionary tunes (James Brown gathers heather) suggest, say, Yeats: on *Common One* Morrison insists on the connection, which means the tunes don't remotely suggest it. With two of the six cuts passing by at more

than fifteen minutes each (making them by far the longest numbers he's ever released), Morrison has time to claim his roots—
he very nearly has time to research them, write up his findings,
publish a book, and watch it go out of print. Instead, he name-
drops. "Yeats and Lady Gregory corresponded, corresponded,
corresponded," he announces, his familiar obsessive repetition
no longer a means to magic but a note on an index card. "James
Joyce wrote streams of consciousness books." "Did you ever
hear about Wordsworth and Coleridge. . . . Did you ever hear
about William Blake?"

Since as a lyric poet, or even as a lyric poetaster, Morrison
is a great soul man, this shouldn't matter: on the hypnotizing
"You Don't Pull No Punches But You Don't Push the River,"
Van was searching for the Veedon Fleece, and no one's ever
figured out what that is. Van's lyrics count, but rhythms and
vocals pitched between heaven and hell can make the most
clichéd phrases new. On *Common One* the singing is so charac-
terless and the sax- and trumpet-led ensemble playing so self-
effacing that the mention of a famous name becomes an event—
something to hang onto. I mean, the highlights of this album
include the ringing of the telephone, and the ringing isn't on the
record. Always a jazz fan, but never a jazz purveyor for more
than a cut every few lps, Van's jazziest outing recalls not Duke
Ellington but the refined and arid textures of the West Coast
cool jazz of the fifties—music that in retrospect captures the
mainstream spiritual emptiness of the Eisenhower era far more
profoundly than such touchstones as "Mr. Sandman" or "(How
Much Is That) Doggie in the Window." Sure, there are hints of
Miles Davis's *Sketches of Spain* and even *In a Silent Way*—
hints buried in a tedium almost heroic in its refusal to quit.

Common One offers a Van Morrison with nothing to say and
a limitless interest in getting it across—to himself. Neither the
music nor the singing makes any move toward a listener. (At a
recent concert Morrison barely acknowledged the presence of
the audience, which is not unusual for him, and compounded the

fifties-hipster persona implicit in his new songs by smoking five cigarettes in the course of nine tunes, which is.) Correctly understood as one of the handful of true and sustaining originals in rock 'n' roll, never enough of a star to fall from pop grace and for ten years sufficiently steady commercially to maintain label support, Van Morrison has access to freedom in popular art—freedom to experiment, freedom from the demands of a fanatic but fickle audience, freedom from the need to go disco—and this time around he's come up with perhaps his most shapely version of freedom. It's most shapely because it's the most false: the purest solipsism.

If solipsism is a dead end for Morrison, it's Don Van Vliet's starting point. Having just released his eleventh album, *Doc at the Radar Station*, the man remains a hermit who complains that lack of promotion has kept him from fame and financial security—as if his cranky, grating music and Captain Ahab voice were ever promotable. Though you can tote up any number of good influences for Van Vliet—the crazed Southern California fifties R&B of the Coasters, the Medallions, and Richard Berry, the city blues of Howlin' Wolf and the country blues of Charley Patton, the flights of Charlie Parker—none holds still long enough for comfort. His lyrics are difficult to follow—even his song titles ("Flavor Bud Living" is a new one) may discourage the curious. Far more than Van Morrison's, Van Vliet's career depends on a belief that the artist molders in his garret (or trailer), forgotten, rejected by his time, honored only by history.

However deeply Van Vliet may hold to these verities, though, his music explodes them. His voice is serious but not solemn, and sometimes his maddeningly dense songs are merely wildly complex jokes, the pun working for him as blind and holy repetition works for Morrison. As with the painter Henri Rousseau, with whom Beefheart may have more in common than any rock 'n' roller, the surreal reveals the prosaic, the prosaic reveals the surreal—Van Vliet's music only seems hard to hear, and were it ever played on the radio it might sound perfectly obvious. And Van Vliet has not been ignored: were it not for his epochal, two-record *Trout Mask Replica*, released in 1969, punk might never have come into being and certainly would never have sustained itself past 1977. Captain Beefheart was the text his followers plundered when they needed to find out how to turn rant into style.

Van Vliet will never be a star in his own country (maybe in Japan). He cannot make his music accessible—when he tries, as he did in 1974 with the hopefully titled *Unconditionally Guaranteed*, he just sounds stupid and worn-out. Either he'll make hermits' records that implode or put together a set of prophecies that will find its listeners no matter how fast it ends up in the cutout bins—and it's the latter that he's done with *Doc at the Radar Station*.

"God, please fuck my mind for good," Van Vliet calls out at the end of this record; it's a harrowing cry, but after *Radar Station*'s twelve songs it doesn't seem likely God could do it. The album is a rampage that pulls back again and again into fragments of synthesized string sections for relief, a breath of air, a new point of view; as he's always done at his best, Van Vliet plays his band like an instrument, every moment apparently thought out, every nightmare fully analyzed. These lines from "Brickbats" ("Brickbats fly my fireplace," it begins, pun in place) catch both the musical momentum and the images that suspend it:

> My mind caught by the corner
> Gradually decides it's safe
> Becomes a bat itself
> Flexes its little claws
> Tests its leather wings with loud hollow pops
> Around the room threatening to dash its brains
> Somehow at the last minute retreats

Beefheart's songs may not be accessible—that is, conventional—but anyone's terrors, and anyone's delight at seeing them plain, are accessible through his songs. What's also accessible (airplay, distribution, and promotion aside) is his commitment to his muse and his demons, bat and God alike. Van Vliet's version of freedom is the mastery of a man who cannot make anyone else's music.

As he has proved in the past, a man who can't make anyone else's music is not the same as a man who won't. His commitment, presented with the force of *Doc at the Radar Station*, can be inspiring, but it can also be a trap: saying no to whoever's making the rules doesn't guarantee vision—and a lot of people simply don't have anything to compromise. Many rockers less talented than Van Vliet—John Lydon, for example—can listen to him, buy his myth, and find themselves seduced by the sentimental, nineteenth-century romanticization of the artist that sustains Van Vliet, but what they'll miss is the fact that while that notion of where art comes from may sustain him, it couldn't interest him less. What interests Van Vliet, perhaps in spite of his better judgment and his peace of mind, is what has often interested artists who make a difference: the fate of humanity, the boundary between dream and waking, the nature of language, the truth of being. Stuff like that.

—*New West,*
28 October 1980

Suspicious Minds

Delta 5 is a band from Leeds, England: three women and two men, all in their early twenties, who come out of the same leftist-punk milieu that produced the Gang of Four and the Mekons. They make pointed, combative, accusatory dance music that sometimes reaches a point of fury and holds onto it for dear life, sometimes steps neatly past fury into a sort of disdainful hilarity, and sometimes inexplicably combines the two. Closing a set with "Where Were You?," a tune borrowed from the Mekons, the three women rail out the seemingly pathetic question

> Would you ever be my friend
> Do you like me?

as if they've got their hands on the neck of the person who can't find time for them—and as if they're squeezing so hard there's no way that person will ever get an answer out.

With just two U.K. singles ("Mind Your Own Business"/ "Now That You're Gone" and "Anticipation"/"You") for London's Rough Trade behind them, Delta 5 arrived in the United States this fall for a twenty-two-date tour. When I first saw them, at the Berkeley Square, one-time cocktail lounge converted into a punk venue, the band was worn down from a day's drive from Los Angeles and unhappy with the club; the show was all hard edges. The smell of vomit rose from the not very crowded dance floor, hardly a smile was betrayed onstage, and every verbal slap in the songs—most of them constructed like quarrels—found its mark. Bethan Peters, bass and vocals, sang with a flat, sullen, unbreaking stare; guitarist Alan Briggs, sharing the attack like Andy Gill of the Gang of Four, cracked or centered the rhythms of the Delta 5's two, sometimes three bassists with grating, shuddering rhythmic noise and tiny comments of his own—and without any facial expression whatever. Kelv Knight, drums, and Ros Allen, bass and vocals, stayed in the background, a rhythm section within a rhythm section. Julz Sale, vocals and occasional guitar and bass, kept the foreground moving.

She doesn't work from the center of the stage, and she's not the lead singer—no one is, and Bethan probably does more of the singing than Julz. (In the Leeds tradition of erasing pop personality cults, Delta 5 use first names only; last names cited above were unearthed solely out of respect for the *New West* tradition of dogged investigative reporting.) But with her hooded eyes and praying-mantis frame, Julz is the most visually striking—the first focus for what the band's songs are all about. Mouthing the beat while bouncing off-mike with one hand jammed in a pocket, or back at the mike and communicating as much of a song in her face as she does with her voice— her expression shifting from desperation to spite to sardonic dismissal to contempt to bitterness—Julz counters Bethan's stare and completes it. The impression left by Delta 5 is one of overwhelming sobriety: a sobriety that excludes not laughter but romanticism.

Delta 5 play love songs—though songs about the situations love creates might be a more accurate way of putting it. They are postpunk love songs: the singers accept the inevitability of love but maintain their suspicions. The music could almost be derived from the little dissertation on The Love Song as a Staple of Pop Language that Andy Gill read out of the murk of the Gang of Four's "Anthrax" ("You occasionally wonder why all these groups do sing about it all the time . . ."). Delta 5 continue questioning the love song without abandoning its form— but they fool with it. The group's tunes are made up of the most prosaic details (errands, getting drunk, no longer having to share a pack of cigarettes, sleeping): details flooded with a flurry of harsh chords, a strident chorus of shouts, a cry of pain or anger, any of which can turn a detail into a touchstone. The performance is like an ongoing argument—though often the words are so sharp they're more like the perfect lines you think up after an argument is dead—and the performance has a startlingly objective quality. Gender is no defense against a Delta 5 love song; as Julz said after the show, there's hardly a line in their tunes that suggests a given character is male or another female.

Delta 5's members are unmistakable as individuals after a couple of numbers, but there's not a hint that the songs are confessional—that is, in pop terms, heartfelt statements protected by the high school homily that if what you say is an expression of your own feelings, no one can criticize it. Delta 5 make critical music, and it is precisely this assumption the band criticizes. The Gang of Four recently put out a song called "Why Theory"; Delta 5 might be asking "Why emotion." That doesn't mean they dispense with it; it means they don't take it for granted.

Delta 5 songs are about distance between people; they don't so much try to close those distances as make sense of them. The way a song can build from resignation to outrage to venom is a tactic here; so is a feel for ordinary absurdity. As with "Mind Your Own Business":

> Can I have a taste of your ice cream?
> Can I lick the crumbs from your table?
> Can I interfere in your crisis?
> No! Mind your own business!

Or "You":

> Who was seen with somebody else?
> (YOU, YOU, YOU, YOU!)
> Who left me behind at the baker's?
> (YOU, YOU, YOU, YOU!)

Who forgot to phone last Tuesday?
(YOU, YOU, YOU, YOU!)
Who took me to the Wimpy's for a big night out?
(YOU, YOU, YOU, YOU!)
Who likes sex only on Sundays?
(YOU, YOU, YOU, YOU!)

On record or onstage, these songs are a lot trickier than they look on paper: assaults on the unfeeling people who suffer the accusations, but also neat parodies of the people who are doing the accusing. In "Mind Your Own Business," the listener is drawn to the supplicant who is trying to break through to a friend or lover with sarcasm too funny to resist, but it is resisted, Alan cuts up the tune with guitar lines that hang the questions in the air, and by the end of the number, with Ros, Bethan, and Julz hammering out "MIND YOUR OWN BUSINESS!" with everything they've got, it's not at all clear which party is victim and which is victimizer. With "You," the petulance of the singers may take the edge off the argument; the delight with which the argument is delivered puts the edge back on. Another song, "Makeup," attacks that very thing, but the women in Delta 5 wear a lot of it.

Delta 5 sometimes encore with one of the Gang of Four's old "ten past one" songs ("It's ten past one and you're gone and I'm all alone," as the Gang of Four's Jon King once put it): "Something they used to do before they decided love songs were ideologically unsound," Ros explained with a grin. Delta 5's own music—which never lets a received idea about love, sex, or friendship through its mesh of rhythms and voices—suggests that the band knew an opportunity when they saw it.

Still, that very rejection of the love song—an overdue pop event, central to the punk discovery of any aspect of life from nature to politics as fit subject matter for a song, a discovery that in most punk or postpunk hands has led mainly to cynicism or misogyny—was probably crucial to Delta 5's ability to make the love song new; the political ferment in Leeds, where "ideology" is not an idle word, was probably no less so. Leeds has long been known for turning out radicalized college students; the University of Leeds (Ros's school) and Leeds Polytechnic (Bethan's), plus the social freedom provided by endemic unemployment and easy access to the dole, have made possible the kind of student/nonstudent bohemia where people can experiment. The Mekons and the Gang of Four, known as smart troublemakers in their college days, were part of this, and Delta 5, before the fact, were part of them: Ros played bass on the Mekons' first single, the wonderful "Never Been in a Riot" (some of them had, though: an anarchist protest against restrictions on foreign students); Kelv spent a week as the Gang of Four's drummer when Hugo Burnham thought he'd go back to acting.

There were many friendships in common; in fact, Ros, Bethan, and Julz started up their group (harmonizing on Parliament-Funkadelic's chant of "Shit! Goddamn! Get off your ass and jam!") because most of their friends seemed to be in bands and they felt left out. Julz, who left her home in Stratford-on-Avon for the Leeds scene after punk arrived, has fond memories of the day she got a copy of "Never Been in a Riot." Dressed in full punk regalia, due at a family wedding and desperate to hear the record, she finally convinced the celebrants to let her put it on, and immediately found her grandmother requesting that she "do some of her punk stuff"—presumably the pogo. She offered to throw up.

Leeds is also the home of the fascist British Movement, which is distinguished from its more famous parent, the National Front, by a complete lack of embarrassment at its Nazi origins. Unemployment and the dole underlie not only bohemia but also the great no-future so trumpeted in 1977, and the ideology of no-future has made it easy for the British Movement, setting up drinks all around, to recruit plenty of punks specifically to harass "Communist" bands. Add an extremely well-

focused consciousness of sexism on the left and a bitter reasser-
tion of male dominance among threatened young men on the
right, and the result is violence.

In such a context, a band with three women and two men is
an undeniable political statement; so is association with an
avowedly leftist band like the suspiciously named Gang of
Four, which gave Delta 5 their first gigs and with which Delta 5
have often played; so is out-front support for abortion rights,
and Delta 5 have appeared again and again at rallies and benefits in opposition to the Corrie Bill, the U.K.'s would-be anti-
abortion statute. And so, for that matter, is patronage of the
wrong pub on the wrong night. The members of Delta 5 don't
go out alone at night in Leeds, Bethan explained, "because we
might be followed and beaten up." It has happened before. One
evening, eight British Movement men, having recognized Ros
as a "Communist witch," trailed the five from a bar and attacked them. Gigs are commonly invaded, and sometimes broken up, by Sieg Heil-ing thugs; one night Bethan found herself
grabbing one erstwhile fascist by the hair and slamming his
head against the stage.

All of this—along with the shadow cast by the Yorkshire
Ripper—has gone into Delta 5's music, though the band may
never write any tunes that say so directly. Just as the punk-
student bohemia that drew the men and women in Delta 5 to
Leeds, and of which they're now a part, is one source of the
critical intelligence and paradoxical humor of their songs, a
wariness in the face of violence, and a readiness for it, is one
source of their music's hardness, its intensity and its quotidian
drama. Such qualities are not exactly beside the point when
what's really wanted is a first-class dance band.

As organized by Rough Trade's recently established American outlet in San Francisco—a combination record store, dis-
tributor, domestic label (Delta 5's first U.S. single, "Colour"/
"Try," will be issued soon), and booking agency—the Delta 5
tour was an almost perfect example of how to present an un-

known band. Choosing small or obscure venues over the larger halls available to a young band supporting a big-name act, Delta 5 headlined every gig, ensuring that those who came, no matter how few, would be up for what the band had to offer. The group spent three weeks on the West Coast, appearing at the Woman's Building in Los Angeles, a gay disco in San Francisco, and punk clubs as far north as Vancouver. With a full seven gigs in the Bay Area, there was time for word of mouth to spread, time for the band to counter the grim if effective show at Berkeley Square with an uproarious celebration of camaraderie at the Savoy Tivoli two weeks later, time for the band to get to know the territory and for the territory to get to know the band.

Those who saw Delta 5 this time around are not likely to mistake their approach for that of anybody else. "There wasn't much of a crowd in Palo Alto," said Bethan, a few days after a show at that town's Keystone club. "And someone kept shouting, 'Why, why are there *five* of you?' I don't know why that bothered him. I said, 'Why are there five of *you*?' "

Continuing the Real Life Rock coverage of domestic politics—despite the complaints of readers who think music critics should know their place—I asked David Geffen, thirty-seven-year-old record company head, why he thought Governor Jerry Brown might have appointed a thirty-seven-year-old record company head to the University of California Board of Regents. There had been a good deal of quid pro quo speculation; Geffen spoke to all of it without my having to bring any of it up. "I don't know why Jerry Brown appointed me," Geffen said. "I don't know him well, and I found out only the day before the appointment was announced. It certainly wasn't because Linda Ronstadt [who records for Asylum, the label Geffen started in 1971 and left some years ago] suggested it, I can tell you that. I suppose he thought I'd do a serious job, which I will, and because he thought I'd be closer to people in college than anyone else on the board, which I probably am. I know there's a lot of talk that I'll be putting on concerts for Jerry Brown, and I'm insulted by that. I don't put on concerts, and I've never raised a penny for Jerry Brown."

A few days later, Geffen's new self-named label released its first record: John Lennon and Yoko Ono's "(Just Like) Starting Over," which is also the first music—and very nearly the first word—to be heard from Lennon in a solid five years. The layoff hasn't hurt John's voice—he's singing beautifully—and the music, if a bit formulaic, is catchy big-beat fifties rock. As for the song itself—well, when John opened with "We have grown, we have grown," everyone in the room groaned. The Lennon/Ono album, *Double Fantasy*, will be out this month, accompanied by interviews, cover stories, and, for all I know, interplanetary holograms. Keep your fingers crossed.

—New West,
17 November 1980

The Next President
of the United States

In October Bruce Springsteen released *The River*, which went swiftly to number one, and began a tour that before it ends, sometime in the summer of 1981, will take him and the E Street Band across the length and breadth of the United States, into Canada, to Great Britain, to Europe, Japan and Australia. As interesting as this event is its context.

Rock 'n' roll is, today, too big for any center. It is so big, in fact, that no single event—be it Springsteen's tour, Sid Vicious's overdose, or John Lennon's first album in five years— can be much more than peripheral. Writing in August 1977, Lester Bangs may have gotten it right: "We will never again agree on anything as we agreed on Elvis."

Rock 'n' roll now has less an audience than a series of increasingly discrete audiences, and those various audiences ignore each other. With the exceptions of disco in the U.S. and reggae in the U.K., blacks and whites have not had so little to do with each other musically since the early fifties, when rock 'n' roll began—and those exceptions are linked to the emergence of hip racism in the U.S. (many discos that play black music "discourage" the patronage of blacks) and of organized racism among white youth in the U.K. The audience that has gathered around punk and postpunk groups may have a grip on the formal history of the music—the account, as written by white critics, of the music's pursuit of new forms and new ideas —but that pursuit has never had so little to do with what most rock consumers actually hear or, for that matter, what they've heard of.

In one sense, this is salutary and inevitable. The lack of a center means the lack of a conventional definition of what rock 'n' roll is, and that fosters novelty. Rules about what can go into a performance and, ultimately, about how and what it can communicate are not only unenforced, they're often invisible, both to performer and audience. That rock 'n' roll has persisted for so long, and spread to such diverse places, precludes its possession by any single generation or society—and this leads not only to fragmentation but to a vital, renewing clash of values. We agreed on Elvis, after all, because he was the founder, because he represented the thing itself; if we will never agree on anyone as we agreed on Elvis, it's equally true that Americans have never agreed on anyone as they agreed on George Washington. But this state of affairs is also debilitating and dispiriting. The fact that the most adventurous music of the day seems to have taken up residence in the darker corners of the marketplace contradicts rock 'n' roll as aggressively popular culture that tears up boundaries of race, class, geography and (oh yes) music; the belief that the mass audience can be reached and changed has been the deepest source of the music's magic and power. The music does not now provide much evidence that this belief is based on anything like reality, and on a day to day basis this means there is no longer common ground for good rock 'n' roll conversation. To find an analogy one must imagine that many Americans who care passionately about baseball would be unfamiliar with Reggie Jackson. Bands with very broad—or at least very big—audiences continue to exist, of course, but they don't destroy boundaries; they disguise them, purveying music characterized principally by emotional vapidity and social vagueness. No doubt the Doobie Brothers have their fans among the Moral Majority as among the ACLU, but that doesn't mean the Doobie Brothers have given such people anything to talk about.

A concert by Bruce Springsteen offers many thrills, and one is that he performs as if none of the above is true. The implicit promise of a Bruce Springsteen concert is that This Is What

It's All About—This Is the Rock. Whether the promise is more than a night's happy illusion is, at the time, less important than whether Springsteen can live up to it.

As songwriter, singer, guitarist, and bandleader, he appears at once as the anointed successor to Elvis Presley and as an impostor who expects to be asked for his stage pass; his show is, among other things, an argument about the nature of rock 'n' roll after twenty-five years. The argument is that rock 'n' roll is a means to fun that can acknowledge the most bitter defeats, that it has a coherent tradition which, when performed, will reveal possibilities of rock 'n' roll the tradition did not previously contain.

Having posited a tradition Springsteen performs as if every bit of it is backing him up—rooting for him. This allows him to hit the boards as if his status as a rock 'n' roll star is both privileged and ordinary, and the result onstage is a unique combination of authority and prank. It means that at his finest, Springsteen can get away with almost anything, stuff that coming from anyone else would seem hopelessly corny and contrived—and that he can come up with stuff to get away with that most rockers since Little Richard would be embarrassed even to have thought of. Such as, in Portland, under the brooding eye of Mt. St. Helens, singing "On Top of Old Smokey."

Two nights later, on October 27 in Oakland, the best seat in the house—front row on the center aisle—was the prize of a small blond woman, a thirty-three-year-old attorney from San Francisco named Louisa Jaskulski. She spent the first hour and a half of the concert dancing in front of her chair—nothing fancy, just the sweetest, most private sort of movements, the kind of dance one might do in front of a mirror. She was so expressive she seemed to add a dimension to every song, and early into the second half of the concert Springsteen responded in kind. He leaped from the stage and, with a gesture of gleeful courtliness, offered Jaskulski his arm, whereupon the two cakewalked up the aisle to the astonishment of everyone in the arena. This wasn't Elvis bestowing a kiss on a lucky female, who then, according to the inescapable script, collapsed in tears like a successful supplicant at Lourdes; prancing down that aisle, Springsteen was not a star and Jaskulski was not a fan. They were a couple. He'd picked up a hint, asked for a dance, and she had said yes.

An hour later Springsteen almost topped that moment. Introducing the band just before heading into "Rosalita," he added a touch to his usual obeisance to Clarence Clemons, the enormous, splendidly decked-out black saxophone player: "King of the World . . . Master of the Universe . . . and . . . the Next President of the United States!" In two seconds it seemed like an obvious thing to do; one second before that it had been a shock so delicious it almost justified the campaign. Then, hard into "Rosalita," Springsteen and the band reached that point when the song hangs in the air—when the pace is most fierce and the question of whether our hero will get the girl most in doubt. At the precise moment when the tension almost cracks the song in half, Springsteen turned to Clemons and kissed him square on the lips.

On Halloween night in Los Angeles, fog covered the stage. Six crew members, dressed as ghouls, brought out a coffin. Springsteen emerged and sang "Haunted House," a 1964 hit by a deservedly obscure rockabilly singer called Jumpin' Gene Simmons. Don't cringe—he could just as well have sung "Ding Dong the Witch Is Dead," a 1939 hit by the Munchkins.

Five days after that, in Phoenix, Springsteen did not introduce Clarence Clemons as the next president of the United States. Instead, he walked onstage and said, "I don't know what you thought about what happened last night. I think it's terrifying." Then he sang "Badlands," the most appropriate song he had to offer—for the time being.

As Jon Landau, now Springsteen's manager, wrote in 1968, an awareness of the Vietnam War could be felt all through Bob Dylan's *John Wesley Harding*; it is an almost certain bet that the songs Springsteen will now be writing will have something to do with the events of November 4. Those songs likely will not comment on those events; they will, I think, reflect those events back to us, fixing moods and telling stories that are, at present, out of reach. Not many rock 'n' rollers can be expected to react on this level. If Springsteen is able to do so, it will be at least in part because of his evident conviction that whether or not rock 'n' roll has a center, someone must act as if it does.

—*New West*,
22 December 1980

1981–1982

Life and Life Only

To hear that John Lennon had been murdered by a fan, that he had been killed for who and what he was, was like watching someone you love being hit by a car. The mind struggles with the contradiction between concrete fact and disbelief, fights off the normal progression of time—stops time, trying to unmake the event. The mind turns the fact over and over, testing the words that convey the fact in order to see if the words really mean what they say.

One reads that the shooting of John Lennon is just one more example of an anonymous nobody seeking notoriety by knocking off a celebrity, but not only does this not seem to have been Mark Chapman's motive, there do not seem to be any other examples. I don't think there are any precedents for the murder of a public figure by a person who was tied to his victim strictly through the roles both played as members of a popular culture. Because this has never happened before, we have to ask two questions: why John Lennon, and why now.

The Beatles and their fans played out an image of utopia, of a good life, and the image was that one could join a group and by doing so not lose one's identity as an individual but find it: find one's own voice. This was an image of utopia that could encompass every desire for love, family, friendship, or comradeship; while the Beatles were the Beatles, this image informed love affairs and it informed politics. It shaped one's sense of possibility and loss, of the worth of things.

At the heart of this cheeky, joyful, shiny utopia was romanticism: the best account of pop hopes and dreams anyone had ever heard. But that utopia was grounded—by John Lennon—

in wit, worry, contingency, doubt, and struggle. John Lennon
was part of the pleasure principle of the Beatles; no one who
heard him sing "Eight Days a Week" could miss that. But he
was also the reality principle of the Beatles, and that is why so
many became obsessed with him. If the Beatles were a common
adventure, John Lennon was its point man and its center. It
was John Lennon who was never satisfied with pop rewards,
who kept questions open and alive while the Beatles continued
—What is the group for? What can it do? When must it be
abandoned?—and it was John Lennon who, once the Beatles
ended, sustained the struggle over an image of utopia. He
broke that image in "God," but a new image of utopia, of what
it might mean to live a good life, to discover what a good life is,
was formed in the impossibly beautiful way he sang the last
few lines of that song: the way he sang, "I was . . . ," the way
he sang, ". . . but now."

Whatever else John Lennon was after that, he was never
again a pop star. Far more than Paul, George, or even down-to-
earth Ringo, John Lennon made himself real. Far more than
they or anyone else in post-Beatle culture, he communicated
the truth that some image of utopia was necessary—be it the
utopia of the great, Brontean passion he pursued with his wife
or the utopia of a song in which he said exactly what he meant
and was understood. This image of utopia was not solipsistic.
Out of reach and all the more precious for that, it always assumed the existence of other people, depended on their presence, be they Yoko Ono, or you, me, or Mark Chapman—and
because of the way John had sung "Anytime at All," "There's a
Place," "Money," "In My Life," or "Don't Let Me Down," and
because of the way he went on to sing "God," "Well Well Well,"
"Oh Yoko," "Stand by Me," or "Just Because," it never quite
lost its force. That is why it was John Lennon who was shot,
and not one of the celebrities now checking out the bodyguard
services.

Why now? Well, that is trickier. Yes, Mark Chapman seems

to have snapped. Yes, after five years John Lennon was speaking to an audience again, trying to find out what he had to say to it and what it had to say to him. Neither fact addresses the overriding truth that nothing like Lennon's killing has happened before. What does address it, I think, is the radical change in the nature of public discourse in the United States over the past year.

The secret message behind the election of Ronald Reagan on November 4th was that some people belong in this country, and some people don't; that some people are worthy, and some are worthless; that certain opinions are sanctified, and some are evil; and that, with the blessing of God, God's messengers will separate the one from the other. It is as if the Puritans have reached across three hundred years of American history to reclaim the society they once founded—accepting the worst vulgarization of their beliefs if it means that, once again, God and his servants will be able to look upon America and tell the elect from the reprobate, the redeemed from the damned.

Such a message likely did not, in any logical manner, inspire Mark Chapman. But such a message, which tells people they are innocent and others are to blame, can attach a private madness to its public justification. It can inform love affairs and it can inform politics. If Klansmen and Nazis had the right to kill Communists in Greensboro, and a jury said they did, then on a certain moral level you and I and Mark Chapman have the right to kill whoever it is that troubles our lives. I think this is why this unprecedented event has occurred now, and not before.

As critic Jim Miller has written, rock 'n' roll works as common experience and private obsession. The two cannot really be separated; indeed, one fuels the other. I have my own reasons for caring about John Lennon—a song, or a moment in *Help!*, that may never have affected you—but you have reasons that are fundamentally the same, and that is why it was other people's reactions to John Lennon's murder that produced in me the most overwhelming despair. To open the door and find a friend whose eyes were red; to see a man going about his business and then to catch the strip of black cloth around his arm; to walk into a friend's store and notice the picture of John Lennon she had placed behind the counter—those were the things that did it, that made the last sixteen years collapse on my head as if now it was time to pay for every moment of pleasure, affection, and friendship they had contained.

Four days after John Lennon was shot, when I woke up to find Beatle music off the radio and the story off the front page, that process by which the mind struggles with a fact it will not accept was still working. I scanned the front page again, to see if I'd missed anything; I ran the radio dial across the stations. Nothing. Does this mean, I thought, that it's over? That he's not dead anymore?

—*Rolling Stone*,
22 January 1981

Songs of Random Terror:
Real Life Rock Top Ten 1980

Since 1963 pop music has had to countenance assassination; now pop music contains it. Before the fact of John Lennon's killing, I tried to fix the place of rock 'n' roll in 1980, and I found myself drawn to Public Image Ltd.; after the fact, PiL sounds like the only band that was ready for it. It's not simply that John Lydon now sings songs of murder, random terror, and self-annihilation. It's also that he has, in the past, been beaten and razored on the streets of London—because he was a pop star, because of what he'd thought and said—and understands that the relationship between the performer and the public has become a matter of lethal ambiguity.

When PiL played to rabidly trendy crowds in San Francisco in May of 1980—crowds that seemed to be trying to prove they were punkier than apostate Lydon—the sound that came through most plainly was that of disdain, and no wonder: when Lydon handed the mike to people in the audience, the only word they gave him back was *fuck*. But on record the story has been very different. *Metal Box—Second Edition* in the United States—was an hour of vengeful, guilty rhythms: a dub abstract, enormous, burdensome. If you kept listening, you could hear Lydon shoulder the weight he'd called into being, hear him drive the weight away with rants that slowly revealed themselves as carefully reconstructed bad dreams, hear him claim triumph or admit defeat—for the moment.

Even more striking, I think, is PiL's new live album, *Paris au Printemps* (by "Image Publique S.A."—as *Metal Box* proved, this band is very big on keeping its concepts straight). With his chilling stare foreclosing even the possibility he might favor the curious with just one more rendition of "Pretty Vacant," Lydon has put himself in an adversary relationship with the audience that clings to the live-fast-die-young punk myth (right now, the only audience he has access to); it's at least as interesting, and as dangerous, as the adversary relationship Johnny Rotten maintained with society at large. In Paris the crowd was hostile, and PiL's response was music that is unrelentingly discomforting and full of emotional clarity: a white boy's version of the reggae concept of dread, which means freedom prized from fear.

"The likes of you and me is an embarrassment," Lydon chants—and what to make of that? The Real Life Rock Top Ten for 1980, offered below, provides no clues. In the case of John Lennon, there are all too many.

1. *London Calling*, the Clash. A double album of grand gestures and good jokes, movie stars and fascists, reggae and rockabilly, punk bravado and a Top 40 hit. For all of its outlaw sentimentality, plainly the album of the year—to be followed, in a few months, by a thirty-six-song package called *Sandinista!* I am not making this up.

2. Single of the year: was it "Call Me," Blondie's fabulous disco lead-in to *American Gigolo*? Tom Petty's "Refugee"? The Clash's "Train in Vain," which seemed trivial when it first hit the radio and now seems timeless? The deep left-field bid by the Anemic Boyfriends (from *Alaska*), whose "Guys Are Not Proud" featured two girls going *Yuuuuck* over such discoveries as "Guys are such creeps/ They'll even do it with sheep"? Nope, it was "Love Stinks" by the J. Geils Band, the funniest 45 since the Coasters' "Poison Ivy"—which, lyricist Jerry Leiber recently admitted, was really about VD. So much for the ocean of calamine lotion. Worst single: Steve Forbert's "Romeo's Tune," which could give smarminess a bad name.

3. The Leeds Faction, being composed of three quirky, in-

tense, politicized U.K. postpunk bands: the three-woman, two-man Delta 5; the one-woman, two-man Girls at Our Best!, who ended the year with the floating, sardonic lilt of "Politics"/"It's Fashion"; and the all-male Gang of Four, who saw the domestic release of their debut lp, *Entertainment!*, and followed it with an EP about the authoritarian personality.

4. *Have a Good Time (But Get Out Alive)*, Iron City House-rockers. Blood, toil, tears, and sweat, plus fantasies about Deborah Harry: the sound of a working-class bar band out of Pittsburgh (actually, they're still in Pittsburgh—the record went nowhere commercially). Signs of life: *Pretenders*, leader Chrissie Hynde's uncompromising account of growing up female in the Midwest; the lust in Dire Straits' *Making Movies*; Black Uhuru's hoodoo reggae breakthrough, *Sinsemilla*; X's fierce *Los Angeles*. Horrors: *Pearl Harbor and the Explosions*; the Roches' *Nurds*.

5. *Dirty Mind*, Prince. Prince is a twenty-one-year-old rude boy from Minneapolis, and as overdubbed one-man-band and inheritor of the falsetto he may be both the new Jimi Hendrix and the new Smokey Robinson. This is definitive postdisco black rock: gleeful funk shot through with punk momentum and shaped by Motown elegance. Subject matter includes a woman's seduction of her younger brother for the purpose of putting him to work as a prostitute, and the younger brother's seduction of a white virgin he meets as she's on her way to her wedding (walking down the street, in her gown, sure, never mind). He persuades her to perform an unmentionable act ("You're such a hunk," she sighs) and comes all over her wedding dress, thus convincing her to marry him instead.

6. The Birmingham Brotherhood, being composed of two racially mixed postreggae bands: the Beat, who delivered the tense dance music of *I Just Can't Stop It* and the dizzy, heartwarming "Stand Down Margaret (Dub)," a plea the prime minister has so far ignored; and UB40, named for Great Britain's unemployment benefits form, whose gray-toned, dully protest-

oriented *Signing Off* was rescued by the thirteen-minute "Madame Medusa." Picture it this way: a slick supper club singer blandly runs through a Gothic ballad inspired by, of all people, the same Tory PM he's heard the Beat damning on the radio; suddenly understanding what he's singing about, he rushes into the audience, shouting warnings. He dashes out of the club and into the street, accosts passersby, takes them by the lapels and screams at them: "RUN FOR YOUR LIFE SHE GONNA EAT YOU ALIVE!" The band shifts out of light reggae and into the darkest, ghostliest dub; the police arrive; the singer flees. He walks the streets for hours, shaken; finally, he makes it home to his bed-sitter, turns on an electric ring under cold coffee, lights a cigarette, and quietly talking to himself, thinks over the all-night odyssey that has changed his life.

7. The discovery of Buddy Holly's glasses, by Jerry Allen, Sheriff of Cerro Gordo County, Iowa, twenty-one years and sixty-four days after the plane crash in which they were presumed lost. Other notable reissues included the Melodians' *Premeditation*, stoic and peaceful reggae from the mid-sixties, and Billy "The Kid" Emerson's *Little Fine Healthy Thing*, early fifties R&B from the Sun studios.

8. *Musical Shapes*, Carlene Carter. The sassiest country and the sweetest rock, joyously produced by Nick Lowe—who, when Carlene made an honest man of him some months ago, became Johnny Cash's step-son-in-law.

9. "Like a Rolling Stone" at Longhi's, Lahaina, Maui, February 22. Longhi's is the ultimate laid-back watering hole; as I sat there that morning, the house radio tuned to KQMQ-FM and playing pop tunes that functioned strictly as unregistered background, Bob Dylan's greatest song came on. The languid crowd slowly turned from its pineapple and Bloody Mary breakfast; feet began moving, conversations died. Everyone *listened*, and everyone looked a bit more alive when the last notes faded. It was a stunning moment: irrefutable proof that "Like a Rolling Stone" cannot be used as Muzak.

As for Dylan himself, his return to the Warfield Theater in San Francisco far outstripped similar appearances in 1979. The previous shows were one hundred percent holy-writ rock; this time the ads promised nostalgia: all your favorites! For Dylan, now so fervently committed to Jesus, it seemed like the first real sellout of his career: a sad concession to his once doting audience, or a pathetic admission that he couldn't live without it. That was not how the music came across. Ending a two-week stand, Dylan gave a gruff, good-humored performance of what, that night, was on his mind: hard and syncopated gospel, an Appalachian ballad complete with autoharp, Little Willie John's "Fever," Dave Mason's startlingly apt "We Just Disagree," a few of his own, older numbers. It was the seventeenth anniversary of John F. Kennedy's assassination; Dylan closed with "A Hard Rain's A-Gonna Fall," which was written during the Cuban missile crisis of 1962—as far as most history books go, Kennedy's finest hour. It was steely, mean, implacable, and forgiving, and it sounded as if Dylan had written it the night before. Maybe ninety-nine-and-a-half won't do, but it did.

10. Most Valuable Player: Prime Minister Margaret Thatcher of the United Kingdom. Raising unemployment and inflation with her right hand, while slashing social services and pressing if-you're-white-you're-right immigration policies with her other right hand, she fostered an upsurge of music made in a critical spirit. From PiL's "Death Disco" to the Beat's wary bop, it was music in which critical energy was directed not only at the powers that be, but also at the seductive conservatism of pop itself: a symbolically crucial institution based on passive audiences, sexist role models, racist categories, banal ambitions, the hegemony of the charts. For some, no-future is turning out to mean take nothing for granted.

—*New West*,
January 1981

Ideal Home Noise

"**P**unk," wrote Isabelle Anscome in 1978, "is a mode of anarchy as much as the dadaist 'Cabaret Voltaire' in Zurich at the end of the First World War, and how many people today are particularly familiar with that?" Quite a lot of people, as it turned out. Punk had good taste in ancestors, and the mostly British artists who can be called the postpunk avant-garde are reaping the benefits: among them, the sense of worth and pleasure one can find in the realization that the past can break open the present, that history contains not only dubious lessons but authentic comrades.

One look at "Eisiger Wind," the new single by the three-woman postpunk band Liliput, tells the tale. In 1916, for a final dada performance, Cabaret Voltaire founder Hugo Ball dressed himself in a bizarre cardboard costume—variously described as the raiment of a "mystical bishop," an alchemist, or a satanist—and chanted a phonetic poem called "Karawane." Grinning on one side of the "Eisiger Wind" sleeve and trying to look serious on the other, the Liliput women—from Zurich, not coincidentally—are dressed in pieces of a virtually identical costume. Or, as a young factory worker caught up in the riots that have split Zurich for the past year put it, when asked by a reporter if she and her friends were Communists: "We are more influenced by British punk, German rockers, and the dada movement. . . ."

Which is to say—what? Fantasy revolution or serious business? Mystical bishop or satanic alchemist? Nothing so much, most likely: simply that out of this surprising cross-cultural milieu is coming the most vital and compelling rock 'n' roll voice of the present day.

Dada and British punk, bent on negation, driven by nihilism and a delight in shock tactics, were cultural explosions that cleared the ground; because they took much of their artistic energy from political symbols, they led people (not least dadaists and punks) to confuse art with politics, and left dreams of inchoate revolution in their wake. As did the New Sobriety artists of postdada Weimar Germany, the postpunk avant-garde faces the question of what to make of a new sense of freedom and a new sense of limits. Anything seems possible, permissible, in the postpunk milieu—any sort of pop voice, one might think, can find some kind of audience to talk back to it. It is equally clear that economic and social forces that require quietude and conformity are more entrenched and ambitious than ever.

The result, as it was for the Weimar artists, is paradoxical. Having served its purpose, nihilism turns into commitment: "I will not *give* up," says John Lydon, Mr. No Future of 1977. "There *is* a future. I will *not* accept the nuclear threat as being the be-all and end-all. I will *not* crawl back into escapism. The nuclear threat is just another form of escapism for the manic depressives." Pop music puts aside its anarchic pretensions and its dreams of revolution. Yet at the same time pop music becomes politicized, because after an explosion like dada or punk "one's own feelings" seem, to some, less sacred than a conceit, less profound than unreal. Pop can then become less a matter of private hopes and romantic fantasies than of consciously shared social facts, less a matter of spectacle than of public speech, less a message than a conversation or an argument. It assumes a public space in which the stuff of pop—romantic fantasies and private hopes, mostly—is changed by the fact of public scrutiny. Private hopes are turned into social facts.

This is a question of voice before it is a question of analytically acute lyrics—rock 'n' roll, after all, is the art of making the commonplace revelatory. The first and perhaps last thing you hear on Liliput's singles, or on British postpunk records like the Au Pairs' "Diet"/"It's Obvious" or the Gang of Four's *Solid Gold*, is a voice that through worry, sarcasm, irony, panic, or humor is manifestly trying to figure things out. It's a distanced voice, antinaturalistic, almost never direct—the voice of an observer or of one observing oneself. Most strikingly, it is an anonymous voice.

What I mean is that Jon King and Andy Gill of the Gang of Four, Lesley Woods and Paul Foad of the Au Pairs, and Klau Schiff, Chrigel Freund, and Marlene Marder of Liliput are not exactly singing "as themselves," not in the way rock 'n' roll has led us to understand the idea. They are not, as would Joni Mitchell or John Lennon, singing to refine an individual sensibility or to project a personality or a persona onto the world. Rather, they are singing as factors in the situations they are trying to construct.

The Au Pairs call their record "Ideal Home Noise": "Diet" is about a housewife who won't or can't think; "It's Obvious" is about sex roles. *Solid Gold* is about the way repression is advertised as everyday life ("Each day seems like a natural fact," says Gill, thus noting that each day is in truth made up of unquestioned assumptions about what's natural). Liliput's songs are about women and the possibilities of play and rant. But they are also about the sobriety of the voice that gets these things across. The voice says, look, this is ordinary life, and you didn't think it was worth singing about; it's not sexy, you walk through it each day. But the voice bears down so insistently, with such a hard sense of bewilderment, fear, bemusement, or outrage, that the ordinary becomes very interesting.

The question Lesley Woods's voice raises in "Diet" isn't that of the plight of the not-conscious housewife—that question is in the lyrics, which are a string of clichés—but the question of how one thinks about the fact that some people don't think. Woods thinks it over: her shifting tones of voice, ultimately, are about thinking itself and a version of it, seen from many angles, acted out.

"I was good at what I did," Andy Gill states flatly in

"Paralysed," the least imposing and most effective cut on *Solid Gold*. It's a song about unemployment and the shock of a displacement that is both social and private. It is so reduced to fact, its claustrophobic, doomy music so reduced to bare rhythm, that the performance seems to turn the singer into a statistic even as you listen: even as the singer makes statistics —in other words, himself—real.

In the Au Pairs' hilarious and somewhat frightening "Come Again," a couple make love. Both are trying hard to get past sexism and to enjoy themselves—or at least convince the other she/he is enjoying it. What you hear, though, is a disjunction between the helplessly addled voice of the man ("AM I DOING IT RIGHT, AM I DOING IT RIGHT?") and the weirdly distanced voice of the woman, who as she fakes her way through the act is judging the action like a cold critic of herself, her lover, and sexual mores in general. You can't help but laugh, and you can't help but feel uncomfortable—it's as if you've been treated to the secret version of every pop sex song you've ever heard.

Liliput (formerly Kleenex) works somewhat differently. Remember the woman Miou-Miou played in *Jonah Who Will Be 25 in the Year 2000*? Liliput has the spirit of that character: frivolous and hard as nails. The three women sing in English but also in bits of pure sound ("Woo-woo-woo-woo" is a big favorite), cacophony, a torrent of squeaks, yells, screeches; they make rhythms that seem crude only until you realize how implacable they are. There's no room for the exposure of an individual personality here, just the sound of women declaring their presence, having fun, making demands, or in rare reflective moments presenting a catchy version of what it means to be accosted by a sailor or while hitchhiking. There's a lot of dada provocation in Liliput. They really don't care what anyone thinks of them, and they'll try anything: "Split" is like a free-for-all at a playground, petulant and full of rule breaking, with cries of (I think) "Hopscotch!" alternating with I don't know what.

They can also force a listener into a confrontation. "Eisiger

Wind" begins with a gorgeously lyrical, almost Hendrix-like
guitar passage; you're set up for a classic rock theme, and then
suddenly the entire structure is collapsed and the song is flung
in your face. The band replaces something beautiful (and recognizable) with what seems to be a shouting match: it's as if a
fight has broken out onstage and in the audience, as if someone
has rushed the band and seized the mike. One word cuts off the
guitar as the melody is trashed and the rhythm sabotaged:
"She's—" But it's a one-word manifesto of, somehow, impossible authority, and it takes over. The new song moves through
furious rhythms, screams, exclamations of delight and triumph,
and finally, in one last surge, whole lines begin to emerge.
You've forgotten "Liliput" (with the guitar intro, you were
thinking, wow, that girl sure can play): this is a public riot.

In such music anonymity highlights the situation, not what
the artist is doing with it: the situation of thinking, unemployment, bad sex, and a score of other ordinary matters. Anonymity means not only that star cults are avoided, and not quite
that the music sounds as if anyone could make it—the music, as
opposed to the singing, sounds much too expert for that. Anonymity means that the music sounds like a conversation in
which everyone is actually taking part: in which the most obvious facts of life are worth questioning, in which every speaker
deserves listeners and a reply. The music works as a kind of
fantasy of good public life, where the affairs of private life—and
in postindustrial society, almost everything seems private—are
given public significance simply by being presented as if they're
puzzling, displacing, and, most of all, held in common. Each day
no longer quite seems like a natural fact.

Everyone knows that the only Grammy award of significance is
that given for the worst performance on the Grammy show itself. On February 25, the occasion of the twenty-third annual
attempt of the National Academy of Recording Arts & Sciences

to prove that nothing interesting is happening in popular music, the competition was especially fierce. Aided by shlock trumpeter Chuck Mangione (greeted as a god by the audience), the Manhattan Transfer—four whites who have rendered harmless more styles of black music than slavers plundered African nations—appeared to have wrapped up the honors early with a gruesome assault on Jon Hendricks's "Birdland"; imagine their shock when singer-songwriter Kenny Loggins, once characterized by Donald Fagen of Steely Dan as "a seal" because of his inability to keep from clapping his hands while onstage, stole the prize. Juxtaposing what he apparently took to be the mannerisms of a soulful black man and a nitty-gritty southern white man, Loggins convincingly demonstrated that he had no identity of his own, and at the same time provided perhaps the first example of simultaneous blackface and whiteface in the annals of American cultural history. For this he gained wild applause.

Completely out of place in these sweepstakes was the great country singer George Jones, who offered a quiet rendition of his hit "He Stopped Loving Her Today." His bearing was wrong: instead of showbiz piety he communicated grace, humility, and sincerity, singing his song as if it were actually about something, and he could hardly have struck a more discordant note if he'd read from the *Communist Manifesto*. Dressed in a baggy, unpressed tuxedo, Jones had already ripped off his tie when he was called back to accept the award for best male country vocal performance; among the many who thanked God that night, he seemed the only one who knew what he meant.

—*New West*,
April 1981

Crimes Against Nature

Father, Mother and Me
Sister and Auntie Say
All the people like us are we
And everyone else is they

—Rudyard Kipling,
"We and They"

The Adolescents are five young men from Orange County who, if their songs are to be believed, hate everything. Neat and trendy: they hate children, homosexuals, girls, politics, their so-called peers, and science class. It's the revenge of the wimps: who else would think to take it all out on an amoeba? "A one-celled creature, a one-celled thing/ It hardly knows it's alive/ You're better off dead."

So why does their music sound so good?

The thirteen cuts on *Adolescents* don't quite stand out from one another, and the feeling isn't exactly that of moral discovery, but the feeling is as convincing as it has to be: you don't *just* laugh. The I'm-mean-and-pissed-and-confused voice of singer Tony Cadena isn't leagues away from those of better-known flag-wavers of lumpen Los Angeles punk—Ron Reyes of Black Flag, Lee Ving of Fear—but it's got its own momentum, because the Adolescents are such a tight, musically precise band. I like the way Cadena turns the Ramones' signature kick-off—that tiresome "one-two-three-*four!*"—into actual lyrics without losing the hurricane beat, but it's a hard trick to give a singer the rhythm he needs to pull that off, and the Adolescents have it down cold.

The Adolescents are also terrific at disguising their skill. They make finely crafted numbers with fairly complex structures sound like found objects, found noise, found rage—the result of too many days spent brooding, cultivating resentment, masturbating (a big theme here). With a British postpunk band like the Gang of Four, Delta 5, or the Au Pairs, an equally harsh, intense music plainly announces itself as thought-out, a matter of a confrontation with a situation that leaves you changed: the point is to acknowledge the process, investigate it, make it real to others. (If punk says, "Life stinks," postpunk says, "Why does life stink?") The Adolescents work in the long, rich tradition of the American's opposition to the effete, overcivilized Old World—a tradition in which Mark Twain's *A Connecticut Yankee in King Arthur's Court* and Henry James's *The American* remain the basic texts. The Adolescents are frankly barbarians, and they create (an essentially effete activity, as opposed to, say, arson) in order to deny the claims of the alternatives.

Which hardly disposes of questions about contradictions between the Adolescents' primitivist, mindless pose ("We're just a wrecking crew/ Bored boys with nothing to do. . . . I could care less about the queers—they suck. . . . I'm just a victim of society/ A slob") and their well-constructed music, between their mindlessness and the jolt their music can deliver to the skeptical listener. The answer may be at once simple and ambiguous: rock 'n' roll based in strong feeling works. It may be in the nature of the music, the terms of which were originally worked out by the earliest blues singers, black men who took a half step away from the feudal constraints of turn-of-the-century Mississippi, men for whom the public expression of rage—against anyone, including their wives and lovers—was a sign of freedom. But strong feeling isn't intelligence. For years women have had to deal with the contradiction, the ugly paradox, of finding themselves captivated by unmistakably sexist rock 'n' roll—and it is specious and sentimental to think that good art is "good": that, say, Nazi rock that is both powerful and seductive is out of the question.

What, then, is the strong feeling that underlies the Adolescents' music? In 1977 Robert Christgau wrote that punk was the first of the U.K.'s many rock-based teenage subcultures to direct its rage where it belonged: against those in power. L.A. punk, which is a U.K. punk spin-off that has chosen Sid Vicious (prophetic thug) over Johnny Rotten (thuggish prophet) as avatar, jumped that track; perhaps because those who make L.A. punk are so often tracked to become those in power, to enjoy money and mobility without purpose, L.A. punk directs its rage against the other, the powerless—and that is a stance no less American than a happy barbarianism.

What this means is not ambiguous. Whoever is not formally like you is an irritant, and therefore the enemy, and therefore a crime against nature. In 1981 this stance is a glamorization of the disinclination to think, or a glamorization of the urge to hit what is vulnerable: to a boy, a girl may function as a crime against nature (his nature); to a white, a black; and so on down the line. Black Flag may explain its "White Minority" ("Gonna be a white minority/ All the rest will be the majority/ Gonna breed inferiority") as an ironic joke on American racism, or as a steely expression of realism, of what people happen to think— but if a politician told us that "something has to be done about the queers, kikes, greasers, dykes, and niggers who are taking over our country," no one would be looking for the irony, and the politician's explanation that he was just trying to "shake people up" or "expose their hidden bigotry" wouldn't be taken seriously. The opening lines of X's searing "Los Angeles" ("She had started to hate/ Every nigger and Jew/ Every Mexican that gave her lotta shit/ Every homosexual and the idle rich") tell us not that the subject of the song has her hangups but that the objects of her rage are types, not like us, deserving of the contempt they get: crimes against nature. The song has enough musical bite to make any nigger, Jew, Mexican, homosexual, or idle rich want to hear the tune again, and then think, "That's not me, I'm not like that" (like *what?*), and that is the true black hole of the number, and of L.A. punk: attacked, one may side with one's attacker, and accept the terms of the attack.

Revenge on the other—how else explain the Asian-American punk in Penelope Spheeris's Los Angeles punk documentary, *The Decline . . . of western civilization*, who graciously informs the camera he wouldn't kill a Jew ("Maybe a hippie . . .")? The kid isn't going to kill anyone, but that's not the point; the point is the attitude, that the question even comes up, and Spheeris's disclaimer that swastika-chic among L.A. punks simply reflects a lack of knowledge about the past doesn't wash any more than that of Black Flag or my imaginary politician. The punk doesn't think he's better than Jews, or even hippies—they're just . . . *not like him*. That's why the question comes up.

Spheeris's movie is wonderfully shot and cut: the opening moments—L.A. punks slamming the shit out of each other with such stylized fury it takes a minute to figure out what's going on—rank with the giant bowling ball sequence in *Raiders of the Lost Ark* for thrills and impact. But that hatred for the other keeps taking you out of the film. Black Flag is more than likable and more than funny in interview segments, but "White Minority" is what it is. Fear's queer baiting and woman baiting are obviously calculated, their "I Don't Care About You" more delightful than it has any right to be, but the band remains repulsive. Contempt for and a wish to exterminate the other is presented here as a rebellion against the smooth surface of American life, but it may be more truly a violent, spectacular accommodation to America's worst instincts. This is the secret Spheeris tells in spite of herself, no matter how much she's cleaned up the scene for public consumption (no heroin, no deaths, no violence against those who don't want it).

This idea—if you want to call it an idea; the idea behind almost every one of the Adolescents' songs (the amoeba is not like you or me)—may well be invigorating: negations usually are, for a time. Certainly, L.A. punk brought Spheeris to life as an artist. A friend of mind saw the movie, laughed her head off, went back to see it again, got the soundtrack lp, and found herself interested in pop music as she hadn't been in years. The action in *The Decline* convinced her that something is going on that knows no limits, and that is a metaphor anyone can use for any purpose, just as those founding Mississippi bluesmen used an attack on their wives and lovers to touch a hatred of their masters, a hatred of those they could not attack head-on.

That is the source of the power of L.A. punk, of the Adolescents' mastery of the form, of their borrowed but appealing detestation of anyone perceived as not like them. The difference is plain: in 1910 a Mississippi bluesman who called for the death of the man who ran his plantation would have found groundhogs delivering his mail. The Adolescents can say what they please. The freedom of Los Angeles punk may be inspiring, it may convince many their world is still to be made, but it costs those who use it nothing. They won't be the ones to pay the piper.

—*New West*,
August 1981

The Au Pairs
in Their Time

NEWS ITEM: London, 4 July 1981. Rioting broke out last night in Southall, a largely Asian section of the city, when hundreds of skinheads, followers of Oi, a reactionary form of punk rock, arrived for an Oi concert at the Hanbrough Tavern. Some of the skinheads —a white working-class cult often identified with the racist National Front—attacked passersby and vandalized shops. Local Asian youths fought back against police and skinheads and burned Hanbrough Tavern to the ground. One of the Oi bands scheduled to perform, the 4-Skins, denied any responsibility for the violence, as did the promoters of an Oi compilation album, *Strength Thru Oi*. . . .

NEWS ITEM: London, 9 July 1981. The disturbances that began in Southall five days ago continued across the nation last night, as blacks, whites, and Asians battled police in several cities. Incidents of skinheads and their usual enemies, blacks and Asians, fighting together against police were again reported. Experts disagreed as to whether the riots could be attributed to a newly emergent political consciousness or disastrous economic policies, or, as official spokespersons suggested, an inadequately developed moral faculty on the part of the lower classes and colored populations or John McEnroe's recent ill-mannered behavior at Wimbledon. The government, whose actions have produced a severe cutback in social services and a seventy percent rise in unemployment over the last year, denied any responsibility for the violence. Home Secretary William Whitelaw expressed "shock" that so many youths were permitted out-of-doors after dark. . . .

> They say our world is built on endeavor
> That every man is for himself

Wealth is for the one that wants it
Paradise!
If you can earn it . . .
My ambitions come to nothing
What I wanted now seems like a waste of time
Can't make out what has gone wrong
The crows come home to roost
And I'm the dupe!
                    —Gang of Four, "Paralysed," 1981

LETTER from my friend Simon Frith, Coventry, England, 3 July
1981: "The daily attacks on Asians/West Indians/leftists/women/
gays by skinheads and right-wing groups are intensifying (two
people killed in Coventry in the last couple of months). . . . The
most disturbing thing about this is how little the establishment as
such acknowledges what is a kind of continuous guerrilla warfare.
At a local level people do have to respond to events, but more and
more I feel I live in a society that bears no relationship whatsoever
to the way it is perceived/conceptualized by Thatcher, Foot, the
BBC, etc. Rock (the Au Pairs' lp, for example) is the *only* medium
that makes any sense of life—aesthetically or politically—at
all."

If the best of present-day pop music is about finding your own
voice and making the act of listening to it worth someone else's
time, then it was clear from the moment the Au Pairs released
their debut single in 1979 that they were bent on reaching the
limits of the process. "You" is as compelling an example of sal-
vation through racket as I've ever heard: it has a giddy energy
that's part celebration, part grim illegal rally, part traffic accident. The Au Pairs play and sing right past their formal ability
to make music—and it's by doing just that that they've gone on
to discover what it is they want to say.
    A lot of bands reverse the story. The Oi groups—which pur-
vey a version of 1977 punk stripped of its humor and vision—

exist only to be followed, which in commercial terms means that whatever they do will be uncritically accepted by their followers: that is, bought. Such groups operate with a panoply of symbols constructed out of received images and trademarks, selling their fans a fraudulent, vicarious membership in the band—a membership that smothers the fan's need to find his or her own voice. The Au Pairs are a rebuke to all that. Listening to their first album, *Playing With a Different Sex*, you can imagine arguing with this band as easily as you can move to them or laugh to them—but try following the Au Pairs and you'll trip.

On one level, the title phrase merely describes what the Au Pairs do: they're two women (Lesley Woods, guitar and lead singing; Jane Munro, bass) and two men (Paul Foad, guitar and backing singing; Pete Hammond, drums). The music itself suggests plenty of other levels. And so does the tone of Lesley Woods's voice.

Birmingham, England, the Au Pairs' gritty, industrial hometown, may be best known to rock fans for all-male, black and white, neo-ska bands like the Beat and UB40, and the Au Pairs are to some degree of a piece with them. But it's a use of musical ideas also shared by two Leeds bands—the Gang of Four and Delta 5—that counts for more.

All of these bands derive some of their energy from an opposition to the attempt of a right-wing government to reorganize their society, and some from a commitment to dance music. All work from a fundamentally Jamaican aesthetic, in which musical (and, in a band that includes both women and men, sexual) hierarchy is bypassed: the bass states and shifts the theme; lead guitar is mostly omitted; rhythm guitar supports or pulls against the theme by jumping off and back onto the main pulse. All are attuned to dub, the reggae form in which instruments and voices continually drop out of a song and then reappear in slightly different shape. The message conveyed is that of a sense of possibility and contingency opposed to—sometimes

fighting off—a sense of fatalism. But where the neo-ska bands
are direct both in words and music—presenting a steady beat,
faded rather than abrupt dub effects, and singer-imparts-
knowledge-or-experience-to-audience lyrics, the Au Pairs and
the Leeds bands work through indirection. Where the singer in
the Beat or UB40 is telling you what he thinks or what he
knows, the singers in the Gang of Four, the Au Pairs, and Delta
5 are creating situations and assuming roles within them. Here,
the dub idea is taken to a certain conclusion: when an instrument drops out, it sounds as if it's been forced out; when it
returns it sounds as if it has recovered its voice after a struggle. But where the Leeds bands posit an abrasive attack,
stressing discontinuities and concealing their sense of pop, the
Au Pairs take the opposite tack. Their tunes have attractive,
sometimes roughed-up Roxy Music-like surfaces; there is a lot
of sardonic vocal comedy. Discontinuities are concealed—and
then revealed through an attack of clatter on a seemingly
unthreatening beat, a rhythmic surprise, a sudden pressure
drop.

The slogan that's usually applied to these groups is that
their music is meant to make you think while you dance—and
while it's hard to imagine a more facile line, with the Au Pairs
and the Leeds bands it actually has some meaning beyond
smart or politicized lyrics. It means that a combination of noise,
rhythm, words, and vocal character makes it very difficult to
know just whose voice it is that you're listening to: you're
thrown off balance, and you have to think yourself back into
position. Jon King of the Gang of Four may sing in the voice of
false consciousness holding off a recognition of the truth; the
women in Delta 5 may sing in the voice of bad conscience.
These are voices of social and psychological displacement:
they make dance an affirmation that things are not as they
seem.

In these bands, a consciousness of sexism works as a third
source of energy. It works as a first principle that continually

forces the questioning of the obvious, and it produces a never-ending argument: nothing can ever be settled, but nothing can be assumed, either.

This is where the tone of Lesley Woods's voice comes in. It's *acrid*—it may be the most acrid voice ever to stake a claim on pop music, and it's precisely the sound pop music has not prepared us to hear from a woman. Up against it, the exhilaratingly cold, analytical voices on Delta 5's debut album, *See the Whirl'* . . , seem abstract, and it's hard not to hear the ebullient, romantic voices on *Beauty and the Beat*, the first album by L.A.'s all-female Go-Go's, as an exercise in British Invasion nostalgia. The only thing comparable to Woods's tone is the back-from-the-dead rasp former Swinging London chanteuse Marianne Faithfull unleashed on her *Broken English* in 1979—a rasp that cut flesh with the murderous "Why D'Ya Do It"—but the comparison is instructive just where it falls short.

No one had ever heard a woman sing as Faithfull sang on that record. But no matter how intimidating Faithfull's voice was, she still told stories that remade her into a conventional, acceptable pop woman: a victim. She didn't understand, she couldn't take it anymore, society had tricked her, men had wrecked her life, some bitch was sleeping in her bed. Woods is no victim. The male and female characters she sings through or about may be victims, but the distance her words and the Au Pairs' music establish between Woods and her characters, and that acrid tone, make it clear that people are perfectly capable of exchanging will and thought for life as a social fact. (It's life as a social fact that the singer in the Gang of Four's "Paralysed" is fighting—and accepting against his will.) Woods is full of humor, but her humor, thanks to her tone, always has an edge that you—and maybe she—can't smile away. Her point of view can change radically within a phrase; it's as if she thinks off the rhythm the way the Au Pairs as a band play off it. The Au Pairs are clearly out to entertain, but Woods's tone makes it impossible for them to put a listener at ease.

On "Come Again" Woods's voice makes sex into an exercise in manipulation and self-deception, though that's the last thing the man and woman in question want; on "It's Obvious," which is about how men and women are "equal/ But different" (isn't that nice), it makes everything dubious; on a version of David Bowie's "Repetition" it makes the bruises a husband puts on his wife's arms seem so ordinary you almost accept them—and then realize Woods has exposed your capacity to accept what you rationally reject. In other words, Woods's voice makes none of these things happen. It merely reveals that they do happen, and denies you a quick way out of the situation. Her voice is so caustic, and yet so seemingly uncontrived—not a tactic, but a voice found in the open arena of postpunk rock—that it pushes you to say no to it, and then wonder if you're wrong.

None of this is unrelated to the fact that a band made up of men and women is patently in the world, a combination representing not fantasy but real life, and none of this is unrelated to the fact that the women in the Au Pairs seem more pointed in their feminism than do other feminists making rock 'n' roll. Jane Munro has said she isn't going to go out of her way to prove she isn't anti-men; Woods has rather perfectly dismissed the notion that the Au Pairs are a "feminist band"—because there are men in it. "I don't believe men can be feminists just as I don't believe men are as oppressed as women," she said in an interview with a U.K. music weekly. "Men can be sympathetic to feminism, and men are obviously victims of stereotyping, but that stereotyping makes them the oppressors, *not* the oppressed." This is the sort of straight thinking that makes the Au Pairs' situational indirection possible. Woods's voice is not, except in the occasional off moment, superior to the situations it renders: she's not giving lessons, she's thinking through or acting out the way people unlearn lessons—or refuse to.

Woods's tone allows the Au Pairs the dispensation of irony

—and makes it impossible for them to settle for it. "Armagh" is about a lot of things: the British occupation of Northern Ireland, a female IRA prisoner, torture as patriarchy, how speech about atrocities can be conducted without the speaker being drowned out by her subject matter. As the tune begins, one line is snapped out over a popping, searing beat: "We don't torture, we're a civilized nation." Other lines fill in the details— grim and graphic details—and the beat turns vague—the Au Pairs as a band can't always keep up with their ideas—but that recurrent opening line rules the song: confronted by Woods's voice, the irony burns off. What's left is contradiction: the idea that civilized nations don't torture is one of the dispensations by which we live our lives. A situation is set up, and then broken down, and the listener is left to put it back together, if the listener can. Because this is not protest music, meanings are not fixed: what those forms of authority are depends on what images the Au Pairs' sounds suggest to you.

And that is why the Au Pairs can carry the weight of England's July days, or the weight of a skinhead attack on a Pakistani or feminist pub, or the weight of a love affair trapped in rules its lovers perceive as nature. The Au Pairs make music of unpredictable rhythms, good humor, nasty revelations, and, primarily, struggle. At its best—the shifting beat of "It's Obvious," driven by a garbled sax; the opening moments of "Armagh," kicked off by Munro's growling bass—the music can sustain struggle, which is to say doubt.

Some of Delta 5's unsettling tunes come across on *See the Whirl'. . ,* especially "Makeup" and "Shadow" (which puts a man in the position of a woman walking alone at night: "It's just a feeling/ In the back of the neck/ Between the shoulder blades"), but all in all the disc is a stunning example of how not to make a first album. Hey, we've got a good, rough little band here—guitar, two basses, drums, our own sound, our own point of view—how about a horn section? Why not some steel guitar? Piano! I know, *sound effects!* Say, doesn't your grandfather play accordion?

—*New West,*
September 1981

Kiss Kiss Bang Bang

The Go-Go's are five women from Los Angeles, and their first album is a hit: *Beauty and the Beat* could be heard everywhere as soon as it was released. The band is also impossibly retrograde. Lead singer Belinda Carlisle once had hardcore credentials, having spent time in the Germs, L.A.'s punk-mort outfit (already an ex-member, she can be heard introducing the band on *Germicide*, a recording of the Germs' first official gig in June 1977). *Beauty and the Beat* now offers Carlisle and the rest of the Go-Go's wrapped in towels and mud packs (front cover), or with bubble bath, chocolates, and champagne (back cover). The inside sleeve collects four coy smiles framing drummer Gina Schock, who's blowing us a kiss. As for the music, it comes off as bright, cheery, bouncy, shiny: pretty much the true sound of Los Angeles, in 1966. The only thing missing on *Beauty and the Beat* is a cover of the Beach Boys' "Wouldn't It Be Nice."

That really is all that's missing. This is a wonderful record; if most good present-day pop music is hard to hear and sets its action below the surface, the Go-Go's' music is easy to hear, and if you never get beyond its surface you can still come away satisfied. "Our Lips Are Sealed," "How Much More," "Can't Stop the World," and even the spooky "This Town" are natural Top 40 performances. You can feel the craft and wit that went into them, and you can also imagine that years of listening to the radio simply brought them into being. Carlisle's voice is high and cute, harmonies are smooth, guitars trade references between the Byrds and the Ventures—the way the rhythm section cuts into solos is made for cutting into the fast lane of a pulsing freeway. The band's sense of timing is exquisite—riding a fast tempo, changes aren't blurred, they aren't hedged, they're thrilling.

But if the music announces itself as all bounce, after a few listenings slap seems like a better word. If at first Carlisle sounds like she's selling mindless optimism in the face of postpunk pessimism (in her happy lilt, in her grin, in lines like "Can't stop the world/ Why let it stop you"), before long that optimism sounds earned, and not anything you can buy. If "Can't Stop the World" and "How Much More" are pure Top 40 tunes, they are also tunes repeated airplay won't blow apart.

No matter how catchy or familiar ("This Town" is more or less based on "This Train"; the guitar solo in "Lust to Love" uses the tuning and the fundamental idea of the solo in the Beach Boys' "Don't Worry Baby"; the piece itself calls up the Electric Prunes' "I Had Too Much to Dream"; and so on), songs do not stand up to airplay unless there's a lot going on in them both musically and emotionally, and unless what's going on isn't fake. Beneath the surface of this music—rather, rising to the surface—is a lot of pathos, nerve, toughness, some bitterness; in a word, experience. *Beauty and the Beat* sounds innocent mostly because we have learned to associate innocence with the sound of joy; if the album has a message, it's that it takes toughness and nerve to make that sound.

You can hear this in the way Carlisle drifts off the last "Oh, yeah" in the choruses of "How Much More"—once you get to know the song, it seems as if the ready-made pop chorus is sung just to give that utterly personal moment its impact. The way the singers bear down on "This Town," a tribute to Los Angeles, goes beyond the number's ironic promise ("This town is our town/ This town is so glamorous/ Bet you'd live here if you could/ And be one of us") and plain cynicism ("We're all dreamers—we're all whores/ Discarded stars/ . . . Litter the streets of this town"). Carlisle, Schock, bassist Kathy Valentine, and guitarists Jane Wiedlin and Charlotte Caffey aren't fashionably juggling moods and concepts, they're aiming at the truth, whatever it is.

Beauty and the Beat is an album of surfaces—and, I think, of very deep pleasure. Partly, it's the pleasure of hearing the world and the music change. The last four years have seen an explosion of female voices into pop music—Poly Styrene of X-ray Spex, Vanessa Ellison of Pylon, the Slits, the Raincoats, Robin Lane, Lora Logic, Lesley Woods of the Au Pairs, Liliput, Deborah Harry, Exene of X, Debora Iyall of Romeo Void, the Anemic Boyfriends, Eve Libertine of Crass, Marianne Faithfull, Chrissie Hynde, Alison Stratton of Young Marble Giants, Delta 5, scores and scores more. They've remade the terms of pop with cattiness, rage, sarcasm, nagging, squeals, sly asides, impatience, pain, acrid dismissals, shouts, antifeminine noise. They've slipped all pop female roles and chipped away at the very idea of what it means to be a woman in public. Pop is about what's new, and to a good degree the surprise and challenge of these voices have been what's new in the music; these voices suggest a world less intractable than some presently imagine. The Go-Go's sing love songs in a manner that is easy to like, but they are as much a part of this change as they are a result of it.

The pleasure of the Go-Go's' music is also the pleasure of hearing people get it right, not cheating, and testing themselves against rock 'n' roll, against its history, and against that enduring piece of conceptual art called Top 40 radio. It is as well the pleasure of responding to what Roland Barthes called "the materiality of the body" in a voice that gets it right and is not cheating, a voice that deflects analysis because it sounds so good and elicits analysis because voices that sound so good are special—a mystery. Yes, Belinda Carlisle sometimes crosses over the line into shlock angst and the band into automatic melodrama—but they always get back. The music is so alive with its own voice that you might think these apparent soft spots are really sucker punches: there to tell you, "Bubble bath, champagne, Beatle notes, and corny rhythms—and you thought we were only kidding!"

—*California*,
October 1981

Charts of the Gods

F ans have been abuzz this fall with word that famed rock
band the Rolling Stones have made a "good" album (*Tattoo You*), as opposed to a "bad" album (such as last
year's *Emotional Rescue*). Buzz aside, however, no one has
been able to explain why *Tattoo You* is a "good" album, save
that it is generally agreed to sound "pretty good." Announcing
the Rolling Stones' current American tour at an August 26
Philadelphia press conference, lead singer Mick Jagger denied
that the good/bad consensus pointed to a "new artistic rhythm"
in the work of the band. "Chacun à son goût, but really," he
said. "All right, *Some Girls* was good, *Emotional Rescue* was
bad, this one's good, I agree—though this one's nowhere nearly
so good as *Some Girls*. But don't forget—between *Exile on
Main Street*, which was a great album, and *Some Girls*, we
came up with four bad albums, and a couple of those were terrible. Consumer Protection Agency investigations, class action
suits, the whole bit. But anyway," Jagger went on, "everybody
will have forgotten about this one in six months. Sure, it sounds
'pretty good,' and it's even got a 'rockin' side' and a 'dreamy
side,' just like those old 'oldies but goodies' lps, but I defy anyone to find a single song on—what's it called again? Oh yeah,
Tattoo You, thanks—with a, as Sartre would have said, raison
d'être. L'enfer, c'est les autres, you know? We could have done
these songs or we could have *not* done them. Who'd know the
difference? What people want is product. To assert that a tune
carefully constructed out of half-forgotten Rolling Stones hits
for the sole purpose of assuaging the listener with a sense
of familiarity disguised as high-tech contemporaneity could

possibly be compared in terms of emotional impact or social metaphor to a record on the level of Elmore James's
'Done Somebody Wrong' is merely to reify the sort of
false consciousness that may well make revolution in our
time impossible," said Jagger, demonstrating the breath control that has made him a singing sensation on five conti-
nents.

Pulling himself together, Jagger pointed out that "the eighties are here" and that he was therefore abandoning his "old-
fashioned sixties habit" of dropping pretour hints that "this
time" the Rolling Stones might surprise their huge audience
with something "new and different." "We're going to do what
we've always done," Jagger said, "and when we're finished,
we're going to do it again. Forever."

The response of KMET, the Los Angeles FM outlet that
was broadcasting Jagger's words live, was all too real. The station immediately scheduled an eight-hour "Stones Special" for
August 28—a marathon that, at least for the two hours during
which I remained within its signal range, was characterized
principally by a nearly complete avoidance of any material
more than five years old. This policy was perhaps predicated on
demographic research indicating that a good proportion of
KMET's audience was not born when the Rolling Stones began
recording in 1963—there being no reason to clutter the airwaves with music that, issuing from a bygone time, might serve
only to confuse many clear-thinking young men and women
with unfamiliar sounds, arcane cultural references, or outmoded
values. As *New Yorker* cartoonist Jack Ziegler put it in his
"Sentiments of a Lost Generation," which pictured three execu-
tives reminiscing about the distant past: "Let the sunshine in"
. . . "All you need is love" . . . "Da doo ron ron."

IN OTHER NEWS: scene watchers have begun to identify more
exemplars of "Republican punk," a new craze first reported in a

July 9 *Rolling Stone* profile of John LeBoutillier, a twenty-eight-year-old right-wing congressman (Republican, New York) who was recently identified by Jack Anderson as one of the "most disliked" members of the House, and whose stated ambitions include outlawing abortion and touring the country as a member of the Eagles.

Republican punks—not all of whom, by any means, are actual members of the Republican Party—may be recognized by their affirmation of traditional morality in a manner that altogether abjures traditional standards of courtesy or decorum, though an authentically original voice, or style of invective, cannot be said to have emerged as of yet. Avatars of the form include the editors of the *American Spectator*, who have perfected a journalistic version of the sneer once used by Hollywood cocaine rockers for album cover art; Young Americans for Freedom (theme song, as reported in the *New York Times*, and while officially unreleased available on numerous bootlegs: "Deck the Halls [With Commie Corpses]"); the black punk/funk singer Prince, who earlier this year went on record in favor of President Reagan's "balls," as opposed to former President Carter's lack of same; former expatriate Iggy Pop, who told *Zig Zag* magazine, "I moved back [to the United States] as soon as I thought Reagan would get elected. I've campaigned quietly for him, asking people at my gigs to vote. . . . I've been waiting for someone who could communicate the joys of liberty as opposed to the joys of equality"; and also Bryan F. Griffin, "a writer of short stories" best known for his August/September assault in the pages of *Harper's* on smut, scatology, vulgarity, flabby literary reputations, and the practice of rock criticism.

While Griffin's articles, provocatively titled "Panic Among the Philistines," have attracted much attention, it has completely escaped public notice that Griffin simultaneously released his apocryphal debut single—a remarkably uncompromising cover of Barry Manilow's "I Write the Songs" backed by an equally remarkably uncompromising cover of Alice Cooper's "No More Mr. Nice Guy" (on the newly launched Harper's Chartbusters label). This is probably because radio programmers are not yet ready for such up-to-date material accompanied by Strauss waltzes. Still, we can expect to hear more from Griffin, if only because a financial loss for his backers is not anticipated—not since the Food and Drug Administration ruling that ground-up 45s can be marketed as "freeze-dried coffee" (a decision on lps is pending), a move concurrent with the Department of Agriculture's approval of the use of such substances in federally supported child nutrition programs.

IF YOU'RE WHITE, YOU'RE RIGHT, ETC.: recently San Francisco FM station KSFX presented "The Rock Years: Portrait of an Era," the era being 1965 through 1980. The series, which ran for fully eight days, was made up of 191 segments, three of which—not four, not twenty-seven, not 111—contained the work of black performers, all of whom were Jimi Hendrix, who indeed shared his final appearance with Janis Joplin. (Presumably, if Hendrix had lacked the good sense to die in tandem with a famous white person, he would not have made it past a second appearance.) Excised from the last sixteen years, in favor of such features as "Deep Purple in Switzerland" and "Stevie Nicks's Writing" (advertised as "Stevie Nick's Writing," but what the hell), were Wilson Pickett, Otis Redding, the Supremes, Curtis Mayfield, the Jackson Five, Sly and the Family Stone, Al Green, the Spinners, the O'Jays, Aretha Franklin, and Marvin Gaye—and, by the by, Creedence Clearwater Revival, which was perhaps omitted because of the influence of Howlin' Wolf, a certified black person, on lead singer John Fogerty's vocal style. One would not be surprised if the series prompted a coveted "certificate of recognition" from the Institute for Historical Review of Torrance, California—an organization that has lately gained notable attention for its claim that the mass exterminations carried out by Nazi Germany never took place.

—California,
November 1981

Food Fight: Real Life Rock
Top Ten 1981

A narchy is where you find it: "Welcome to Der Wienerschnitzel," says a polite little counterman. "May I take
your order, please?" "Yeah," answers the customer, "I
want—" and suddenly a torrent of desire mixed with hysteria
rises from his throat, gets caught somewhere in the esophagus,
and then bursts free as unfettered Southern California
hardcore: "TWO LARGE COKES! TWO LARGE FRIES!
CHILE CHEESE DOG! LARGE DR PEPPER! SUPER
DELUXE WITH CHEESE AND TOMATO!" The counterman
ought to be hiding behind the soft-drink dispenser after this; he
hasn't even blinked. "Would you like incomprehensible on
that?" he asks (some people hear "bull sperm"). The customer
doesn't blink either. He expected this. He's been to Der
Wienerschnitzel before. "NO!"

The customer—the singer—is one Milo, described in a press
release as "skinny . . . with tense face and one hand gripping
his pants leg." The band is the Descendents—since Milo sounds
like a drill sergeant, ancestors include not only Little Richard
but, presumably, Sgt. Barry Sadler—a four-man combo from
the Redondo/Manhattan Beach area. "Weinerschnitzel" (the
spelling varies on the disc) lasts fully eleven seconds, as does "I
Like Food," another tune from the Descendents' *"Fat"* EP, and
if a more perfect disc has appeared this year, I haven't heard it.

Which brings up the Real Life Rock Top Ten for 1981. I
regret to announce the final appearance of the Journey Award
for the worst album by a California band. Having released two
lps in 1981—*Captured* and *Escape*—Journey accomplished the

astonishing feat of tying itself for the prize, which has therefore been retired for reasons of gross redundancy.

1. "Jessie's Girl," Rick Springfield. The moment I first heard Kim Carnes's "Bette Davis Eyes" remains the high point of the year for me, but endless airplay brought the calculation of that great single to the surface, and buried its mystery too far beneath it. "Jessie's Girl" is all surfaces—classic teenage music from a thirty-two-year-old Australian-born Angeleno who makes his rent playing Dr. Drake on *General Hospital*—and after well over six months on the radio the disc comes across with more punch than ever: fast, funny, anguished, sexy—and that drum sound! and that guitar solo! Still, it may live in history more for these lines, as naturalistically odd as anything by Chuck Berry: "And I'm looking in the mirror all the time/ Wondering what she don't see in me." A hit that should have been a smash was Rosanne Cash's painful, fated "Seven Year Ache"; a smash that should have been a hit at one of the year's many devil's music bonfires was Starsounds' "Stars on 45," a disco medley of Beatle tunes that stands as the most commercially effective exploitation of John Lennon's death—so far.

2. Prince at the Stone, San Francisco, March 29. Fronting a band of three blacks and two Jews from Minneapolis, Prince stormed into town on the heels of last year's breakthrough *Dirty Mind*, was greeted by the most excited and diverse crowd (black and white, punk and funk, straight and gay, young and old, rich and poor) I've been part of in a long time, and sent everyone home awestruck and drained: "That was the history of rock 'n' roll in one song!" a friend shouted before the last notes of "When You Were Mine" were out of the air. All barriers of music, sex, and race were seemingly trashed by Prince's performance, and leering organist Lisa Coleman walked off with the 1981 Most Valuable Player award—edging out Junior Walker, whose sax work on Foreigner's "Urgent" is the closest he's come to hoodoo in a twenty-year career.

All barriers were in place when Prince opened for the Rolling Stones at the Los Angeles Coliseum in October. He was roundly jeered and taunted with racist catcalls, and after inaccurate reports appeared in the news that he had been "booed off the stage" (Prince left after twenty minutes, all his contract allowed), he and his band were pelted with garbage at a second Stones show two days later. A correct account of the situation given by Ken Tucker in the *Los Angeles Herald-Examiner* brought this anonymous response in the mail: "You obviously are a fan of that faggot nigger group our you wouldn't of lied about it. I just wanted you to know that us W.A.S.P. Rock n rollers pay to see white performers and not niggers, faggots our tawdry critics like yourself President Reagan has proven once and for all that liberals, niggers, fags and minorities are out. Thank god for that. I can sure bet your ass on one thing, prince wont open up for the stones next time around."

3. *Beauty and the Beat*, Go-Go's. Reet petite.

4. "Eisiger Wind," Liliput. Three Zurich women leave off rioting in the streets for a day, change their clothes, and flaunt their hometown roots in the Cabaret Voltaire. A furious manifesto, thrilling, alarming, probably the most radical sound of the year, in English, and I still wish I could understand more than four of the words.

5. *El Rayo-X*, David Lindley. Los Angeles rock announced itself in the early fifties as novelty R&B, narratives about trouble with the white power structure that could be made public only as jokes. Whether Lindley—longtime Jackson Browne guitarist and in the sixties a member of the definitively eclectic L.A. band, Kaleidoscope—learned the music from the Robins (later the Coasters) or Jan and Dean, he caught its spirit on this debut solo lp: a goof with a sting in it. In other words, this breezy romp through personal renewals of old faves (the Temptations' "Don't Look Back," K.C. Douglas's "Mercury Blues," Huey "Piano" Smith's "Tu-ber-cu-lucas and the Sinus Blues") and addled street-life originals (such as "Pay the Man," in which a hooker throws her baby in the river—"Now Sally is a

happy girl," Lindley explains earnestly) may in truth be a concept album about pain, poverty, and the absurd. The music is surefooted white rhythm and blues cut with zoot suit reggae—an eighties version of what used to be called folk rock—and Lindley's playing, so offhand, can take your breath away.

6. "Start Me Up," Rolling Stones. There really isn't much happening on *Tattoo You*, which will likely top most polls for album of the year—and on lp this crude and rangy piece of rhythm was soon disarmed. It found its place only in the Top 40 mix, where its roughness disarmed everything around it—and forced DJs to rush back to the mike to drown out the last line, the one that followed the final chorus of "You make a grown man cry": "You make a dead man come."

7. Bruce Springsteen at the Sports Arena, Los Angeles, August 27. I was there because I wanted to hear him sing one line: "Take a knife and cut this pain from my heart." He didn't just sing it, he did it.

8. "I Feel Like Going Home," Charlie Rich. In 1973, after more than sixteen years as a little-known country soul singer, would-be bluesman, hopeful rocker, and secret jazz pianist, Rich was on the verge of the success that has since made his fortune. Thus he sat at the piano and, rolling his fingers over the keys until he found the deepest, plainest gospel chords, recorded a song he had just written about failure. It remains the strongest moment of Rich's career—a match for Ray Charles's "Georgia on My Mind" or Otis Redding's "Try a Little Tenderness," and somehow more indomitable than either—and it went unheard until this fall, when Epic stuck it on at the end of an undistinguished various-artists anthology called *Rockabilly Stars, Vol. 1*.

9. *Re • ac • tor*, Neil Young & Crazy Horse. Leave it to the hermit of La Honda to put out an album drenched in no-nukes iconography (as with the lp title, all song titles are broken down into syllables, a typographic conceit apparently symbolizing the

splitting of the atom) that nevertheless reaches its high point with a gloriously mindless epic called "Sur • fer Joe and Moe the Sleaze." Yes, it's the same Surfer Joe you knew and loved when the Surfaris sang his praises up and down the coast in 1963, now grown up and wondering what to do with himself—a dilemma made irrelevant by "Shots," *Re • ac • tor*'s last cut. This is the most powerful evocation of all-out war since the Sex Pistols' "Holidays in the Sun," and every bit as horrifying, and exciting: for six minutes, phrase after phrase, Young's guitar drives smack into a volley of machine-gun fire. If this sounds like a cheap sound effect, it isn't—the machine gun is used as an instrument, and before long it has as great an aesthetic charge, is as listenable, as any other here. Twelve years after they first broke loose with "Cowgirl in the Sand," Neil Young and Crazy Horse have produced what their music has always implied: a nightmare so intense only the fact that it ends seems false.

10. "That's the Joint," Funky 4+1, and "The Adventures of Grandmaster Flash on the Wheels of Steel," Grandmaster Flash & the Furious Five. The conservatism of mainstream radio doubled back on itself in 1981, and the proof was that rap— aural graffiti, or South Bronx dada—was heard principally in the form of soft-drink commercials. That is, Madison Avenue admen knew they could catch the ear of the public with this stuff, but program directors didn't believe it. The results fit no demographic printouts. Opening for the Clash in Manhattan, Grandmaster Flash was chased from the stage with a barrage of paper cups—perhaps less because Flash is black (though, given the white crowd, that surely helped) than because his sound cutups on twin turntables ("the wheels of steel") produced the response that has obtained throughout the twentieth century when the avant-garde has met an audience that doesn't know much about art but knows that it likes. At the same time, the Clash was heard throughout black New York as "The Magnificent Dance," their own rap twelve-inch, blasted from giant

radios. And the Funky 4+1 played the Kitchen, the SoHo performance artists' space, to wild applause. Stay tuned, if you can
find the station.

—*California,*
January 1981

Life After Death

W e've all been transported by music—swept away, taken out of ourselves. It's what the Lovin' Spoonful meant in "Do You Believe in Magic" when John Sebastian sang about "a smile on your face and you don't even know how it got there"; it's part of what Pentecostal preachers mean when they damn rock 'n' roll as devil music; it's what theorists mean when they bump into the limits of their theories and start talking about the ineffable. When you step back from the experience and try to make sense of it, nothing is sufficient; any attempt to break down the effect through an examination of a musician's genius or a lyricist's profundity seems like so much desperate irrelevancy. Not long ago I saw a new band that raised this question, and read a new book that offered a clue to an answer.

In *Sound Effects*, a study of how pop music is used by its listeners, Simon Frith takes up a point made by the late French semiologist Roland Barthes. Barthes argued that the thrill of music is not a result of one's conscious or subliminal response to "significance" (the rendering of an important idea, emotion, moment in time, or whatever—think of how you've tried to make sense of your response to "Like a Rolling Stone" or "Gimmie Shelter"); rather, the thrill comes from one's response to *signifiance*. This odd and intriguing word has baffled Barthes's translators (some, as if to say the hell with it, have rendered it *as* "significance"), but Frith handles the word best: *signifiance* refers not to a sign but to "the work of signification"—not to meaning, but to "the making of meanings." We do not respond to symbols (doom in the dark chords and apocalyptic lyrics of

"Gimmie Shelter," escape and release in the rising choruses of "Like a Rolling Stone"), though we seize on such symbols and connect them to historical events or personal situations in order to explain our response; we respond to symbol creation.

The moment when we feel music taking us out of ourselves, Frith writes, is a moment when "the terms we usually use to construct and hold ourselves together suddenly seem to float free." If this is so, then that moment can be understood and fitted back into daily life: music on this level deconstructs the frame of symbols we use to represent both ourselves and the world, and thus confronts us with the prospect of making new symbols. Frith's example is startling, and perfect: "Think of Elvis Presley—in the end this is the only way we can explain his appeal." We can never understand that appeal, that explosion of response, "in terms of what he 'stood for,' socially or personally." Instead, "Elvis Presley's music was thrilling because it dissolved the signs that had previously put adolescence [or, one can argue, American identity] together." Because it dissolved those signs, or symbols—symbols, one might say, of conformity, restraint, and limits—Presley's music was a celebration of the possibilities of signification, of "symbol creation itself." The best writers on Elvis speak of the sense of freedom one can hear in his music, but Frith may be closer to the mark.

This whole matter of *signifiance*, of symbol making, seemed to be at stake in the show New Order gave on 9 November 1981 at the I Beam, a disco in San Francisco—though the context was not adolescence (you have to be twenty-one to get in, after all). The context of New Order's performance was more like that of dread and resistance.

New Order emerged from the ruins of a late-1970s band from Manchester, England, called Joy Division—a name Nazis gave to the concentration camp brothels they stocked with female slaves. Joy Division's lead singer was a young man named Ian

Curtis. He sang on the edge, and not as a metaphor: his strongest numbers conveyed the feeling that he was fighting against
all odds either to back away from the edge or to go over it. The
nihilism of the Sex Pistols' singles that had inspired Joy Division's more measured music had been recognized from the start
as a political negation; Curtis personalized that nihilism. He
hung himself in May 1980 at the age of twenty-two.

Immediately Joy Division's albums—*Unknown Pleasures*
and *Closer*—topped the U.K. charts. The band's final singles,
"Love Will Tear Us Apart" and "She's Lost Control," headed
the major U.S. critics' polls. Instant legend, but what to do with
it?

The three remaining members of Joy Division—Bernard Albrecht, guitar and melodica; Peter Hook, bass; and Steve Morris, drums—were joined on keyboard and synthesizers by Gillian Gilbert; Albrecht took over the singing. Going against all
necropop cult tradition (Johnny Burnette died in 1964, but an
album of newly recorded material by "Johnny Burnette's Rock
'n' Roll Trio and their Rockin' Friends from Memphis" was issued in 1981), the four gave themselves a new name and
dropped most of their old material. Joy Division's music had
always communicated chaos, despair, doubt, and fear: *The Myth
of Sisyphus* with the pages on why you shouldn't kill yourself
ripped out. New Order deepened that sensibility and superseded it with a shining, haunted debut single, "Ceremony." The
show I saw went past the single.

New Order presented itself as ordinary life: there was an
occasional smile but mostly quiet faces, few extra gestures, no
flourishes. These were four people doing their work. At the
same time, the presence of both sexes on the stage conveyed a
subliminal sense of real life. Since 1976, the most interesting
groups have formed on the basis of one's wanting to be in a
band rather than on the basis of one's musical skills; over the
past two years so many male-female bands have emerged that
an all-male or all-female band can seem as much like an artifi-

cial construct, or a conceit, as a one-sex movie. A one-sex band now raises an image that bypasses, or evades, the world people actually live in, whether in their houses, in their fantasies, or in the supermarket. New Order began from these premises, this everyday credibility.

One step past that first impression, the band's music was primarily dramatic—and the music's drama, set against the band's ordinariness, was an immediate, delicious shock. What was dramatized was exclusion. The drama squeezed out various elements of life: fun, frivolity, transcendence, anything casual. It squeezed them out not as possible responses to the music, but as subjects for it.

Gillian Gilbert built a drifting orchestral frame, often a distantly vamping, syncopated pattern that seemed to loom up before a listener's eyes. Within this frame, textures took shape and fragmented. Though the music was neither improvised nor abstract, the abstraction Simon Frith insists on was there in the difficulty one had in precisely associating what one was seeing with what one was hearing. Bernard Albrecht's melodica drew on the otherworldly tones of dub master Augustus Pablo's *East of the River Nile*; Peter Hook's structured bass lines led the sound, taking over the role one expects guitar to play. Gilbert's synthesizers and Steve Morris's drums—and, at times, a drum machine or syndrums (the latter creating hard, riflelike cracks that seemed to come from some invisible fifth musician)—further skewed the image of a band that New Order presented. Sometimes the music seemed to move of its own accord, and sometimes it was as if the music were being pulled by an offstage force or an overriding idea: say, the secret intentions of the world outside the I Beam, intentions that overrode those of any mere musicians.

Music is fundamentally ambiguous, which is why its symbol-making (as opposed to symbol-imposing) power is so great. Music can make the dumbest lyrics sound profound, but ultimately it can support no specific message: its symbol-making power is the power of making the ambiguous symbol. If a piece of music is musically alive, if it has its own momentum, it will undercut, it will question, whatever explicit images or symbols it is supposed to carry—which is why in folk protest music (Joan Baez's "There But for Fortune") or punk protest music (Dead Kennedys' "California Uber Alles") obvious melodies and debilitated rhythms function like a demagogue's rhetorical tricks. Thus a piece of music with words is a contradiction—not a cancellation, but a contradiction that can lead to a synthesis unintended by whoever wrote the words and music—and from this contradiction comes tension, the source of a song's ability to dramatize the process by which a symbol is created.

This is what I saw in New Order's performance. That night, lyrics were mostly more sounds—after a score of listenings to a tape of the I Beam show, I've picked up only a few phrases ("No reason ever was given" is a current favorite). But at the I Beam, Albrecht's voice had its own function. It was hard, monochromatic, antirealistic—seemingly lacking an object, and a violation of the conventional postpunk conversational voice. But because the music did include a voice, and thus forced a listener to confront an individual who was singing specific words, even words one could not quite make out, one responded as if a distinct message were there. Albrecht's voice broke up the lines he was singing as if what he was trying to talk about was the impossibility of speaking clearly, and this, not paradoxically, intensified the possibility of response—of response to sound, to the process of symbol making, to the act of signification. It led the listener to begin to find symbols: to free-associate within the structured, dramatic, excluding frame of the music.

One got no idea of who Bernard Albrecht was from his singing. There wasn't a hint of confession, of autobiography, of personal struggle. But one got a sense of the singer's—and one's own—role within the context of dread. Simply because Albrecht's voice was a voice, which implicitly carries thoughts, arguments, ideas, he presented the possibility of response to dread: resistance. Otherwise, one's sense of action said, he would not have been there.

Albrecht's voice was, more than anything, determined. It had, perhaps, something of the tone of Ian Curtis's voice, but none of its expressionist character. Albrecht's voice was itself an idea, the idea of symbol making within the dissolution of received symbols—the symbols one brought to the show of a band, of a concert, of Joy Division gloom, or real life—and that dissolution was the burden of the music. If it is true that Elvis Presley celebrated the act of symbol creation, then the four people in New Order did something subtly, vitally different: they argued that symbol creation was possible.

Pennies from Heaven was the strongest American movie of 1981—perhaps the first noir musical. Directed by Herbert Ross, written and conceived by Dennis Potter, the film is perverse, and willing to set its perversity against irresistible sentiment—that's what happens when Vernel Bagneris, as the destitute Accordion Man, steps out of a diner and mimes his way through Arthur Tracy's terrifyingly impassioned 1937 version of the title song. Moving with almost feral wariness through the Depression rain—which turns into a shower of golden coins—and "singing" straight to Steve Martin, who as the go-getter sheet-music salesman believes every song he sells, Bagneris's face is all menace, all secret knowledge, but with Tracy's huge voice coming out of his mouth it's impossible to tell what he really knows. See the movie, listen to Tracy on the soundtrack —and wonder if 1982 will produce a moment half so grand.

—California,
February 1982

Dial Twisting

If pop music is about love or money, the Gang of Four make music about the wish to love money. Flat, accepting images are shot up with complex puns and disjunctive guitar-bass-drums rhythms; singer Jon King's everyman embrace of the commodity is exposed as fear and his identification with the status quo as hysteria. Thrilling on *Entertainment!*, this was more than a little boring on the band's 1981 second album, *Solid Gold*: the rhythms were stabilized. Without the constant questioning—or disruption—of each element of the music by every other, the band's drama came too close to agitprop. Argument became point of view and contradiction was reduced to irony.

Sound is the metaphor that supports and translates the Gang of Four's themes, and on *Songs of the Free* the sound is texture. The clash of elements is replaced by a constant shifting of the distance between the singer and the music—or the singer and the singers. Guitarist Andy Gill's dour attempts to talk-sing his way through mystification—"No-man's land surrounds our desires," he says, but desires are located in "the space between our work and its product," which makes that space itself a no-man's-land—frame King's melodramatic angst, an angst at times so fierce it dissolves the melodrama; the cold, hard soprano of an uncredited female singer cuts the ground out from under King's hopeful narrative in "I Love a Man in a Uniform" with the same strength new bassist Sara Lee uses to hammer out the offbeat against Hugo Burnham's kickdrum. "Time with my girl, I spent it well," says King as a man about to join the army in the face of economic redundancy. "Oh, man," says his girlfriend to herself, "you must be joking!"

The elements in the Gang of Four's music work differently on *Songs of the Free* because what the band is now putting on its stage is not only the isolation of almost indecipherable alienation but the piecemeal recognition of a common predicament; not just the false consciousness of acceptance but the doubt and willfulness of resistance. Resistance—saying no, and then groping for a way to act on the negative—is presented as a struggle for consciousness. What you can hear in "I Will Be a Good Boy," "The History of the World," "Of the Instant," and in the devastating "We Live as We Dream, Alone" is the struggle to think; what you hear in "I Love a Man in a Uniform" is the absurdity and submerged panic of failing even to try. The deliberate, thought-out textures of the sound—and the sometimes devious, sometimes baleful punning of the lyrics, which you don't catch right off—seem to symbolize, to act out, thought as such. The result carries an almost cinematic suspense: hearing the singers try to think, hearing the band add and subtract force from the adventure, you can't help but wonder, will they make it?

Rock 'n' roll is a metaphorical arena. In early 1964, Lesley Gore made the Top Ten with "You Don't Own Me," celebrated ever since as a proto-feminist manifesto. Less well known is that Gore (or her managers) immediately backed off: the follow-up was the all-accommodating "That's the Way Boys Are." Message: he may treat you like garbage, but they're all like that, and we love 'em for it!

Metaphors die: today Joan Jett is the queen of Top 40 punk, and her teeth-bared version of "You Don't Own Me" is devoid of tension; she sings as if the matter were never in doubt. And metaphors are turned around: Y Pants are three women from New York, off-market art punks who play "toy instruments," and their version of "That's the Way Boys Are" (from their first album, *Beat It Down*) puts more tension into the tune than the tune or the world it speaks for can hold. With the nicest, most innocent a cappella vocal, a woman relates the sad facts of romantic love while her sisters confirm there is no way out: "That's the way boys are." It's lovely—like listening to the Fleetwoods. And then the screaming starts, edging its way up out of the speakers, louder even as the girls keep singing, *horrible* screaming, twenty-years-in-the-snakepit screaming, screaming that decent people *should not have to listen to*—

Rock 'n' roll is a metaphorical arena, and that is why you can find the abyss in a harmless old pop song.

The implacable griminess of the San Francisco hardcore band Flipper conceals its artiness: the group is as close to pure concept as a group can be and still move. Tempos are sludge, riffs unrelieved, but explosions of scorn keep an emotional pace. Songs range from wordy (though if Quaaludes are the drug that can turn English into a second language, Flipper is the band) to nearly wordless. The complete lyrics to the seven-minute forty-five-second "Sex Bomb"—Flipper's recent single and a highlight of *Album/Generic Flipper*—are "She's a sex bomb . . . my baby—yeah." That's "Wild Thing" boiled down to a burnt pot, unless you count the music: the sound of bombs, naturally, but also car crashes, planes taking off, trains pulling into a station, D-Day, the 1906 earthquake, old Blue Cheer records played backward. The post-Beat caterwauling of "Life Is Cheap" is essential Flipper: negation as non sequitur. "Life is pretty cheap," say two pissed-off, resigned voices. "It's sold a decade at a time." Go argue with that.

The flip of the "Sex Bomb" single, "Brainwash," isn't on *Generic Flipper*, but it sums up the band. Coming off a thudding beat (I guess I have to call it a beat—it's more like the rhythm of a car trying to start on a cold morning) is this heartfelt message: "Uh . . . Okay. When— S-s-see, there was this— And— What, and then, uh— Never mind. Forget it. You wouldn't understand anyway." Then it all stops. Then it starts again. And again. And again.

The response to this record is unvarying: "What *is* that? What are they *doing? When* does it *end?"* It might be the most conceptually extreme bit of anticommunication (or the most conceptually extreme shaggy-dog story) punk has yet churned up, but it's equally accessible to ten-year-olds and Mohawked pit divers—an old-fashioned novelty record. To announce a change in call letters, a San Francisco Top 40 station once played "The Purple People Eater" for twenty-four hours straight; maybe somebody in Flipper was listening.

Since 1978 the all-female Zurich band Liliput has lived by their singles. *Liliput,* their first album, isn't bad, but from a combo so dada-brazen and riot-toughened, it seems tame. One exception: "Do You Mind My Dream," which with a typically Liliputian chant offers a typically Liliputian sentiment: the equation of "weight control" and "thought control."

Oh Ok, a two-woman (voices, bass), one-man ("he just plays drums") band from Athens, Georgia, uses the white, suburban, chirpy girl-group sound of the Kalin Twins ("When," 1958), the Angels ("My Boyfriend's Back," 1963), and everyone's high school cheerleading squad. Stripping that sound of its outdated themes and emotions ("Love me or I'll die"; "Get that ball and fight"), Oh Ok makes it modern—or at least as timeless-rootless as a day spent in a shopping mall.

If there is such a thing as a generic white American voice, Oh Ok may have found it—and found what to do with it. The four songs on *Wow Mini Album* come off like a conversation you might overhear while standing in line for a matinee of *E.T.* The skimpy dance rhythm is firm and tight, never calling attention to itself; the tone of voice is appealing, thoughtful, earnest, sunny. What's surprising is that the voice is as sure of itself, as determined, as it is aggressively ordinary: all those years of cheerleader practice have given this voice muscle. "I-I-I-I-I am a person," says Oh Ok's Linda or Lynda (the band has one of each). "I speak to you. I am a person, I am a person, and that is enough." It's sweet, it's flirtatious, and in its own way it's probably as much of a challenge as X-ray Spex's "Oh Bondage Up Yours!" was in the punk heyday of 1977.

The Nig-Heist's "Walking Down the Street" speaks as clearly for white male California anticulture as Moon Unit Zappa's "Valley Girl" did for the female version. That's mainly because there's about the same amount of art in this blithering piece of Redondo Beach hardcore as there is in a teenager's decision to drink enough to make himself throw up. Don't worry, you won't hear it on the radio.

—*California*,
June and September 1982

from Elvis Costello Repents: The *Rolling Stone* Interview

Declan MacManus was born in London in 1955 and grew up there, attending Catholic schools. For his last two years of secondary or high school he moved to Liverpool to live with his mother, by that time divorced from his father, Ross MacManus, a big-band singer and solo cabaret performer.

I graduated from secondary school in 1973. It was the first year of one million unemployed in England in recent times—in Liverpool, anywhere up north, it was worse. I was very lucky to get a job. I had no ambition to go into further education; I just went out and got the first job I could get. I went along to be a chart corrector, tea boy, clerk—because I wasn't really qualified for anything. I got a job as a computer operator, which happened to be comparatively well paid: about twenty pounds a week. I'd just put tapes on the machines and feed cards in, line up printing machines—all the manual work the computer itself doesn't have arms to do.

I had something of an ambition to be a professional musician. I was already playing guitar in high school—playing in folk clubs on my own. I was writing my own songs—dreadful songs, performing them more or less religiously. I didn't think the songs were worth recording—but the only way you get better is to play what you write. Then you have the humiliation of being *crushed*—if they're obviously insubstantial. If you don't put them over you quickly learn from experience.

I stuck out the first computer job for about six months; at the same time, I got into a group in Liverpool, a sort of folk group—we'd do a few rock 'n' roll tunes, and songs of our own,

but we weren't getting anywhere. The Cavern was still there—
and that's where I met Nick Lowe, just before I came to London, in '74. He was still with Brinsley Schwarz; it was the *au-
tumn* of their career. We'd do a few of their numbers in our set;
we had a show at a little club, they were playing at the Cavern,
and we went along and met in the bar and started chatting. He
was in a real proper group that recorded records! That was the
first time I'd ever spoken to anybody that was in a group—and
his attitude *even then* has been reflected in the way he's been
since. When we've worked together, it's been, "I can't see
what's so difficult about it, it's just four chords"—and he'd bang
them out. He always had that attitude—it was quite a revelation to me.

What was the beginning of your life as a fan?

My father was with Joe Loss—the English Glenn Miller, I suppose. He was with him from about 1953 to 1968, and then he
went solo; his instrument is trumpet but he's a singer. After
the years with Joe Loss he went out as a cabaret artist; he does
social clubs and nightclubs and cabaret, drives around himself.
    The first records I ever owned were "Please Please Me"—
and "The Folksinger" by John Leyton. I was at a little bit of an
advantage because my father was still with Joe Loss then—he
used to get quite a lot of records because they would cover the
hits of the day. He'd often have demonstration copies, even acetates; as late as 1966, Northern Songs would still send Beatles
acetates out to the orchestras to garner covers for [live] radio
play. I've got them at home. As my father was the most versa-
tile of the three Joe Loss band singers, I was fortunate—he got
the records and just passed them on to me.
    I was just into singles, whatever was on the radio—the
Kinks, the Who, Motown. It was exciting . . . I was in the
Beatles fan club when I was eleven; I used to buy the magazines. The one kind of music that I *didn't* like was rock 'n' roll—
as a distinct [classic] form. The girl next door loved the Shad-

ows and Cliff Richard—I thought that was really old hat. Someone who lived across the road from my grandmother liked Buddy Holly—I thought that was terribly old-fashioned, I couldn't understand why anybody liked it. It never occurred to me that someone as *archaic* as Chuck Berry could have written "Roll Over Beethoven"—because I was quite convinced that George Harrison had written it.

The only time it changed, the only time it went a bit peculiar, where it maybe went a bit *clandestine*, was when I went to live in Liverpool. I was never very taken with psychedelic music—but my dad went a bit psychedelic around the edges, about 1968. He grew his hair quite long; he used to give me Grateful Dead records, and *Surrealistic Pillow*. I'd keep them for a couple of weeks, and then sell them at the record exchange and buy Marvin Gaye records. When I went to live in Liverpool I discovered everyone was still into acid rock—and I used to *hide* my Otis Redding records when friends came around. I didn't want to be out of step. To the age of sixteen it's *really crucial* that you're *in*—and I tried hard to like the Grateful Dead or Spirit. I tried to find somebody of that sort that I could like that nobody else did—because everyone would adopt his group, and his group would be *it*: someone weird like Captain Beefheart. It's no different now—people trying to outdo each other in extremes. There are people who like X, and there are people who say X are wimps; they like Black Flag.

I actually "saw the light" when I was already playing—coming back to London, seeing a lot of groups, Nick Lowe and the Brinsleys, pub-rock groups. I think you get very earnest when you're about sixteen to eighteen, and everyone at school was listening either to the psychedelic groups or singer-songwriters: it was all very *earnest*, pouring out *your inner soul*. In London I discovered that all the music I liked secretly, that I'd been hiding from my friends—that was what was great fun in a bar: Lee Dorsey songs! Suddenly it was all right to *like it*; that was when I saw the light. There was nothing wrong with it.

In England, now, there's a prejudice against that era, the prepunk era; the bands tend to get ridden down: "Oh, that's just pub rock." I'd much rather any day go and see NRBQ playing in a bar than I would the most illustrious of our punk groups in England, because I don't think they have anything to do with anything. They're horrible—and *phony*, and *dishonest* as well.

Who are you talking about?

The Exploited—and the whole Oi business.

Bands like the Anti-Nowhere League?

Now, the Anti-Nowhere League, I quite like them, because they're just *animals*: they drive around in a van that says, WE'RE THE ANTI-NOWHERE LEAGUE AND YOU'RE NOT!—I mean, that's great.

The Damned were the best punk group, because there was no art behind them; they were just enjoying themselves. There was no art behind them that *I* could see. They were just— *nasty*. I loved them from the start. I liked the Pistols as well— but you could see the concern behind it. It's dishonest to say, "Oh, yes, we were just *wild*"; they weren't just wild. It was *considered* and *calculated*. Very art. The Clash as well.

While all that was going on, I had a little group in London. I'd moved from one computer job to another; it was a total bluff, really, I knew nothing about it, but I knew enough of the jargon. It was ideal: waiting for the machine to do the work, there's a lot of free time for writing and reading. In the evenings we'd try to play rock 'n' roll, R&B numbers, some country songs—a real pub-rock mixture. There was no focus to it; it was aimless. We could get through the usual bar-band repertoire—but I remember Pete Thomas, now the Attractions drummer and *then* a drummer in a quite successful pub-rock band, Chilli Willi, coming to see us—he was a *celebrity* to us—

and he walked out after about thirty seconds. I think he came to see our worst-ever gig—but with no offense to the guys, we weren't very good.

It was the usual thing—trapped in mediocrity. So I went out on my own again, solo. That's very hard, because there's no real platform for solo singing unless you sing traditional music or *recognized blues*, doing re-creations—you know how *reverent* Europeans are.

It was difficult to develop an original style. I have no idea who it was I might have been imitating, whether consciously or unconsciously. I was playing on my own, trying to put my songs across. I suppose I should have had a band behind them—but playing alone did build up an *edge*. I did the odd show just to keep up, to keep trying to *improve* the ability to play. You'd soon know if a song was bad if you were *dying* in a club; you'd have to put more edge on it. Playing on your own, you'd have the tension—you could increase the tension at will, not relying on anybody to pick up the beat.

MacManus made a guitar-and-vocal demo and hawked his songs to various record companies. The one that responded was Jake Riviera and Dave Robinson's new Stiff label, emerging in 1976 out of the pub-rock scene and bridging the gap to punk.

On the first demo tape that I sent to Stiff, that brought me the *gig*, as it were, there were only two or three songs that ended up on *My Aim Is True*. There were a lot of raw songs—and looking at them now, rather precious songs, with a lot of chords. Showing-off songs. I was very impressed by Randy Newman, and wrote a lot of songs with that ragtime feel. I was very impressed with those funny chord changes that he used to play and I was emulating that on guitar. They came out convoluted; they weren't poppy at all, they had pretensions to a sophistication they didn't have.

That exactly coincided with punk. But I was working—I didn't have the money to go down to the Roxy and see what the bands were doing: the Clash, the Pistols. I just read about them in *Melody Maker* and *NME* the same as anyone else. Joe Public. I was living in the suburbs of London, I couldn't afford to go to clubs uptown. They were open until two o'clock in the morning, I couldn't afford taxis—the tubes are closed just after midnight. All these bands were playing in the middle of the night. I don't know who went to the bloody gigs—I can only guess they were rich people with cars and lots of drugs.

I got up at seven in the morning and so I couldn't go. I was married with a son; I couldn't take the day off. I took enough time playing sick, taking sick time off of my job, just to make *My Aim Is True*.

Then I started listening to the records that were coming out, because I'd got this snobbish attitude: so *little* of any worth had come out for a few years. When the first few punk records came out, I suddenly started thinking: "Hang on—this is something a little bit different."

I mean, I spoke with someone the other day who said that when the first Clash album came out, he was *outraged*. I remember being outraged, and thinking, "If *this* is what music's going to be like"—I remember Joe Strummer describing their sound as a sea lion barking over a load of pneumatic drills, which *is* what their first album sounds like when you first hear it—I remember hearing it and saying, "If that's what it's going to be like, *that's it*. I'll quit before I've done anything."

Then I listened to that album on headphones—we lived in a block of flats and we couldn't really play music at night—and I listened right through the night. I thought, "Well, I want to see what this is about. And I'll listen to it until I decide it's rubbish, and I'll probably *quit*, if that's the way music's going to be, or else I'll see something in it." I listened to it for thirty-six hours straight—and I wrote "Watching the Detectives."

We were all living in this block of flats, and nobody had an awful lot of money—I don't want to sound like my-deprived-background, but nobody did. And there were all these people in 1977, when the Jubilee was on, *wasting their money* on a bloody street party for the Queen. Perhaps it sounds small-minded now, but I used to really enjoy playing "God Save the Queen," *loud*, because all the little old ladies would be so outraged.

"God, did you see the Sex Pistols on the TV last night?" On the way to work, I'd be on the platform in the morning and all the commuters would be reading the papers when the Pistols made headlines—and said "fuck" on TV. It was as if it was the most awful thing that ever happened. It's a mistake to confuse that with a major event in history, but it was a great morning —just to hear people's blood pressure going up and down over it.

I wrote a lot of songs in the summer of 1977: "Welcome to the Working Week," "Red Shoes," "Miracle Man," "Alison," "Sneaky Feelings," "Waiting for the End of the World," "I'm Not Angry," all more or less in one go, in about two or three weeks.

Your first single was "Less Than Zero." When did you write that?

Earlier in the year. I saw a program with Oswald Mosley, the leader of the British fascist movement of the Thirties. And there he was on TV, saying, "No, I'm not anti-Semitic, of course I'm not—doesn't matter even if I was!" His attitude was that *time* could make it all right! It was a very English way of accepting things that used to really irritate me, really annoy me. The complacency, the moral complacency there—that they would just *accept* this vicious old man: not string him up on the spot!

This was the time when the National Front and the British Movement were recruiting with great success—and they derived directly from Mosley's old British Union of Fascists.

They were the same old bastards, the same old weirdos like
Colin Jordan that kept reappearing, and denying they had any
fascist overtones, and then there would be pictures taken of
them dressing up in pervy Hitler Youth uniforms. They're really *sick* people. If there wasn't a danger that some people of
limited intelligence would take them seriously, they'd be sad
and you'd feel sorry for them. But you can't. There are people
gullible enough and there are enough problems—the same way
as you've got here. You can point fingers and say, "These are
the people who are the source of all your problems: it's the
black people." It's the same as saying, "It's the Jews. . . ." I'm
English, but my ancestry is Irish, and they used to say the
same about the Irish as well. My wife's Irish. Sooner or later,
we'll probably have to leave England—because I'm sure the
people of England will try and send the Irish back.

We cut the first singles without any impact. My immediate
reaction was, "Well, maybe I haven't got it." If I'd been somebody like Johnny Cougar, signed to a major label—someone
with a five-album deal for a million dollars—I suppose I would
have felt, "Well, I'm secure now, I can write some songs," but I
wasn't sure. Stiff was running from week to week—we were
totally independent, we weren't licensed, we had no national
distribution: it was mail-order. We finished the album in six-
hour sessions; there were no days in the studio. Jake said,
"Well, we're going to put it out"—but one moment it was going
to be Wreckless Eric on one side, me on the other, as a way of
presenting two new writers. There were a million ideas a day
floating around; it was all improvised and all governed by a
very limited budget.

You had picked your name well before that?

I hadn't picked it at all. Jake picked it. It was just a marketing
scheme. "How are we going to separate you from Johnny This
and Johnny That?" He said, "We'll call you Elvis." I thought he
was completely out of his mind.

Riviera was right, perhaps because he knew Declan MacManus could live up to his new name. With My Aim Is True, *Costello stepped out as a central figure in British new music; the follow-up was the far stronger* This Year's Model *("A ghost version of* After-math," *Costello says, noting that he'd never heard the 1966 Rolling Stones lp until a few months before making his own album). In 1979 came the even more ambitious* Armed Forces—*originally and more appropriately titled "Emotional Fascism." It was a tricky, allusive set of words, voices, and shifting instrumental textures, primarily influenced, Costello says, by the music he and the Attractions, the three-man combo he'd worked with since just after* My Aim Is True *was issued, had been able to agree on as listening material while touring the U.S.A. in a station wagon: David Bowie's* Low *and* "Heroes", *Iggy Pop's* Lust for Life *and* The Idiot, *Kraftwerk's* Autobahn, *and most of all Abba's* Arrival. *(" 'Oliver's Army' was most successful," Costello says of the lp's U.K. hit, a bright, poppy cut that would have been released as a single in the U.S. had Costello been willing to take out the line characterizing army recruits as "white niggers"—the whole point of the tune. "That was the aim," he says. "A grim heart in the middle of an Abba record.") As Jim Miller wrote of* Armed Forces, *"personal relations are perceived as a metaphor for relations in society at large. . . . [Costello's] stance may begin with private refusals, but it ends with public references."*

In a bizarre manner, that truth was acted out, backward, during Costello and the Attractions' 1979 U.S. tour, when one night in a bar in Columbus, Ohio, at odds with Bonnie Bramlett and other members of the Stephen Stills Band, Costello suddenly denounced Ray Charles as "a blind, ignorant nigger," said much the same about James Brown, and attacked the stupidity of American black music in particular and America in general. Bramlett decked him; the incident quickly made the papers, then People *magazine, and the resulting scandal forced a New York press conference— Costello's first real face-to-face encounter with journalists since 1977—where he tried to explain himself, and, according to both Costello and those who questioned him, failed. This, from a man who had produced the first album by the Specials, the U.K.'s pio-*

*neers of interracial music? Who at some risk had taken on the
National Front with "Night Rally," had appeared at Rock Against
Racism concerts—and who, again to quote Jim Miller, is plainly
"obsessed with the reality of domination wherever it occurs"? What
happened?*

It's become a terrible thing, hanging over my head—it's horrible to work hard for a long time and find that what you're best
known for is something as idiotic as . . . this.

*Do you really think that this incident is what you're best
known for?*

Yes. The first thing that a lot of people heard about me was
that incident. I think it outweighs my entire career. I'm absolutely convinced.

Fred Schruers wrote a piece about it in *Rolling Stone*—a
sort of "tenor of the tour." About the fact that we went around
with CAMP LEJEUNE on the front of our bus—Camp Lejeune,
where they train the marines. He said it was like an exercise in
paranoia. To an extent, it was. The antijournalist thing we were
doing, the antiphotographer thing, had reached an almost ex-
cessive level by that point. Schruers said that the press were
looking for something to crucify me with, and I fed myself to
the lions. There were words to that effect. I remember them
distinctly. And I couldn't help but agree, to a certain extent,
looking—aside from the incident itself—dispassionately at the
effect of what happened.

What actually happened was this: we were in the bar—
Bruce Thomas [of the Attractions] and I were in the bar after
the show in Columbus, Ohio. And we were *very* drunk. Well, we
weren't drunk to begin with—we were reasonably drunk. And
we started into what you'd probably call joshing. Gentle gibes
between the two camps of the Stills Band and us. It developed
as it got drunker and drunker into a nastier and nastier argu-

ment. And I suppose that in the drunkenness, my contempt for them was probably exaggerated beyond my *real* contempt for them. I don't think I had a real opinion. But they just seemed in some way to typify a lot of things that I thought were wrong with American music. And that's probably quite unfair. But at the exact moment—they did.

Things such as what?

Insincerity, dishonesty—musical dishonesty.

How so?

I just think they're— This is difficult, because this is getting right off the point. Because now I'm getting into mudslinging.

But now we're trying to talk about what it was really about.

What it was about was that I said the most outrageous thing I could possibly say to them—that I *knew*, in my drunken logic, would anger them more than anything else. That's why I don't want to get into *why* I felt so affronted by them, because *that's* not important. It's not important because . . . they don't mean *anything* to me. They don't even mean anything *now*—I don't feel any *malice* in the way I feel they probably *exploited* the incident to get some free publicity.

My initial reaction—I can tell you now—to seeing Bonnie Bramlett get free publicity out of my name was, "Well, she rode to fame on the back of one E.C., she's not gonna do it on the back of another." But that was before the consequences of what had happened had sunk in—that was a flip way of dismissing it.

Did you have any idea how dangerous, or how exploitable, or how plainly offensive, what you'd said would be in a public context?

No, because it was never intended—if I hadn't been drunk I would never have said those things. If it had been a considered argument, I probably would have either not pursued the argument to such extreme length, or I would have thought of something a little bit more coherent, another form of attack, rather than just *outrage*. Outrage is fairly easy. Not in terms of dealing with the consequences, but in terms of employing it as a tactic in an argument.

With the press conference in New York a few days later, the situation reminded me of nothing so much as the "We're more popular than Jesus" blowup with the Beatles.

It had approximately the same effect on our career. The minute the story was published nationally, records were taken off playlists. About 120 death threats—or threats of violence of some kind. I had armed bodyguards for the last part of that tour.

And not since?

For one tour since. Not armed, but—

But not now?

We take more care with security than we did before.

Were records taken out of stores?

I don't know—there may have been. Just like people won't sell South African goods. I mean—quite rightly so! Until there was an explanation.
  The press conference was unsuccessful because I was *fried* on that tour. This is aside from the incident; now I'm talking from a personal point of view.

It was at that point that everything—whether it be my self-perpetrated *venom*—was about to engulf me. I was, I think, rapidly becoming not a very nice person. I was losing track of what I was doing, why I was doing it, and my own control.

In your first interview, in 1977, with Nick Kent, you made a famous statement: words to the effect that all you knew of human emotion was revenge and guilt. Those words have been endlessly quoted—I've quoted them, they're irresistible. Now you're describing that as venom—as if your artistic venom, what you put into your music, had taken over your life.

I think it did. You see, I think that after a while—apart from anything else, looking from a purely artistic point of view—it started to become a problem for me to incorporate the wider, more compassionate point of view that I felt; I was trying to put that forward in some of the songs, and it was so much at odds with the pre*conception* of the image.

When we were playing, the frustration of that just ate me up. And with my lack of personal control of my life, and my supposed emotions, and drinking too much, and being on the road too much—

I'm not saying I wasn't responsible for my actions; that sounds like I'm trying to excuse myself. *But I was not very responsible.* There's a distinct difference. I was completely irresponsible, in fact. And far from carefree—care*less* with everything. With everything that I really care about. And I think that, inasmuch as it was said that we fed ourselves to the lions, you could say that *whatever* the incident was, it was symptomatic of the condition I was in, and that I deserved what happened regardless of the intentions of the remarks.

But it was only quite recently that I realized that it's not only the man on the street, as it were, who's never heard of me otherwise, who's only read *People*—that it's not only people like that who know only this about me. When we were record-

ing *Imperial Bedroom,* Bruce Thomas was in the next studio
while I was doing a vocal. Paul McCartney was there, and Michael Jackson came in to do a vocal—everything was very nice.
Everyone was getting along fine until somebody introduced
Bruce as my bass player. And suddenly—there was a freeze-
out. Michael Jackson was—"Oh, God, I don't dig that guy . . .
I don't dig that guy."

He had heard about it thirdhand, from Quincy Jones. Two
guys I have a tremendous amount of admiration for. It de-
pressed me that I wouldn't be able to go up to him—I wouldn't
be able to go up and shake his hand, because he wouldn't want
to shake my hand. *Or* James Brown, for that matter. But what
could I say? What could I say? How could you explain such a
thing? But there is nothing I'd like more.

—Rolling Stone,
2 September 1982

Badlands

We must mobilize every asset we have—spiritual, moral, educational and military—in a crusade for national renewal. We must restore to their place of honor the bedrock values handed down by families to serve as society's compass.

—Ronald Reagan,
9 September 1982

*In the summer all the lights would shine
There'd be music playin' people laughin' all the time
Me and my sister we'd hide out in the tall corn fields
Sit and listen to the mansion on the hill.*

—Bruce Springsteen, "Mansion on the Hill"

. . . schools can avoid taking attendance [as a requirement for the receipt of] federal per-pupil monies. This last provision will put the farmworkers' and coal miners' children back to work without cost to local schools.

—Mary C. Dunlap, *The Sentinel* (San Francisco),
10 July 1981, on the Family Protection Act, an
omnibus bill endorsed by Ronald Reagan

*Now mister the day that lottery I win I ain't never
gonna ride in no used car again*

—Bruce Springsteen, "Used Cars"

The republic's assertion that "all men are created equal," which Lincoln regarded as a stumbling block to tyranny, is also a stumbling block to National Renewal. That we are created equal has never meant that Americans were supposed to live alike. What it does mean, what it has always meant, is that the citizens of this republic cannot be treated in law and by government as mere social and economic functions. Yet this is exactly how the Reaganites propose to treat the citizens of the commonwealth. The administration intends to bestow wealth upon the wealthy because it is their function to invest in productive enterprise. The administration intends to impoverish the poor because it is their function to perform menial services and not be a drag on investors. . . .

What the Reaganites really care about is this: they want capitalism in America to become what Karl Marx thought it would be by nature—the transcendent force and the measure of all things, the power that reduces free politics to trifling, the citizen to a "worker," the public realm to "the state," the state to an instrument of repression protecting capitalism from the menace of liberty and equality. . . . Marx's description of capitalist society is the Reaganite prescription for America. This is the meaning of National Renewal.

—Walter Karp, *Harper's*, October 1981

I've interwoven lines from Bruce Springsteen's new solo album with words on Ronald Reagan's U.S.A. because any separation of the two would be a fraud. *Nebraska*—recorded in January 1982 in Springsteen's New Jersey living room with acoustic guitar and harmonica, with a bit of synthesizer and an occasional backing vocal added later—is the most complete and probably the most convincing statement of resistance and refusal that Ronald Reagan's U.S.A. has yet elicited, from any artist or any politician. Because Springsteen is an artist and not a politician, his resistance is couched in terms of the bleakest acceptance, his refusal presented as a no that doesn't know itself. There isn't a trace of rhetoric, not a moment of polemic; politics are buried deep in stories of individuals who make up a nation only when their stories are heard together. But if we can hear their stories as a single, whole story, they can't. The people we meet on *Nebraska*—the 1958 mass killers Charley Starkweather and Caril Fugate; a cop who lets his brother escape after a barroom killing; the kid who watches as his father is patronized by a used-car salesman; the man who loses his job, gets drunk, shoots a night clerk, is given life and begs for death; the man who dumps his soul and goes to work as a hit man for the mob; the mill workers who've grown up in the glow of the mill owner's mansion—can't give their lives a public dimension because they are alone; because in a world where men and women are mere social and economic functions every man and woman is separated from every other.

Two songs here outstrip anything Springsteen has written: the title tune, about Charley Starkweather ("From the town of/ Lincoln, Nebraska/ With a sawed-off .410/ On my lap/ Through the badlands/ Of Wyoming/ I killed every/ thing in my path"— the pace is barely there at all, you can feel the wind blowing in the grave), and "Highway Patrolman." With the voice Bob Dylan used in "With God on Our Side"—a young man's voice with hundreds of years of unwanted knowledge in it—Springsteen's patrolman, Joe Roberts, tells us who he is, what he does, what he's about. Then the story is twisted, just a bit, a turn at once offhand and purely ominous: "I got a brother named Frankie/ And Frankie ain't no good." With a timing too delicate to measure, Springsteen barely rushes the first two words of that last line, and then steps back from the last three. The words curl; he hooks the story right in your heart, and then pulls just slightly: not to reel you in just yet, simply to make sure the line is fast. The same touch is there in "Used Cars," as the boy in the backseat watches the car salesman looking over his father's hands, watches his mother nervously twisting her ring; it's there when the music rises, almost secretly, as it becomes clear that generations of workers, not just one boy who's singing, will spend their lives in the shadow of the mansion on the hill.

The countless details of craft and empathy that underlie this album portray a world of meaningless killings and state executions, a world in which honest work has been trivialized and honest goals reduced to a bet on a state lottery; a world where the rich live as a different species, so far above the aspirations of ordinary people as to seem like gods. But the only acts of rebellion presented on *Nebraska* are murders. They are nihilistic acts committed in a world where social and economic function have become the measure of all things and have dissolved all values beyond money and status. In that context, these acts make sense. And that is the burden of *Nebraska*.

—California,
November 1982

1983–1985

The Mekons Story

A man stands in a room, bare save for a mattress, a few bottles, a few books. From his window he can see a crowd gathered before a huge, new, domineering public building; we can't tell if this is taking place in the present or in some distopian no-future, or if the queerly distant reverberations in the scene locate the action well back in the past. A dignitary steps down from a reviewing stand to snip a ribbon. As the crowd presses forward for a better look, the man in the room begins a keening sound; it's the strangled no of someone who's spent too much time talking to himself, a voice that gives off not the slightest hint of winning a response. The scene below the window plays itself out; stamping one foot to keep a rhythm going, the man edges toward hysteria, then escapes it as his curse takes on a hint of form. He's screaming quietly at his walls, railing at the spectacle that confronts him, wishing that the crowd were somehow a community and that he could join it, no matter that with his every jagged intonation—"And we bow to re-pub-lic . . . we bow to em-ploy-er . . . we bow to *God*" (a horrible, helpless loathing for that last word)—he drives himself away from any possible community, or any possible communication. He loses his breath for a moment, loses his place, then regains it; the listener (who feels almost ashamed to be listening, feels like a peeping tom) begins to realize that, at least to the man in the room, this cry is some kind of song, a set of obsessions, reaching toward shape, which have developed since the man started to sing and which he is desperate to hold on to.

The singer has made his way down to the square; he stands

at the fringes of the crowd, peering from behind a corner of the
new building. *Don't look at him*, says a mother to her ten-year-
old. *Fucking drunks*, says her husband. The man leans his body
out from behind a corner, as if expecting that someone will actually acknowledge his presence. The way he carries his voice
—this is now a public assault, no matter how the public ignores
it—tells how he carries his body: ready for abuse, maybe hoping for it. Abuse is a sort of communication: a perversion of
community that in an inverted sense nevertheless suggests
community when nothing else does; an intimation of utopia to a
man almost silenced by the polite noise of domination. "Little
girls, lit-tle girls, *we're innocent until pro-ven guilty*," he keeps
saying, and you can't tell if he sounds more like a priest than a
child molester. There is some hint here, some fragmentary cultural memory, of the Ranters, the possessed and sometimes naked heretics who defined the farthest reaches of extremism
during the English Civil War; they established a tradition, severed from history almost before the tradition took shape, of
absolute negation, a tradition communicated ever since through
ritual gestures, drunken curses, catchphrases deaf to their
sources: "Thus saith the Lord," pronounced the ranter Abiezer
Coppe in 1649, ". . . *that I overturn, overturn, overturn . . .*
[I] who am UNIVERSALL LOVE, and whose service is perfect
freedome, and pure Libertinisme. . . ."

Who hasn't witnessed a version of this scene in the last few
years? I see it almost every morning, outside a Berkeley coffee
store where former mental patients funneled onto the streets
force themselves on the honest bohemian bourgeoisie, demanding quarters, standing silent, speed-rapping, calling down the
wrath of God. (I once witnessed the performance of a man who,
madly free-associating, assumed the identity of every well-
known rock 'n' roll musician the name of whose group, or whose
first or last name, began with the letter *J.*) But if evading such
a scene is the task of most of us, making it into a piece of music
—taking it away from its banal context of socialized mental ill-

ness and playing with its possibilities as history, and as art, and as politics—was the task of a now-defunct English punk band, the Mekons of Leeds. The account above—the ranter in the public square—is merely my version of "The Building," one of twenty cuts on *it falleth like the gentle rain from heaven: The Mekons Story, 1977–1982*, an album that functions almost as a map of hidden impulses in pop music.

A free-floating aggregation of anarchists, students, and provocateurs (perhaps two dozen sometime or onetime members circling around a core of three or four), the Mekons came out of the same University of Leeds leftist milieu that later produced the Gang of Four and Delta 5. They formed in 1977, when the emergence of the Sex Pistols in London (and no one was a more natural inheritor of Abiezer Coppe than Johnny Rotten) seemed to have overturned all the rules of pop: all the rules governing pop as sound, and all the rules governing it as marketplace. They disbanded in 1982. The Mekons were never particularly famous even in the U.K., and they remain almost completely unknown in the U.S.; they played, I think, a single American show, supporting the Gang of Four at a Manhattan New Year's Eve date. In the drunken, electronically slurred narration that links the tunes and fragments of *The Mekons Story* into a story that tells itself, a phrase like "internationally famous number one hit" means "noticed."

Hung on such bare bones, the group's tale is hardly different from that of any of the thousands and thousands of bands to have appeared in the wake of the Sex Pistols, and to have set about trying to act out the clues to freedom each thought it heard in the Sex Pistols' nihilist manifestos, manifestos that by the time of "Holidays in the Sun" had taken on a complexity most would ignore—clues to freedom that have been interpreted by groups from Warsaw to Berlin to Teaneck to Azuza as promising everything from lotsa money to the seizure of state power.

"My first article in the review *Philosophies*, published in

1923 or 1924," said the Marxist sociologist Henri Lefebvre in 1975, "[was] a portrait of dada. This article brought me a lasting friendship with Tristan Tzara. . . . I had written: 'Dada smashes the world, but the pieces are fine.' . . . each time I ran into Tristan Tzara, he'd say to me: 'So? You're picking up the pieces! Do you plan to put them back together?' I always replied: 'No—I pick them up in order to finish smashing them.' " Sex Pistols manager Malcolm McLaren, 1983: "The Sex Pistols created a tremendous amount of debris, and that was very rewarding. It's like a child who loves to destroy something in order to find out what it's made of . . . smash everything . . . they just weren't able to construct anything from the debris. [But] that was just the beginning." D. H. Lawrence, 1923: "The furthest frenzies of French modernism or Futurism have not yet reached the pitch of extreme consciousness that Poe, Melville, Hawthorne, Whitman reached. The European moderns are all *trying* to be extreme. The great Americans I mention just were it." From the Sex Pistols on down, the pursuit of extremism has constituted the burden of the most interesting rock 'n' roll performers of the last seven years: extremism as a modification of the rock 'n' roll form, and extremism by means of rock 'n' roll as an attempt to intervene in the symbol system of a listener's everyday life. (And, if a band lasts long enough, a pullback from extremism in an attempt to maintain the pursuit of extremism as a form of paying work within the commodity economy—perhaps a killing contradiction in terms, perhaps not.) In a recent issue of *Artforum*, Kim Gordon of the New York band Sonic Youth memorialized the 1982 antiart nonperformance of PiL at the Ritz in New York City: that the crowd rioted (echoes of the premiere of *Rite of Spring* or *Nude Descending a Staircase* at the Armory Show—they hoped, they hoped) confirms the conceit of stars charging $10 for a show in which stars went-to-the-farthest-extremes and smashed-their-stardom by standing behind a screen instead of playing to an audience, a ruse staged sixty-two years previously by Berlin dadaists Walter Mehring and George Grosz. The Mekons, as acquainted with dada as anyone in the punk world—which is saying something—never performed behind a screen. One could say that they just were extreme—that they gathered up the debris left by the Sex Pistols just to finish smashing it.

Of course, in the domain of twentieth-century art practice, the word "just" is always suspect. " 'Culture,' " Harold Rosenberg quoted a May '68 Paris wall slogan, " 'is the inversion of life.' " He commented: "But this statement is itself culture, since it is inherited from the radical art movements of fifty years ago." "The Building" may seem like the opposite of self-conscious, or just conscious, cultural production—it's so naturalistic it sounds like a field recording ("Documents of the Industrial Revolution, Gott textile mill, Leeds, 1802; Ranter survival section")—but the piece, far from being an early Mekons stumble toward profundity, was made by Mekon Mark White, just voice and stamping foot, in the Mekons' sixth and final year. Beginning their career as a band notorious for their ur-punk inability to organize an ensemble of instruments in an acceptable manner, the Mekons' six years taught them how not to.

Rock 'n' roll as "the only form of music which can actually be done better by people who can't play their instruments than by those who can" (critic Mary Harron, quoted on the sleeve of *The Mekons Story*) functioned as a concept. The apprehension of ordinary life—drinking, all-night arguments, wage labor, jealousy, political dread, sloth, blocked desires, consumerism, friendship, fatigue, love, good times—was put into practice, through the use of technologically complex tools, both as a version of ordinary life and as an aesthetic. The crudity of technique on which the Mekons insisted ("Those who couldn't play tried to learn and those who could tried to forget," as one writer put it) allowed the blind impulses of ordinary life to destroy the specialness of the performer—no screen was necessary—and the crudity of technique validated ordinary life as subject matter.

This is the idea behind "Letter's in the Post," the first,

shortest, and almost the earliest ("recorded in a room above the Fenton Hotel in Leeds 1978") song on *The Mekons Story*. Mark White of "The Building" is credited with "concept," and no instruments or vocals. Remember Elvis's 1962 "Return to Sender"? A rejected lover sends a note to his ex-girlfriend, but it comes back, again and again—"No such number, no such zone"—she won't accept it. The song works because write-to-order tunesmiths Otis Blackwell and Winfield Scott were so good at intricate lyrical touches (that pre-zip-code "zone" reference) and equally intricate pop melodies. "Letter's in the Post" is basically the same idea, reduced to I-sent-it-you-better-read-it. The band hammers out the number; the guitars are one big scratch. The intensity is fabulous; the song's thirty-four seconds seem to go on for minutes. The music and the vocals are so plain, so unshaped, that you can't not believe something is at stake here; you can't ignore the noise. Someone has grabbed you by the throat and is talking to you. The road that took the Mekons to that public square, and the debris they found along the way, becomes visible.

The Mekons' first singles, also from 1978—"Never Been in a Riot" (a riot they were in, sometime later—a neofascist attack on their radical-gay pub—is detailed on *The Mekons Story* in "Frustration"), "Where Were You?," and "32 Weeks"—were preposterously rough, left-handed screeches about, respectively, a wish for a political situation that could force participation, the wish for an affective situation that could force contact, and the number of weeks of labor required to pay for a given everyday object—like a refrigerator. They're the shouts of people who have invaded the bandstand during someone else's tuning up, a confrontation in the cafe that can't be denied: "Would you ever be my friend, do you *like* me?" Those 45s were on Fast Product, an Edinburgh independent label; they got the Mekons a contract with Virgin, a London corporate record company. There the Mekons made one failed-compromise lp—and if in 1979 *The Quality of Mercy Is Not Strnen* (chimp typing out

Shakespeare on the cover) sounded as if the Mekons had sold out to their hopes for stardom and mass acceptance, today it sounds as if the concept, not merely its execution, was beyond them. The record didn't sell and Virgin soon dropped the band. In 1982, with the independent Red Rhino, the group produced *The Mekons* (a shining reproduction of Caspar David Friedrich's *The Wanderer Above the Mists* alone on the sleeve), so odd and rattled few could hear it. *The Mekons Story*, on the leftist CNT label, is almost exclusively made up of material not released before; it junks everything together, out of chronological sequence, and everything sounds of a piece. There is nothing that comes off as rock 'n' roll, in the sense that the phrase denotes the institutionalized international culture of pop music; there is nothing on it that is conceivable within the framework of any other currently functioning international popular culture.

it falleth like the gentle rain from heaven—with *The Mekons Story* picking up the quote from *The Merchant of Venice* that was skewed for the title of the band's first album— begins from the premise that expression is a natural right with no obligations to world-historical significance ("Letter's in the Post") and moves back and forth across a terrain where that self-exculpatory idea attaches itself to an obligation to discover what it is one really wants to say—and an obligation to discover the most interesting ways to say it, and who one wants to say it to. In other words, expression turns into politics. That might be "Bomb Train," another 1982 cut: a muddled, uncertain rhythm, voices burbling incomprehensibly in the background, until after a minute or so someone shouts, "There's no time! Look! Over there!," and a guitar breaks in like a blessing with chords that say, *there's nothing you can do about it*. It's a perfect rendering of the fear behind the warning signs in every London subway train, of the fantasies every London subway rider must either entertain or repress as a matter of daily habit.

The Mekons began with slogans—"Anyone can do it!," the 1976 punk rallying cry against the oppressions of rock stardom —and moved to something like poetry—"Little girls, lit-tle girls, *inno-cent until proven guilty.*" When Mekon David Spencer reads the narration to *The Mekons Story* (quoting from the band's Virgin contract, detailing the advance specified for the never-approached third Virgin album, explicating Canadian rights), he sounds like an old man laughing into the night: what fools we were! (What fools *they* were, to have bet on us in the first place!) Following the album's last song, Spencer comes to his last lines—"The Mekons . . . finally folded . . ."—and he seems so far away, the alcoholic haze so thick, you can hardly believe the band ever existed. For that matter you can hardly believe that all those fifties joke songs and doo-wops that established the expressive power of rock 'n' roll ever existed, if the fact that they existed means that they ultimately gave birth to something so strange, and in its way so much older than rock 'n' roll, as "The Building." But they did; and it was only last year.

—*Threepenny Review,*
Summer 1983

In the Fascist Bathroom

*C*lick click. *Click click.* There's a bloodlessness to the punctuating handclaps on Elvis Costello's "Pills and Soap" that is almost entirely self-effacing—an odd detail for a song about fascism in Margaret Thatcher's England, after five years still on track as harbinger for Ronald Reagan's U.S.A. But perhaps not so odd when fascism is denied its image-bound, pornographic dimensions, and represented on the level Hannah Arendt brought into view in 1945, with "Organized Guilt and Universal Responsibility."

The transformation of the family man from a responsible member of society, interested in all public affairs, to a "bourgeois" concerned only with his private existence and knowing no civic virtue, is an international modern phenomenon. . . . Each time society, through unemployment, frustrates the small man in his normal functioning and normal self-respect, it trains him for that last stage in which he will willingly undertake any function, even that of hangman.

Costello's device doesn't sound much like rock 'n' roll handclapping, a grand tradition. (In the midst of the Preston Sturges-like confusion of Floyd Mutrux's 1978 film *American Hot Wax*, a frantic fifties record producer trying to get a dead "Come Go with Me" off the ground grabs the black janitor: "You've got big hands, get in here!" History is made.) In "Pills and Soap," a tune based on "Sing a Song of Sixpence," the handclapping sounds alien, like a joke that isn't funny: a hipster snapping his fingers in front of a firing squad, maybe. Costello's refusal of rant or melodrama in a performance that doesn't hedge its bets—pills and soap are what (in the remarkable Thatcherist neologism) "redundant" occupants of the U.K. are to be melted down for—ultimately isolates the clapping, raising it out of the background, until it echoes about as subtly as Boris Karloff's footfalls in a haunted house. No one is clapping; someone is counting.

"Pills and Soap" is catchy. And yet it is very nearly too well written, too artful, to sidle its way into a listener's day, which is what it means to do—so that days or years later one will recall its whole, unfragmented vision, as bits and pieces of that vision begin to come true. There are striking, displacing lines in this song, but they are not allowed to call attention to themselves. The sure, sensual, somehow natural sway of the music, and Costello's insistence on singing to the music, not to the words, make his words communicate like real talk, make the singer seem like a real person, make the situation he is singing about seem like a real situation.

If there is such a thing as the fascist personality, it comes not from "the dim No-Man's Land between the Bohemian and the Pimp" (where Susan Sontag was still locating it thirty years after Arendt had coined the phrase to kill the sociological cliché), but from "the normality of job-holders and family men." The bathroom in the fascist utopia is made of plaster and ceramic tile, not rubber and leather; it contains pills and soap, just like any other bathroom, not arcane sexual aids. Life goes on. To be presented as horrifying fascism must be made to seem ordinary.

If the presentation itself is ordinary, though, it will evaporate on contact with the listener. Poetry is necessary, and in the case of Elvis Costello—a family man interested in all public affairs—this means wordplay, puns, diverted homilies, distorted slogans. As a pop pantheist, Costello is too captivated by the possibilities of his chosen form to settle for didactic protest art. He won't play the blessed demagogue; he won't use the demagogic artist's nonspecific paranoid "they." "Give me the needle, give me the rope/ We're going to melt them down for pills and soap"—whatever happens here leaves neither the singer nor anyone else the privileged out that is the most specific benefit of protest art. No doubt without having read it, Costello works from Walter Benjamin's dictum: "the tendency of a literary [we can say 'aesthetic'] work can only be politically correct if it is also [aesthetically] correct."

Now a track on Costello's *Punch the Clock* lp, "Pills and Soap" was originally released in the U.K. in 1983, not long before the election that returned Thatcher to office; it was released pseudonymously, credited to "The Imposter," and withdrawn from circulation on election day. It never mentions or even refers to Thatcher, but a good subversive pop song is like a disease—in terms of what it truly means to say it arrives silently. The song begins with some sort of nightly-news tragedy, reporters poking their microphones into the faces of a sister, a mother, and a father—this could be a war death, or something much more private, a suicide, a fire victim, even an accused murderer in the family. None of which makes direct sense of the chorus that follows: "What would you say, what would you do/ Children and animals, two by two/ Give me the needle, give me the rope/ We're going to melt them down for—" The quiet, repressed way Costello sings the word "soap" is so erotic he seems almost to be swallowing it: the soap, not the word.

The song is seductive; it begins to sound like something Peggy Lee might sing, until Costello makes a tiny rip in the smooth, curling fabric of his music with the phrase "Lord and Lady Muck." They are, you realize then or later or never, the Prince and Princess of Wales. The singer's acceptance of his new fascist personality is immediately replaced by hatred: "They come from lovely people with a hard line in ·hypocrisy/ They are ashtrays of emotion for the fag ends of the aristocracy."

The calm of the performance is so strict that the slightest increase in pressure is like a bomb. For these lines alone Costello clips his syllables, his thick tone sharpens, and you can imagine a guillotine hitting home. The lines are not ordinary: if "ashtrays of emotion" is meaningless bad poetry, it sets up "the fag ends of the aristocracy," the words rushed as they're sung, the sort of line that needs only to be heard to be understood, the sort of lyric that is never fully absorbed.

This is the only moment of the song when Costello sings to the words, not the music—and as the pills-and-soap chorus pulls the singer into a secret fantasy of regicide, the man who is singing is comforted. The man who is singing—and the "singer" is no less a representation, a construct, than any image in the number—sings only this chorus freely, happily, but by the final chorus the energies liberated by his fantasy will be turned away from their sources and back upon their mandated objects. The man who is singing is singing in the voice of a man who in 1945 Hannah Arendt cited in a story about an SS member recognized by a Jew upon his liberation from Buchenwald. As Arendt told the story, the Jew stared at his former classmate, and "the man stared at remarked: 'You must understand, I have five years of unemployment behind me. They can do anything they want with me.' " That "they" is not nonspecific; after "Pills and Soap," you can hear the tune's handclaps behind it.

If Costello is wrong about the future he has lined out in "Pills and Soap" he will seem like a paranoid fool, but that risk has never bothered him in the past. It is worth remembering that people can be melted down to pills and soap—melted down, within the stated limits of the Thatcherist or Reaganist project, to utensils, to their social and economic functions. Which is to say that a long listen to Costello's song can convince you that he is not singing about the future at all.

—*Artforum,*
January 1984

Free Speech, #1

Cyndi Lauper's "Girls Just Want to Have Fun" was the across-the-board hit of the new year—if you haven't heard it you don't own a radio. The day after Lauper sang it on *Late Night with David Letterman*, a woman in San Francisco called up her favorite FM station to complain. "I had the TV on and I just drifted off, you know? And then, oh, it was hours later, there was this, this *noise*. I mean, that woman woke me up out of a sound sleep!"

If Cyndi Lauper accomplishes nothing else in the years to come, she can savor that moment. It calls for headlines:

TOP FORTY SONGBIRD REALIZES AMBITIONS OF MODERN ART

Painters in Shock
Suicide Rate Jumps in NY, LA
NEA Halts Museum Construction Grants

Heater, Calif., March 15. Famed video sculptor Ras Matass (Arnold Brodsky) was discovered today hiding in this tiny desert hamlet. Matass agreed to speak to reporters only on the grounds that he "might be able to help" other victims of "Lauperism."

"Suicide is for quitters," said the 1971 winner of the Bypass Award. "It's just what she wants. I'm not taking the easy way out. I came here to think it over. Everybody has to think it over. TURN OFF THAT RADIO! The use of pastiche, there's nothing new in that, noise is nothing new, but I heard the story about the woman on the radio station, everybody heard it, and before anyone knew what was happening everything began to fall apart. You understand, don't you? I've been trying for twenty years just to get people to blink!"

What is there in "Girls Just Want to Have Fun" to threaten anyone? Lauper is cute, her songs are catchy, and she wears interesting clothes. Combined with her Slavic features, her gypsy outfits seem more shtick than weird. Her debut lp, *She's So Unusual*, is so shiny, so well produced, that it's easy enough to write her off as this season's Galatea. The record's cover, on the other hand, where Lauper can be seen dancing in some New York City street, is queerly lacking in movement. Lauper is anything but possessed by the surrealist abandon promised by the back-cover montage, where, against the Coney Island Parachute Jump, bobby-soxed feet in white shoes fly through the air with van Gogh's *Starry Night* on their heels. On the front of the album Lauper looks worried; she's holding a bunch of flowers the way a tightrope walker holds a bar, for balance. She looks like she's trying not to fall down.

Put the record on and Lauper sounds like she looks. The woman on the radio was right: you can't use Lauper for Muzak. The saturation airplay given "Girls Just Want to Have Fun" is beginning to get on people's nerves. Maybe it's the froufrou sexism of the lyrics (written by a man); maybe it's the squeaks and blips in the mix and the vocal; maybe it's that there's so much pathos and desire secreted in this piece of squeaky blippy froufrou sexism it calls for a redefinition of the word "fun," if not "girls," if not "just." I don't know—let's ask Elvis Costello. "My ultimate vocation in life," he once said, "is to be an irritant. Someone who disrupts the daily drag of life just enough to leave the victim thinking there's maybe more to it all than the mere humdrum quality of existence." This is a real vocation. Is it why so many are happy to dismiss Lauper as Betty Boop, Olive Oyl, Ethel Merman, or Pia Zadora?

Criticism in rock 'n' roll is generally as compartmentalized as criticism everywhere else; thus Lauper is only talked about in terms of other women. No, she isn't much like Joni Mitchell/ Carly Simon/Pat Benatar. She shares more than a bit with London punk Lora Logic, but the singer she brings to mind most is Buddy Holly. Twenty-five years after his death Holly remains fascinating because the composite image created by his reassuringly ordinary appearance and the strangeness of his vocal sound remains unresolved. His silly/violent vocal shifts from midrange to high to low and back again were never set up, were never called for by the song, never seemed to make musical or emotional sense; in 1957 they made people laugh, and since then they've brought forth every response from delight to terror.

In pop music high and low voices signify different emotional languages, and it's the clear transition from one to the other that signifies the signifiers, that allows them to communicate in an orderly way. Holly leaped over the process and confused the categories; so does Lauper. Her music doesn't wake people up because her voice is scratchy and piercing, though sometimes it is. She wakes people up because, in the context of arrangements that are as reassuring in their familiarity as Buddy Holly's glasses were, she so relentlessly demolishes the expectations that would seem to follow from whatever it is she's just done.

The Brains, a male combo from Atlanta, released "Money Changes Everything" in 1978. It never made the *Billboard* charts, was played often on the independent stations that ignore them, and got the Brains a major-label contract, which quickly led them back to Atlanta, where they broke up. "Money Changes Everything" was their one moment, and they made it stick. As a stately, bitter, hopeless account of idealism and innocence ground into dust, it was a perfect example of the punk impulse to reveal the world-historical (here, more or less the "all that is solid melts into air" section of the *Communist Manifesto*) in ordinary life. It was hard, it hurt, and Cyndi Lauper's version makes the original sound compromised. She makes you wonder if Brains composer and singer Tom Gray even knew what he was talking about.

"Money Changes Everything" opens with a woman leaving her man for a prospect with a thicker wallet. Gray sang as the man, remembering what the woman said to him as she left; with right on his side, he won your sympathy automatically, put you in the song. Lauper sings as the woman, remembering what the man said.

> I said I'm sorry baby, I'm leaving you tonight
> I've found someone new, he's waiting in the car outside
> Oh honey how can you do it, we swore each other everlasting
>   love
> I said yeah I know, but when we did there was one thing
> We weren't thinking of
> And that's money
> Money changes everything

"It's all in the past now," runs the most chilling line of the song, even worse than the frigid "yeah" in the fourth line, which is no happy improvisation: Gray wrote it. He gave the word a sardonic curl; Lauper seems to dump her girlhood in the course of saying it. You might realize she didn't have to take this role—she could have easily turned the song around, made the victim female. But then she wouldn't have had the chance to stamp her foot through her old lover's porch.

You don't hear any of this right away. You hear a celebratory instrumental pastiche, a mnemonic tease—the synthesizer fanfare is from the Brains, the rhythm guitar from the 1964 British Invasion-era Searchers, the lead guitar part from Barry McGuire's 1965 "Eve of Destruction," the bass from Fleetwood Mac's 1977 "Go Your Own Way"—a typical recycling of the old to hide the absence of anything new. In the middle of it all is a mindless warbler seemingly more bent on hitting notes than singing the song. The production is attractive and the vocal almost repellent. But soon the attraction of the pastiche begins to fade, to separate into its parts, and by then the warbler is beginning to explain herself. She takes over the composite sound until it seems not as if this were a neatly constructed bid for airplay (which, among other things, it is), but as if all the radio music of the last twenty years were being brought to bear in a single five-minute performance.

Lauper never does completely explain herself. She moves too fast to keep a fix on, there's blood all over the song, but finally the reassuring composite of the arrangement works as the anchor necessary to translate Lauper's free speech, her instinctive version of Futurist parole in libertà. She sings at least half of "Money Changes Everything" from hell—you can hear her get there, learn its rules, and then rip her fingers trying to crawl her way out—but she comes off the instrumental break, which is played on a hooter (I don't know what it is; the name is perfectly descriptive), like the devil on a recruiting drive, or a girl who can't wait for the clock to strike on New Year's Eve. She communicates philosophy with a flounce, self-loathing with a screech. When, to end the number, she holds a note for a good eleven seconds, you can't tell if she's showing off or possessed by the song.

Whether or not money changes everything, it's patent that singing this song has changed Lauper, if only into more of a singer—which is to say that a confrontation with questions of value intensified her will to ignore the rational transitions of song texts, to the point that the radio may be unable to transmit that will without suffering damage in the process. And that is finally to say—as, driving around town, I twist the dial in search of another Lauper media shock—that the likely reason she can wake people up is that she can herself be wakened.

—*Artforum,*
May 1984

Imperial Margarine

"Imperial Boredom," Eric Bonaventura called the Elvis Costello lp that won the *Village Voice* 1982 Pazz & Jop Critics Poll, the album that everywhere brought forth shouts of "masterpiece"—even in full-page CBS advertisements, even before reviewers had time to provide the quotes, though the ad department did append a smart "?" There's nothing imperial about the boredom of *Goodbye Cruel World*, Costello's latest. It's the sort of record you stop hearing halfway through a side. The music quietly settles on the tables and chairs, like dust.

The title is the best thing about this album, and also the worst, because it promises so much: a set of performances so negative and tough (" 'Revenge and guilt'?" you can almost hear Costello say. "That was the word seven years ago, when prospects were *good*") they'd make you wonder how he'd ever follow them, make you nervous waiting for his version of what the world would follow them with. "*How* cruel, Elvis?" "Well, you've heard the one about the Khmer Rouge day-care center, right? Now I'm going to do a little tune about . . ."

The problem with *Goodbye Cruel World* is not cosmic. It's in the bass-drums-keyboards accompaniments and the way Costello fits his guitar into them. That is, it's in the arrangements —arrangements which don't shape the songs but muffle them. Between *Imperial Bedroom* and *Goodbye Cruel World* was the super *Punch the Clock*, which should have won the 1983 Pazz & Jop poll but didn't come close ("No one's going to call *this* a masterpiece," wrote one notably stupid reviewer, as if the title could tell him how to write about a record without listening to it). This was a package of straightforward rhythms so jittery and full of worry that the tension of Costello and the Attractions (and horns, and backing singers) pressing against the formal musical limits of the material made the songs inexhaustible and finally irresistible on the radio. The arrangement of "Let Them All Talk" was so tightly coiled that loaded up with sound effects for a twelve-inch remix—a dozen broadcasts in as many languages, a shortwave radio with a loose tuning dial—it sounded not just more ambitious but more passionate. Within restricted, Stax-Volt structures, Costello really could let everybody talk—in English or Swahili, it hardly mattered.

Here he can't talk. As on *Imperial Bedroom*, the songs are purposely detached from rock, country, or R&B rhythms, tending instead toward the more diffuse territory of cabaret, Billie Holiday, Frank Sinatra. It worked on the 1983 "Pills and Soap" because the melody and arrangement (pretty much Holiday's "Strange Fruit") were familiar enough to be taken as simple aesthetic facts and then left alone, thus leaving enough empty space in the sound to put the burden of the performance directly on Costello, as a singer, and he outdid himself. The new songs are tricky, shifted back and forth by melodies keyed to the ironic metaphors and allusions of the lyrics. The songs are so tricky Costello and the Attractions seem to settle for versions that are merely coherent—or merely gussied up.

The result is that the arrangements don't carry the ironies (let alone question them), they underscore them, thus killing them. Worse, in order to allow the band to follow the busy, flitting, insensately self-referential tunes, Costello pulls in his voice. He pulls back from his own songs, until what you hear in his voice is simply another instrument in a merely coherent arrangement of something that has become beside any point he might have started out to make.

When Costello closed an Attractions-plus-horns-plus-backing-singers show last year with a solo rendering of a then-unrecorded song called "The Great Unknown," the moment was so saturated with desire and uncertainty I could barely stay in my seat for the edginess. He seemed to have taken all the great rock 'n' roll "Great" songs (the Platters' "The Great Pretender," the Fleetwoods' "The Great Imposter," John Prine's "The Great Compromise," and, I swear, "The Great Snowman," a record about Colonel Tom Parker that I heard in the fifties and have never been able to track down), to have fixed them as a fan's mini-tradition, and then to have superseded the tradition with a world-historical cry. Listening to "The Great Unknown" on *Goodbye Cruel World*, I can't imagine what I heard. It's just another blur, without an instant of instrumental or vocal frisson to pull your ear toward the words being sung—and it joins the mini-tradition of terrible rock 'n' roll "Great" songs, the only other example being Van Morrison's "The Great Deception," an ode to the evils of mixing art and commerce so pious it almost made you glad "the great Rembrandt . . . didn't have enough money for brushes."

Elvis Costello is a typical first-rate rock 'n' roll singer with a third-rate voice: almost no physical range, little coloration. Sam Cooke might have been able to bring life to the three-piece-suit-with-watch-and-chain arrangements on *Goodbye Cruel World*; given Costello's limits, diffuse phrasing on top of diffuse melodies and diffuse instrumentation produces only a nullity. As with Bob Dylan, Costello's true—and vast—range as a singer is primarily conversational: pauses, emphases, gestures, asides, bursts of rage or compassion, an argument in which values are weighted, weighed, and found wanting. As a man who means not only to bring the bad news but to make sense of it, he needs something hard to play off of—not a cornered chump who can't do much more than mumble, flatter, ask the time, and name-drop, which is more or less what the music on *Goodbye Cruel World* does. The one exception here is "Peace in Our Time"—save for a pretentious French horn on the choruses, against the story Costello tells (a British version of Dylan's "With God on Our Side") there is nothing but a bitter, echoing pulse, a restraint that gives the death-time words Costello is singing an impact all out of proportion to their literal meaning, which is what argument, or rock 'n' roll, is all about. And for "Peace in Our Time," you don't need *Goodbye Cruel World*—you can get it as an import single, credited to "The Imposter" (of course he's heard the Fleetwoods).

On Costello's recent solo tour, he accompanied himself on acoustic or electric guitar, acoustic or electric piano, and sang for more than two hours a show: a cover of James Carr's obscure "Pouring Water on a Drowning Man" so soulful it was hard to believe Costello didn't write it, numerous other borrowed tunes, a dozen of his hits, a dozen of his buried treasures. He made it clear that his purpose as a singer was not only to change the way the world looked, but to change the way his records sounded—the new versions of his own songs spoke to their recorded versions, wrestled with them. The songs that would turn up on *Goodbye Cruel World* punched the clock, did the job, and stuck around.

—*Village Voice*,
26 June 1984

Gone with the Wind

Seventeen is a made-for/rejected-by public-television documentary by Joel DeMott and Jeff Kreines about working-class high school seniors in Muncie, Indiana. No-big-deal dope-smoking, a pervasive sense of no-future, black boys with white girlfriends, and a lot of obscenity made all the more obscene by its casualness are what got the film excluded from the Public Broadcasting Service's *Middletown* series, but that's not likely what you'll take away from the movie if you see it.

The most striking scenes in *Seventeen* grow out of an ordinary party. It's held in the house where Lynn Massie—white, seventeen, and the central figure in the film—lives with her parents and two brothers. The hand-held camera shots and the ambient noise are confusing at first; soon, everything begins to revolve around another teenager, Keith Buck. He seems so much a part of the family it can take the credits to show that he's a friend, not one of Lynn's brothers. He's that comfortable with Lynn's parents, that much not a guest. The viewer doesn't feel like a guest either; the feeling in the crowded rooms is very intimate.

The party finds its rhythm, and Keith gets drunker by the frame. The Massies don't appear concerned—no doubt they've seen him like this before. But it's an amazing, ugly drunk: a rant, where the drunk locks into a couple of phrases and can't let them go. Keith is raving about his best friend, who's been in an auto accident. There's a terrible incoherence to his speech; though every word is clear, no emotion is. *He's gonna pull through*, Keith says, *'cause he's tough as nails. He's tough as nails. He's tough as nails. He's tough as nails just like me so he's gonna pull through. He's gotta pull through 'cause he's tough as nails just like me. He's tough as nails just like me.*

Watching, I was sure it was the beer talking—that Keith's friend wasn't really badly hurt, that this was an act, adolescent mythmaking, a buildup to a fake event which, years later, could be talked about as if it had actually happened. *Man, remember when you almost bought it? I knew you'd pull through and you did, 'cause you're tough as nails, man*—forty-year-old fist punches forty-year-old beer belly—*just like me.* This wasn't a study in teenage crisis, or a study in teenage friendship—it was a study in teenage drinking. But that shift from "gonna pull through" to "gotta" should have tipped me off.

In the next scene, still at Lynn's house—it's the next day—we see Keith calling up a radio station, asking the disc jockey to dedicate a song to his best friend, who's just died. Keith wants Bob Seger's "Against the Wind." A cut: we see Lynn, a girlfriend, and Keith sitting in Lynn's room, chatting, the radio playing. "Against the Wind" comes on. "That's it!" shouts Lynn, though the disc jockey says nothing about a dedication. In the same voice she'd use if the party were still on and the disc jockey were spinning her number one dance tune, Lynn shouts again: "Crank it!"

Keith sits by the radio; Lynn and her friend are on the bed. Lynn's mother looks into the room and leans on a doorjamb. Suddenly, the whole film changes. Its language changes, and the language of the people in it: both become utterly unreal. Earlier—in schoolrooms, cars, in other homes—we've seen people glance out of the corners of their eyes at the camera, where other documentaries have made us expect camera subjects to appear "natural"; we've seen people talk directly to the camera, though the documentary never acknowledges itself as such, and the interviews come onto the screen as ordinary conversations with an unseen listener. But a different sort of self-consciousness has now taken over, and it has nothing to do with the camera. It has nothing to do with the fact that this incident, in

which a death has fixed a moment in time, will be made into a
series of images to be received by film viewers whom the people experiencing the event directly will never meet. It has
nothing to do with the filmic process of displacement, which
makes real events into narrative representations—though this
is a scene of extreme displacement, whose source is in representation.

As the song plays, the film turns theatrical for the first time
—or rather the people in it do. Lynn, her mother, her friend,
and Keith display emotional reactions familiar to the viewer, so
familiar that the viewer realizes they are re-presentations of
reactions that have in the past been represented to those who
now display them. These people are performing, not for the
camera, but for each other, and most intensely for themselves.
From the moment Keith calls the radio station we see only the
most detached, free-floating, meaningless gestures; with the
first notes of "Against the Wind" Lynn reacts as if a dedication
were marking merely her birthday, or a six-month boyfriend
anniversary—"Crank it!"—nothing more. The gestures we've
seen have never referred to the dead friend; they weren't bur-
dened. Now grief erupts: sobs, moans, Lynn and her friend hug-
ging and hiding their faces, Lynn's mother crying, Keith holding his head in his hands. But for all the noise, and the gestures
that now carry the full weight of the dead friend's corpse, the
scene does not come off the screen. It seems to recede into
it.

It becomes obvious that the actuality of a friend's death is
being sealed by the radio. The event cannot become real until it
is sanctioned by an agency of representation, until it is removed
from those who have experienced it and represented to
them, until they can perceive it as a representation and then
act it out as a performance scripted by people they have never
met.

The song Keith has chosen is perfect for the moment, which
suggests that he is at least a coauthor of the script. "Against

the Wind" follows the tale of a rock 'n' roll singer. Through years of obscurity and temptation he fights his own sense of failure and the world's definition of success—and even now, a star, he's somehow "still running against the wind." It's a wonderful elegy: sentimental, soothing, and uplifting in its melody, beautifully sung from deep in the chest. But compared to "Night Moves," the allusive, tricky, blazingly personal song that in 1976 made Bob Seger the star he is now singing about, the mythical/autobiographical "Against the Wind" is a song written less by Seger than by other heroically sentimental uplifting songs. It is a set of cues—cues picked up first by Seger, and then by the people in the Massie house.

The song finishes; the spell of grief is broken, or its performance simply ends. Keith raises his hand in a hard fist, shakes it, and lets go with a great "UHHH-WOOO!," precisely as if he were at a Bob Seger concert. Rituals cross over: one, of how you are supposed to behave when a friend has died, another of how you are supposed to behave when a star has played your favorite song. It seems inescapable that the latter ritual has contained the former. It's less that the song, with its mnemonic power to unleash hidden emotions, has allowed these people to acknowledge their grief than that their ability to make the radio acknowledge a grievous event has allowed them to dramatize and stylize their grief.

What hangs in the air when the scene is done is not grief, but Seger's song itself. Up against the event it has orchestrated, it begins to break down once severed from it. Now it is no more than Bob Seger promising that after ten years of struggle, and a few years of stardom, he has not sold out and never will. With Lynn and Keith, in the film, off to other concerns, the scene of their grief reshapes itself: one looks back and sees them promising that they won't sell out, that they have not sold out the right of their friend to smash himself to death, that they won't sell out their chance to do the same. The whole complex of entreaties and responses has been so fabu-

lously removed from anything directly lived you might begin to
wonder what would have happened if, when Keith phoned up
the radio station, the line had been busy.

—*Artforum,*
October 1984

Four More Years

America's future rests in a thousand dreams inside your hearts. It rests in the message of hope in songs of a man so many young Americans admire: New Jersey's own Bruce Springsteen. And helping you make those dreams come true is what this job of mine is all about.

—Ronald Reagan, 19 September 1984

There's a line from a Bruce Springsteen song so fierce I've never been able to get past it: "Take a knife and cut this pain from my heart." I hear "The Promised Land" on the radio, instinctively turn up the sound, forget what's coming—and once that red moment arrives, whatever follows only chases its echo. Listening to Springsteen's voice takes you out of yourself: it connects you to the singer and to everyone else. Hell is not other people. The world is suddenly remade into a utopia of what it would mean to speak so plainly and be understood so violently, a utopia in which one immediately loses one's way. Driving, you could run into a tree. Shaving, you could cut your throat.

A couple of years ago Springsteen put the knife in and left it there; then he stood still and watched the wound rot. That was *Nebraska*, the guitar-and-vocal lp he'd recorded in his living room. The record began in the voice of Charley Starkweather, the number-one mass killer of the fifties, on the night of his execution; then it got worse. Save for two tunes in which the singer pleaded for the deliverance of hearing the right song come off the radio at the right time, the album described, it felt out, it transmitted the collapse and the corruption of all values. The final number was called "Reason to Believe," and critics fell over themselves in a rush to assure their readers that this last word testified to their hero's unbroken optimism. "At the end of every hard-earned day," he had sung, "people find some reason to believe." Especially if you don't see what you're looking at, or listen to what you hear. The situation from which Springsteen had gleaned his moral was this:

> Seen a man standin' over a dead dog
> Lyin' by the highway in a ditch
> He's lookin' down kinda puzzled
> Pokin' that dog with a stick
> Got his car door flung open
> He's standin' out on Highway 31
> Like if he stood there long enough
> That dog'd get up and run

Remember *Time* magazine's special issue on "National Renewal," the one that followed Ronald Reagan's election to the presidency? Not only would Carl Sandburg rise from the dead to sing the song of humming factories, the very grass would grow greener beneath your feet. *Time* read the signs correctly: the newly empowered had bided their time, and what they had waited for was nothing so trivial as a change in regime, but the chance to create a whole new epistemology, a whole new set of rules governing what it meant to live and die. Springsteen read the signs as clearly; *Nebraska* was his response.

Now we are in the midst of the next election. Released in that setting, *Born in the U.S.A.*, a full-blown rock record, came forth as a triumph, all metaphors in place, an instant number-one hit. It reached me as a piece of cheese. The record was a retreat; it replaced refusal with malaise, with a merely disillusioned acceptance, an acceptance that had no edge. The car

door flung open in *Nebraska*'s "Reason to Believe" was a fragment that made the whole scene real, and reduced your sense
of belief to a belief in the stick in the man's hand. On *Born in
the U.S.A.* the eye and ear for detail that animated *Nebraska*
drifted into a contemplation of motifs.

You could see what was wrong with *Born in the U.S.A.*
when you turned on the television and saw Springsteen in his
first in-the-flesh video, live onstage in St. Paul at the start of
the year's tour, singing his top ten single "Dancing in the
Dark." On record, the song is about blind faith and struggle;
here, as the comic Bob Goldthwait put it, Springsteen looks like
a member of Up with People. He looks made up. Moving across
the stage in seemingly choreographed, marks-on-the-boards
jerks, he grins like a supper-club singer doing "Gloomy Sunday" while communicating boundless love for the crowd. One is
made to see a wide-eyed girl pressing against the stage;
Springsteen takes her hand, lifts her up, and dances with her as
the video fades out. From show to show, he really does this—
but this girl is too cute, and the routine makes something that
actually happens into something that could never happen. The
next time you pay your money, enter a hall, and see Springsteen sing his songs, it will make you think the woman whose
hand he takes is a plant.

All in all, as the songs from *Born in the U.S.A.* took their
turns on the radio, I'd rather have heard the Beaver Brown
Band imitating Springsteen on the soundtrack to *Eddie and the
Cruisers* than Springsteen imitating himself. Then "Born in the
U.S.A." came on—not the album, just the title cut. Written and
recorded about the same time as *Nebraska*, the song is the tes-
timony of a Vietnam veteran. "*Born* . . . in the U.S.A.,"
Springsteen sings over and over; drummer Max Weinberg provides a single thudding beat for each word. Born in the U.S.A.,
born in the U.S.A.—a lot of people have complained the song
doesn't go anywhere. What was it supposed to do, provide a
solution to the national debt?

Precisely. The song is about the refusal of the country to treat Vietnam veterans as something more than nonunion workers in an enterprise conducted off the books. It is about the debt the country owes to those who suffered the violation of the principles on which the country was founded, and by which it has justified itself ever since. In other words, the song links Vietnam veterans to the Vietnamese—or rather (because when he is on, Springsteen personalizes everything he touches), one veteran tries to make that link.

In Joe Klein's book *Payback: Five Marines After Vietnam,* the story begins with an account of an appalling 1967 battle between American marines and North Vietnamese regulars as it was experienced by Klein's five subjects. It ends in 1982 with a hypnotist leading one of the five to finally remember what happened during the battle, to achieve catharsis. "You know," the ex-marine says when the moment is over, "I wonder if any of the North Vietnamese are in hypnosis, reliving the same battle. . . ." This possibility seems never to have struck Klein, and when it presents itself he does not wonder how the Vietnamese version of the battle might read, let alone try to find out—a gesture one might think could have occurred to him even before he witnessed the ex-marine's revelation. In Klein's book, the Vietnamese are only the enemy, a cipher, and because zero times five is zero, the wealth of biographical detail Klein has amassed falls away, leaving the story a void. Springsteen's veteran shouts at an unseen judge: "Sent me off to a foreign land/ To go and kill/ The yellow man." He was, he knows, sent off to kill a cipher, and he knows that he was sent as a cipher. The furious irony in his voice, ten years building, turns the racist phrase inside out and makes both ciphers real.

Springsteen begins "Born in the U.S.A." with a great scream. Not only does he maintain it throughout the performance, he somehow modulates it, makes it talk, so that each shift of line and rhythm tells a whole truth. It's not easy to maintain a scream, and a scream is the hardest voice to inflect.

I don't know how Springsteen does it; it may be that the monolithic drumbeat gives the most imperceptible shift in Springsteen's voice tangible power. "I had a brother/ *wham/* At Khe Sahn/ *wham/* Fighting off/ *wham/* The Viet Cong—They're still there/ *wham/* He's all gone"—this is a series of negations that says more about the rightful loss of the war than any page in Klein's respectable book.

The song moves on like a landslide. It carries the tension of clandestine communication in a Stalinist country, the power of the argument paradoxically multiplying in a country where no censorship is necessary; Springsteen keeps screaming, and as he does, he catches, for the only time on the album, details as quick as any on *Nebraska*. With every line Springsteen increases the pressure. The song never does explode. "I'm a long-gone daddy in the U.S.A.," the singer says finally, as Springsteen's scream takes on a hint of syncopation, of fun—"I'm a cool-rocking daddy in the U.S.A."

Cool rocking—the ability to respond to the right song at the right time, coming off the radio without warning. It's easy to believe that little else is left. The one truth the album *Born in the U.S.A.* tells is that to take a knife and cut the pain from your heart you must be prepared to leave the knife in. And anyway it is already there.

—*Artforum,*
November 1984

400,000 More Years

With the election long gone, all the rap records featuring all the Ronald Reagan soundalikes are just so many Mondale buttons. All but one—the one the man made himself.

Everybody heard about it, but not too many people heard the thing itself: "My fellow Americans, I'm pleased to tell you today that I've signed legislation that will outlaw Russia forever. We begin bombing in five minutes." Hearing it is indescribably more chilling than reading it on the page. My first chance came a few days after the fact, on KALX-FM, the Berkeley college station. Certain it was a fake, I pulled over at the first phone booth, called, asked what it was. "The real McCoy," said the DJ. I couldn't believe it, and I didn't want to believe it. But they played it straight through the next fifteen minutes, over and over, adding echo and reverb here and there, and by the end I had the Mondale spot designed.

Black screen; hold. Voice-over and white letters on screen: Ladies and Gentlemen, the President of the United States. Reagan on, voice and white letters: "My fellow Americans, I'm pleased to tell you today that I've signed legislation that will outlaw Russia forever. We begin bombing in five minutes." Reagan off. Black screen; long hold. Tag, white letters, no voice: Ronald Reagan Thinks Nuclear War Is a Joke. Do You? No such ad ever ran, of course; it would have been unseemly. It might have lost votes.

A few weeks before November 6, Bootsy Collins of Parliament-Funkadelic and Jerry Harrison of Talking Heads released

"Five Minutes" under the name Bonzo Goes to Washington. The credit was the only cheap shot—the only note that linked this twelve-inch to the other Rappin' Ronnie discs, all of which were merely funny or not funny, which were made out of liberal condescension, from the idea that the president is not a serious man, and which in any case had only one effect: they made Ronald Reagan seem likable, even hip. Here, in a spirit of horror and glee, Collins and Harrison let the man speak for himself.

They ran a few scratch cutups over the lines to keep them pumping. And they isolated the words to force you to catch the nuances, to become aware of the phrasing, to feel the rhythms. The production was nothing special, but save for Collins's bass line the music was in the vocal, and that was remade into a work of art. The whole point was to make sure you listened until you believed he'd really said it.

Reagan starts out slowly, but then his voice changes, blurs a little. He rushes the ending. He rushes it because while this really is a joke—you can hear people laughing in the background—it is also unmistakably sexual. The lust in the passage is what makes it so terrifying. It's anything but unknown for soldiers to fuck the corpses of women killed in search-and-destroy missions; they're turned on by death. That, that exactly, is what you hear. Again and again, shifted, speeded up, slowed down. It's viva la muerte turned into la muerte, l'amor. It's sickening.

I have a fantasy that, by some kind of luck, this record will last, if only because enough people will buy it to transform it into an artifact. Not a historical artifact—just the sort of thing that ends up in attics or basements, packed away in trunks. I imagine that someday, a dozen or a hundred or a thousand years from now, one last surviving copy will be found, and the technology will be there to decipher it. And I imagine our inheritors, those many who built their society on the abolition of total destruction, or those few who burrowed out from underneath it, laughing, one way or another. "That's it," they say. "It was such a joke, nobody could take it seriously."

—Village Voice,
18 December 1984

Corrupting the Absolute

Sue got off work and drifted down the midway in a wet heat, past the American-flag petunia gardens. Screamers rammed circles in the Whirl-A-Gig cars, pasted in stand-up Roll-A-Turn cages by their own gravity. They whistled and moved in droves behind raw hot dogs. At night she lay in the top bunk naked with the lights off. Fan on full aimed at her crotch while janitors lounged in front of the garages watching the rows of windows. Rod Stewart, scratchy and loud, combed his hair in a thousand different ways and came out looking just the same.

That paragraph is the last of three in a Jayne Anne Phillips story called "What It Takes to Keep a Young Girl Alive"; the title is a play on a line from Rod Stewart's "Every Picture Tells a Story," the tune drifting through Sue's window. I sometimes wonder how good a song has to be to make its way into fiction like that—into a life like that. I wonder what the song does there. This isn't the old soundtrack-of-our-lives routine: you know, when Sue gets older and "Every Picture Tells a Story" comes on the radio as an oldie she'll remember working at the amusement park. Something is happening in Phillips's story, to her character and to the song. It isn't clear what; maybe the contact itself is all that can be dramatized. Beneath the drama, though, there's an ugly, blank feeling, as if, lying on her bed in the heat, a girl with a dead-end job has found herself humiliated by Rod Stewart's wild-oats ramble from Paris to Peking—or as if the facts of her life have humiliated the romanticism of the song. Or has the girl ignored the tale Stewart tells and stolen a moment from it, a moment that comforts because it tells her she's not the only one who can't change her life? Fuck you, Rod Stewart, who gives a shit how your hair looks? Maybe none of that matters here; maybe the point is simply that Stewart was right. If a song is good enough, one story leads to another.

As it happens, "Every Picture Tells a Story" is Rod Stewart's greatest performance. That means either Phillips has good taste in pop-song references or that the capacity of the song to enter a situation, transform it, and be transformed by it confirms its quality. Or it means neither. The thirty-year winnowing-out of rock history by oldies programming has more or less proven that quality talks and bullshit walks—Jimmy Gilmer's "Sugar Shack," the top single of 1963 and, according to a private survey, one of the five most loathsome records ever made, has disappeared—but bad records too enter people's lives, and just as easily as good ones. What do they do there? Just because a bad record has been removed from the airwaves by the common critical work of mass taste doesn't mean the bad record disappears from the life of whoever absorbed it in the first place.

Now, by a good record I mean one that carries surprise, pleasure, shock, ambiguity, contingency, or a hundred other things, each with a faraway sense of the absolute: the sense that either for the whole of a performance (as with the Rolling Stones' "Gimmie Shelter"), or more often for a stray moment, someone (the singer, the guitarist, the saxophonist) wants what he or she wants, hates what he or she hates, fears what he or she fears, more than anything in the world. The wonder of "Every Picture Tells a Story" is that such absolute moments occur all over the place: in the acoustic guitar licks after each verse, in the drum roll at the end of the first, in Maggie Bell's answer to Stewart's "Shanghai Lil never used the pill" with an out-of-nowhere "SHE CLAIMED THAT IT JUST AIN'T NATURAL!," in a dozen of Stewart's lines, in the unmatched openness of the rhythm—which somehow shuts up tight for the long instrumental coda, exactly as if a bunch of studio hacks had been brought in to finish the number because, after shaking the world off its axis, the original musicians were kind of worn out. By a good record I mean one that, entering a person's life, can enable that person to live more intensely—as, whatever else it does, "Every Picture Tells a Story" does for Jayne Anne Phillips's Sue.

By a bad record I mean one that subverts any possibility of an apprehension of the absolute, a record that disables the person whose life it enters into living less intensely. Words like corrupt, faked, or dishonest suggest themselves, but there are plenty of corrupt, faked, or dishonest records with moments just as deep and powerful as any in "Every Picture Tells a Story"—not just honorable let's-get-rich records like Freddy Cannon's "Palisades Park," but this-is-a-load-of-shit-but-let's-get-rich-and-maybe-change-our-names-and-not-have-to-tell-our-mothers records like the Diamonds' 1957 white-boy rip-off of "Little Darlin'," which was originally made by the noble black rhythm and blues group the Gladiolas, whose version wasn't as good. As Kim Gordon of Sonic Youth once put it, in "rock 'n' roll, many things happen and anything can happen." (Who knows what happened to the Diamonds? I saw them more than fifteen years ago in a Reno casino, singing evergreens, pretending, even though by then their mothers were probably dead, that they weren't even the same group that had recorded "Little Darlin'," which was still on the air.) By a bad record I mean a record that is so cramped and careful in spirit that it wants most of all to be liked.

I'm thinking of Julian Lennon, his album, *Valotte*, his hit single, "Too Late for Goodbyes," and a letter in *Rolling Stone* where a mother wrote in with her my-kid-said-the-darndest-thing: "Mom, you had John Lennon, and now we have Julian." Good luck, kid, I thought: what kind of wishes will be sparked in you, what kind of life can you make, out of these pathetic little Family Favorites tunes about nothing? It hurt to read that letter, not because Julian Lennon is corrupt, fake, or dishonest, but because he is probably worthy, sincere, and true.

Julian Lennon is so promotable it makes you wonder if he really is John Lennon's son. Yes, his voice sounds just like John's—it's uncanny, and that's the hook. He looks like John. But just as John's bright sneer is beyond Julian's smooth, sad-eyed face, the endless emotional complexities in the dumbest lyrics John ever sang are beyond Julian's Xerox voice. Even on the earliest Beatle records, when John Lennon sang badly, which is to say emptily, you could hear failure; on *Rock 'n' Roll*, released in 1975, his last album before the 1980 *Double Fantasy* lp which ended his life, you could hear self-loathing and doubt. When Julian sings badly, emptily, which is all he does, you hear success. It's the success not of carrying off some intimation of the absolute, but of carrying a phrase to its completion. It may seem pretentious to throw around an idea like "the absolute" in reference to such music—or even to "Every Picture Tells a Story," a hilariously crude set of rhymes about a guy trying to get laid—but that is what rock 'n' roll is all about. Can anybody argue that Jerry Lee Lewis's "Whole Lotta Shakin' Goin' On" was hedged?

What happens when a song like Julian Lennon's "Too Late for Goodbyes" enters a life as easily, as mysteriously, as unconsciously, as "Every Picture Tells a Story"? What happens when such a song frames, defines, the possibilities of life? When Julian Lennon's songs enter a life I can only imagine that they reduce it. His songs reduce it because, in the immediate context, they say that that person's parents had something richer, and lived in a better time. They made or turned away from better choices, and their successes and failures can be more fully dramatized. They had the real thing, which unfortunately is no longer on the market. But it is in the context of time passing that the real process of a bad song in a real life begins to function. A bad song is absorbed whole, in the moment, unconsciously. The person whose life it enters barely knows it's there—it's just part of the day. But as time goes on, and the song fails to live up to the life of the person carrying it, it starts to break down. It reveals itself as a tumor in the psyche. Never saying its name, it frames the bits and pieces whoever absorbed the song was willing to settle for—and that's all there is.

Of course, almost everyone settles. No one wins. The absolute was denied in the Garden of Eden, and the defining characteristic of human beings remains their ability to want what they know they cannot have. That contradiction produces rage, desire, hate, and love, and real art brings all those things to life. Art that quiets or buries those cultural instincts can't survive the human faculty—it falls apart. But as it does, it humiliates whoever carries it. If Jayne Anne Phillips's Sue was humiliated by Rod Stewart's "Every Picture Tells a Story," that humiliation made her realize what she had given up, and made her want it even more.

—*Artforum*,
April 1985

Number One with a Bullet

The late Lester Bangs on the 1976 Second Annual Rock Music Awards telecast, hosted by Alice Cooper and Diana Ross:

The highlight of the evening was the Public Service Award. Alice complained that "rock music personalities are foremost and basically people—contrary to rumor. People with the same dreams, desires and feelings as everyone else. They're ambitious but they're not selfish or self involved—but caring! . . . and I can't read this card. Their careers are time-consuming, but they still invest whatever time they have in—" Diana: "—what we in the industry are most proud of—the Public Service Award." They gave Public Service Awards to Harry Chapin for contributing to World Hunger Year, and to Dylan for helping get Rubin "Hurricane" Carter out of jail. . . . Then Diana administered the *coup de grace*: "But seriously, folks, there's an incredible movement growing in the United States; concerned citizens who believe that whales have the right to life. And through words and through music the team of David Crosby and Graham Nash express their own concern, by giving a special concert so that the whales are still alive. I think that is absolutely incredible and we honor them with our fifth Public Service Award. Well, once again, I don't think they're here, but we'll accept it for them."

Alice made a crack about Flo and Eddie being there, speaking of whales, and Diana continued: "No, seriously, I do know that a lot of my friends are concerned about this area and it's something that I personally would like very much to be interested in."

Things haven't changed much since then. Rock stars still invest whatever time they have in what they are most proud of.

The only difference is that the Rock Music Awards have been replaced by the American Music Awards, and whales have been exchanged for Ethiopians.

Following the AMA telecast in January, more than forty performers gathered to make a record to raise funds for Ethiopian famine relief. AMA host and big winner Lionel Richie had already written the song with Michael Jackson; Quincy Jones produced. Diana Ross, Bob Dylan, Bruce Springsteen, Tina Turner, Willie Nelson, Steve Perry, James Ingram, Kenny Rogers, Paul Simon and the rest "checked their egos at the door" and, under the name of USA for Africa, cut "We Are the World." As Oscar Wilde might have said, it takes a strong man to listen without laughing. Or throwing up.

As I was cleaning the floor, I had to admit that as a tune "We Are the World" isn't at all bad—but a more vague composition about specific suffering could not be imagined. Small print on the sleeve claims "United Support of Artists for Africa ('USA for AFRICA') . . . has pledged to use . . . all profits realized by CBS Records from the sale of 'We Are the World' . . . to address immediate emergency needs in the USA and Africa, including food and medicine," but there isn't a word in the song about how or why this might be necessary. In the first verse one is told that "There are people dying" (STOP PRESS); in the last verse, that "When you're down and out" (the Ethiopians are "down and out"?) ". . . if you just believe there's no way we can fall." Literally, that means if Ethiopians believe in USA for Africa the stars will realize their own hopes. That's it for Ethiopia.

While grammar is no help, contextualization comes to the rescue: certainly the superstars of USA for Africa knew their efforts would receive such overwhelming media coverage that their proximate inspiration would be clear to all. Thus once past "There are people dying" the rest of the song can fairly be about not the question but its answer—a celebration of the rock music personalities who are singing.

"There's a choice we're making/ We're saving our own lives"

—those are the key lines of "We Are the World," repeated again and again. Dylan sings them, Cyndi Lauper sings them, Springsteen sings them, Ray Charles sings them, Stevie Wonder sings them. Within the confines of desperately MOR music, Charles is magnificent, Wonder sounds fine, Springsteen sounds like Joe Cocker, and Dylan—well, if a comedian attempted a Dylan parody this broad he'd be laughed off the stage. But that's irrelevant. Here recognition is all: objective parody is more recognizable, more salable, than subjective performance. The point is voracious aggrandizement in the face of starvation —a collective aggrandizement, what those in the industry are most proud of. Melanie Klein posited the infant's projection of itself on the world, and its instinctive attempt to devour the world; beneath perfectly decent, thoughtless intentions, that's what's to be heard on "We Are the World." Forget the showbiz heaven of "We are the world, we are the children/ We are the ones who make a brighter day"; listen to the way that, projecting themselves on the world, the USA for Africa singers eat it. Ethiopians may not have anything to eat, but at least these people get to eat Ethiopians.

Obviously, I think the subliminal message of "We Are the World" is destructive. The message is, ye have the poor always with you; that there is a "We," you and I, who should help a "Them," who are not like us; that as we help them we gain points for admission to heaven ("We're saving our own lives"); that hunger, whether in the U.S.A. or in Africa, is a natural disaster, in God's hands, His testing—His testing, perhaps, of those Americans who are homeless and starving "by choice," and if they aren't, how in God's name did they reach such a fate? And if they are, aren't the Ethiopians? For that matter, small print and small USA for Africa contributions to American hunger relief (ten percent) aside, doesn't the spectacularization of Ethiopian suffering trivialize American suffering and hide its political causes in a blaze of good will? Bad politics, which can be based in real desires, can produce good art; bad art, which can only be based in faked or compromised desires, can only produce bad politics. Such carping is as vague as "We Are the World"—but there is a message hidden in the song that is more specific than anyone could have intended.

As with Michael Jackson in 1984, the highlight of the 1985 Grammy telecast was the unveiling of the new Pepsi commercial. Lionel Richie, earning $8.5 million as a Pepsi spokesman, strolled through a three-minute spot, advertised as the longest network TV advertisement in the history of the medium. The theme was pressed hard. "You know, we're *all* a new generation," Richie said, "and we've made our choice"—most notably, he was saying without saying it, the choice of Pepsi over Coke.

Pepsi first tried this theme in the sixties, when it pushed "The Pepsi Generation" as a slogan. In the time of the generation gap, of seemingly autonomous youth, the line didn't work. As based in abundance as the sixties were, the ideology of the era was antimaterialist; the corporate cooptation rubbed raw. But the new generation of Richie's commercial really was new —the post-sixties generation, which is all-inclusive, which indeed has room for anyone from that passed time; a generation whose members, according to media wisdom, have traded utopianism for self-realization, but nevertheless look hard for quality time to spend on family, friends, and areas they personally would like very much to be interested in, so long as those areas are sufficiently distant, say, eight thousand miles distant.

Actually, the 1985 Pepsi commercial was a lousy commercial: a stiff combination of a Lionel Richie video and an insurance-company ad. Compared to the 1984 Mountain Dew breakdancing commercial it was merely long. But "We Are the World" is a great commercial. It sounds like a Pepsi jingle—and the constant repetition of "There's a choice we're making" conflates with Pepsi's trademarked "The Choice of a New Generation" in a way that, on the part of Pepsi-contracted songwriters Michael Jackson and Lionel Richie, is certainly not intentional, and even more certainly beyond serendipity. As pop music,

"We Are the World" says less about Ethiopia than it does about Pepsi—and the true result will likely be less that certain Ethiopian individuals will live, or anyway live a bit longer than they otherwise would have, than that Pepsi will get the catchphrase of its advertising campaign sung for free by Ray Charles, Stevie Wonder, Bruce Springsteen, and all the rest. But that is only the short-term, subliminal way of looking at it. In the longview, real-life way of looking at it, in terms of pop geopolitical economics, those Ethiopians who survive may end up not merely alive, but drinking Pepsi instead of Coke.

As American singers came together for the USA for Africa sessions, Canadian performers gathered to make their own Ethiopia record. Among the contributors was Neil Young. "You can't always support the weak," he had said in October 1984. "You have to make the weak stand up on one leg, or a half a leg, whatever they've got." But the Ethiopia benefit session? Hey, it was something he personally very much wanted to be interested in.

—*Artforum*,
May 1985

Less Than Zero

I n *Less Than Zero*, a first novel by Bret Easton Ellis, rich
kids in Los Angeles do what the Manson family did on the
same terrain in 1969. Swimming in dope, they watch murder 'n' castration films (Manson had them made), engage in
gang rape, fetishize corpses: when the kids find a dead boy in
an alley, everybody goes to gawk, and someone sticks a cigarette between the blue lips. Leaving a party where a twelve-
year-old girl tied to a bed is being shot up and raped, the narra-
tor, Clay, remembers "a party that somehow got out of hand."

A young girl from San Diego who had been at the party had
been found the next morning, her wrists and ankles tied together.
She had been raped repeatedly. She had also been strangled and
her throat had been slit and her breasts had been cut off and someone had stuck candles where they used to be. Her body had been
found at the Sun Air Drive-In hanging upside down from the
swing set that lay near the corner of the parking lot.

The things that go on in this book lack the apocalyptic aura
of the Manson crimes. This is fin de siècle stuff. Manson received messages from the Beatles, or so he thought, but in *Less
Than Zero* pop music is just weather—everybody talks about it
but nobody does anything about it. You don't know what Clay
or his friends get from it, what they want from it, why he turns
on MTV every chance he gets. The constant pop-song references bounce off the flat surface of the prose: no song ever
plays. Clay goes to a club to see X, a founding L.A. punk band
whose music contains all the loathing and fury Clay can't touch

in himself, can't talk about. He wants to hear them do "Sex and Dying in High Society," but it's no accident that he leaves before the number comes up; otherwise he'd have to respond to the song.

Clay walks out of the room where the twelve-year-old is being raped.

> "Why?" is all I ask Rip.
> "What?"
> "Why, Rip?"
> Rip looks confused. "Why that? You mean in there?"
> I try to nod.
> "Why not? What the hell?"
> "Oh God, Rip, come on, she's eleven."
> "Twelve," Rip corrects.
> "Yeah, twelve," I say, thinking about it for a moment.

There are a lot of good novels without a pause, a suspension, as perfect as that in Clay's last line: a pause that so precisely constitutes a void. "I don't think it's right," Clay finally mumbles. "What's right?" Rip shoots back. "If you want something, you have the right to take it. If you want to do something, you have the right to do it." As philosophy it's pure Manson—or pure Aleister Crowley, the English satanist who helped clear L.A.'s moral ground before Manson showed up—but stripped of any pretense of taking over the world or even changing it. When the Manson gang seized a Beatle song and wrote "HEALTER SKELTER" on the wall of the LaBianca home in the blood of Leno LaBianca, the sign was rich in meaning. In the world at large the sign was meant to sow terror and confusion; to the Mansonists it was the key to a complex scenario which was to end with their emergence from a hole in the earth to rule the world. In 1969 the signs the Mansonists raised were partly contained by police explanations marking them as extrapolations from Beatle texts: a sign that has been explained cannot communicate freely, because the subjective relationship between the sign and viewer has been demystified. On their own, though, as headlines, the signs communicated directly. Among other things they said that pop music was more dangerous than even its most besotted fans or opponents—those who, in 1969, were plotting concordances of Beatle lyrics or burning Beatle records—ever thought it was.

Pop music is a sign system, most powerful when its autonomous signs float above a terrain on which they can touch down and take root. Manson could crystalize an apocalyptic aura in 1969 because in 1969 that aura, as a generalized will to violence, was present in the culture at large; the terrain was there. The rub is that when autonomous signs touch down on a terrain where real people actually live, the signs change the terrain ("Helter Skelter" justifying the slaughter of various men and women), but the terrain does not necessarily change the sign. It's possible to listen to "Helter Skelter" today without recognizing, on any level of consciousness, that photos of a dripping "HEALTER SKELTER" were once flashed all over the world, and it's possible today that someone might listen to "Helter Skelter" and—connecting to the violence in the music to the void in the song's false ending—use the sound and the phrase as a call to murder.

It may be that the autonomy of signs is a paradox, that the autonomy is empowered only by the existence of a social terrain on which the signs can light. It may be that without the sort of new Merrymount maypole that allowed Manson to sanctify himself, and the general public to demonize him—the aura that in the late 1960s guided the president of the United States and various political assassins no less than a hippie shaman—the sign cannot signify at all. And it may be that the impotence of the sign in the absence of such a terrain, or such a maypole, is what *Less Than Zero* is about. Why was the corpse of the girl who was raped, strangled, and mutilated hung upside down? It could have been hung right side up, or just dumped.

But hey, let's hang it *upside down*. Why? Well, it's ah, more weird. At most this is a blind reference to what by Ellis's time, the early 1980s, had become the Manson myth; that, or a mute gesture toward a meaning that will never be defined. Anything that weird ought to mean something.

Fin de siècle means a malaise that by definition can't be focused. Time just fades away. History exists only in the past. The terrain of *Less Than Zero* is an antiterrain, just as one of the L.A. clubs its characters would be going to if the book were set in 1985 rather than in '82 or '83 is called the Anti-Club. The book is named for Elvis Costello's first single, released in March 1977, a TV viewer's reaction to the rehabilitation of 1930s British Nazi leader Oswald Mosley: if Mosley could appear as just another chat-show guest, Costello sang, then "everything means less than zero." The song is never mentioned in the novel, but Clay has a poster for Costello's 1982 *Trust* lp over his bed. His psychiatrist has a framed *Rolling Stone* cover on his wall: one featuring a 1982 interview, and headlined "Elvis Costello Repents." The use of the headline seems to be the psychiatrist's way of suggesting that even angry young punks grow up and accept the ways of the world. It's meant to stop the patient in the tracks of his or her own willfulness. But to Clay it is "Elvis Costello Repents" that signals "everything means less than zero," not the song itself, or the angry young punk who sang it. When he damned the violation of certain moral limits, Costello affirmed that moral limits were necessary, and their violation a crime. The sign on the psychiatrist's wall reduces the social dimension Costello insisted on to neurosis. To the psychiatrist, Elvis Costello has become a therapeutic, but to Clay, if Costello is no longer willing to say no, all that's left is a yes, endlessly diffused. It is a yes that allows for the gang rape of a twelve-year-old tied to a bed; a yes that makes it impossible for Clay to really say no to such an obscenity; a yes that, to Clay, contains a more practical nihilism than Elvis Costello's "Less Than Zero" ever hinted at.

Or so it seems to me. I stay fixed on "Elvis Costello Repents" on the psychiatrist's wall because in a way I put it there. I conducted that interview, in which, along with tracing his early years as a musician, Costello offered apologies for various violent or offensive incidents in his career. I tossed off the headline as a wisecrack; great, said the editor. No, I said, it's all wrong, it's a complete distortion of— Come up with something better in three words by tomorrow or it runs, the editor said. I didn't and it did. Costello, Bret Ellis may be happy to learn, was appalled, but Ellis isn't Clay. Clay's life is bounded by the covers of *Less Than Zero*, and for him "Elvis Costello Repents" will stand. The sign floats free, and lights on the antiterrain Ellis has laid out, a terrain that perhaps exists only in a novel, which gives life a form it doesn't really have.

—*Artforum*,
September 1985

The Last President
of the United States

Rock 'n' roll, as anyone will tell you these days, is now simply mainstream music—pervasive and aggressively empty, the sound of the current sound, referring to nothing but its own success, its own meaningless triumph. For the first time, rock 'n' roll really is everywhere: Madonna's wedding and Bruce's tour are hard newsbreaks. Old hits spout ad-agency lyrics every time you hit the dial or change the channel. With Michael Jackson's purchase of Beatle copyrights, Beatle music may soon be run through a commercial revival that will definitively erase whatever mnemonic power the songs still retain. Imagine:

> She's leaving home, she's leaving home . . .
> *Is she? Has she? Call National Childwatch, Inc.*
> *We can help—and you can*
> Get by with a little help from your friends.

And that's just the public service version—a Jackson tax credit.

All this is obvious. Less so is the way the shapeless main-streaming of pop music has produced a perfect, balancing compensation: the process by which the pop milieu, now merely the milieu of everyday diversion, is continually reorganized around a single replaceable figure.

Since 1984's Jacksons tour, performer after performer has been brought-forth-to-come-forth as a unitary, momentarily complete symbol of individual fulfillment and public conquest. As Michael Jackson was replaced by Prince, Prince was replaced by Madonna, who has been replaced by Springsteen. At the given moment, their faces appear on every magazine cover (Bruce on the cover of the *Star* in the supermarket: "HOW MARRIAGE HAS CHANGED HIM." Inside: "IT HASN'T"). Every single and lp, every tour, sets "records," generates "unprecedented" amounts of money. The Guinness people can't keep up with the ever-lengthening number of hours logged by fans camping in lines for tickets. It's no matter that much of this is pure hype; what counts is the result, and the result is a sort of consumer-fan panic, a Konsumterror (the phrase was Ulrike Meinhof's) that suspends one's very identity in the fear of missing out on what's happening, or what is said to be happening. It's a social version of the TV quiz show where contestants are asked to guess not the true answer to a question, but the answer that polls have shown most people believe is true—or is it the answer most people believe most people believe is true?

Whatever signs and meanings a performer might bring to this process are nothing compared to the process itself. Meanings are dissolved, or attached to the dominant sign systems of the moment ("BRUCE—THE RAMBO OF ROCK," reads a bumper sticker), or trumpeted as spurious, glamorized oppositions to fake versions of the dominant sign systems ("DO YOU WANT YOUR DAUGHTER TO GROW UP LIKE MADONNA?"), making real opposition incomprehensible. And as their meanings are dissolved, so are the performers. They're used up, exiled into the wilderness where dwell those who, once, were. Jackson was not just replaced by Prince; exposed at the height of his fame and power as a celibate zombie, he was discredited by a world-class fucker. But then Prince was revealed as a megalomaniac, and so he was discredited by a down-to-earth slut, who was discredited by a man who stands for the values that made this country great, who was discredited by—

It's true that this voraciously entropic process has a constant need for weirdos, for people who in pre-rock times would have been inconceivable as public icons. "Anarchy had moved in," wrote Nik Cohn of the mid-fifties. "For thirty years you couldn't possibly make it unless you were white, sleek, nicely spoken and phoney to your toenails—suddenly now you could be black, purple, moronic, delinquent, diseased or almost anything on earth, and you could still clean up." Thirty years later, though, that touch of anarchy has turned out to be a legitimating principle of control. This is the rock 'n' roll contribution to mainstream hegemony.

Think of the sense of freedom and resistance Cyndi Lauper must have wanted to communicate. The sensual social pluralism of her "Girls Just Want to Have Fun" video, its affirmation of the pleasure of self-invention, became a reifying star turn in her following "Time After Time" piece, where her boyfriend didn't like her new haircut. What happened to all those people on the "Girls Just Want to Have Fun" screen, whose discovery of their own autonomy created a dance in the street? They were shoved back into the same anonymous crowd that may soon receive Cyndi Lauper, and from that crowd they will watch whoever comes next, and wonder where she came from, who he is. They will stand in line for a record-breaking number of hours, pay a record-breaking number of dollars, to find the answer, or anyway what most people are said to think the answer is.

Just as, in the pop milieu, there is at any given time only one real star, in the U.S.A. today there is only one real person: Ronald Reagan. Behind all the replaceable center figures of pop is an irreplaceable center: product of grand historical forces, function of his time and place and all that, but also a unique individual with his own goals, his own fears, his own way of using his institutional power to take social power as a supercelebrity. An autonomous individual, Reagan seals the autonomy of all others, and also seals the limits of that autonomy, since all autonomy must finally be returned to him, and to what he chooses to represent. He is omnipresent, as naturalistically at home dancing the night away on the cover of *Vanity Fair* as he is, through the magic of electronics, chatting with the winners of the Superbowl, making their victory his.

Making their victory his—in its primitive form, that's how the process seems to work. In its fully realized form—the 1985 Superbowl, say, where Reagan actually appeared in the locker room as a video hologram—it is apparent that the supercelebrity does not take, but gives. In 1985 it was made to seem as if the 49ers had not won until Reagan had joined the event—in other words, until he made it real.

This is altogether a pop process. Yes, Ronald Reagan has never said a public word about Prince or Madonna, only had Michael Jackson to the White House and appropriated Bruce Springsteen for a campaign speech. But by those acts and thousands like them, he validated the process by which stars are validated. He became bigger; so, for the moment, did they. The difference is that he is not in it for the moment.

—*Artforum*,
November 1985

1986

Alone and Forsaken

In *Minima Moralia* (1951), which may be the gloomiest book ever written, Theodor Adorno described social totality as a system that "would suffer nothing to remain outside it," and then went on to prove that nothing did—save perhaps the hopelessly feeble impulse to remain outside. All people, he insisted, generals and civilians alike, had become objects of history. There was no chance left to be a subject of history—to subjectively make it. Philosophy, once "the teaching of the good life," had turned into pure method; there was no longer any good life to be taught, only production to be increased and managed. Facing the new postwar world, Adorno wrote as a bitter sentimentalist:

He who wishes to know the truth about life in its immediacy must scrutinize its estranged form. . . . To speak immediately of the immediate is to behave much as those novelists who drape their marionettes in imitated bygone passions like cheap jewellery, and make people who are no more than component parts of machinery act as if they still had the capacity to act as subjects, and as if something depended on their actions.

Thus Adorno set about his book of aphorisms: "If today the subject is vanishing, aphorisms take upon themselves the duty 'to consider the evanescent itself as essential.'"

In the pop milieu today, the blinding illumination of rock megastars makes the evanescent not only inessential, but almost inconceivable. The network of communication that is the pop mainstream has expanded to the point where everyone feels he or she must occupy a place in it; in everyday terms, that means he or she must contrive a response to whatever megastar is currently the object of the network's organization. The replaceable megastar, the replaceable number one, dissolves all other numbers. You sit watching a merry-go-round spin, and each time your eyes light on a single wooden horse, you believe with all your heart and soul that that horse is the only horse in creation: "All horses are white." "All horses are black." "All horses are zebras." "All horses are frogs." As an all-encompassing logical absurdity, it makes perfect social sense.

In the mainstream rock 'n' roll of the mid-sixties you could hear an eagerness to reach other people. In present-day mainstream pop music you can hear a confidence that people will be reached. But reached with what? With a proof that people can be easily reached. The all-star jamboree of USA for Africa's "We Are the World" was a structuralist's dream, because its true content was structure itself: order. It brought new order to the pop world; checking the invitation list, one knew who counted and who didn't. But it brought an even stricter order to the world at large. Bypassing its putative objects, the starving Africans, the performance completed a circuit that erased all differences between performers and spectators, objectifying both in the face of objective good. Through the simple act of buying the record, you too could become part of the world.

Of all the totalistic pop centers of the past two years—Michael Jackson, Prince, Madonna, "We Are the World"—Bruce Springsteen has worked hardest to resist the mechanism. If many of his songs are about people who have been turned into objects of history, the songs were written to remind a listener that those people could have been, should still be, subjects. Yet just as every record made today that is not patently aimed at the mainstream is a "novelty"—that is, an aphorism, a sterile oddity—Springsteen's music, like Madonna's or Michael Jackson's or "We Are the World," is, among other things, a vast, grand, utterly coherent world-historical thesis: the thesis of the popular mechanics of domination. This is not the thesis Springsteen plays, but the thesis he plays out: what he says is subsumed into a celebration of his ability to say it.

When Springsteen plays in a coliseum filled with sixty thousand people, what is at issue is not the size of the audience, but the intensity of its desire to be confirmed as an audience. When Springsteen sings about dispossession in contemporary America, when he violates the ruling political fantasies of the nation, there are many in the audience who do not believe a word he says, and many more who will never, not even in their most private thoughts, live out a word he sings. Yet not a single person says no. When, between songs, Springsteen speaks even more eloquently (and, without the comforts and supports of music, far more riskily) about dispossession in contemporary America, there is respectful silence. That silence—the absorption of a pop moment that is also a deflection of its content—is the enemy: the silence is an affirmation that the structure of the event has contained, has swallowed, its contents.

Sitting in the midst of sixty thousand people, thrilled by Springsteen's "I'm Goin' Down" and "Cadillac Ranch," I wondered what would have happened, what could have happened, if he had exchanged his pointed metaphors for denunciation. What would have happened if he had said what I like to imagine he believes: that those who currently rule the country are evil people, with evil motives, doing evil things? Most likely Springsteen does not believe that—does not, at least, believe in that kind of speech. But I don't think he was saying all that he believes. I think he was saying all he thought he could get across. What would have happened if Springsteen had said no with rage instead of forgiveness, tried to blow away the empowerment of stardom and stood on the stage as a crank? I can't help wondering if the solipsistic hysteria surrounding Springsteen's show—a process that turns the star even more than the fan into an object, that robs his every subjective word of its particular meaning—could have been breached.

The Mekons' new *Fear and Whiskey* was made in that breach—which is to say that the record is a novelty, a sterile oddity, an aphorism as opposed to a thesis, an insistence that the evanescent is the essential. To bring it back to life you have to drape it in old jewelry. The record was made by cranks: formed in 1977 as the first punk band in Leeds, the Mekons quickly blew their first and only chance to sell out to a major label. Wending ever deeper into the pop wilderness, enduring countless splits and death notices, even their own, they have persisted ever since.

If *Fear and Whiskey* can only be heard as an aphorism, what evanescence does it consider essential? A bitter sentimentality. This is the music of a small group of people who, in a pop moment now almost a decade gone, once thought all things were possible, and who now live in a society where nothing they want is possible as more than an evanescence. They still wear the old jewelry of the punk ideology of 1976: no-future, which was somehow turned into an adventure, which got the Mekons a major-label contract. If anything, their music today is stronger than it ever was, but against the confidence of mainstream music, it carries an unmistakable undertone of self-mockery, of humiliation, of shame, because it cannot count. *Fear and Whiskey* is just fear and whiskey, nervousness and oblivion; it is the music of people who are sure that the world they cannot change will never find a place for them, that what they have to say will never be heard.

Still, there is no objectification in the Mekons' music. One hears a small group of people talking to each other; one enters a conversation. Its content is bitterness; sentimentality, the severed wish for a good life, is what keeps it going. These people are waiting, not for the world to change, but for their lives to end. In the meantime, they will talk. Their talk is like anyone's talk: What's new? Not much. Come on, it's been months since I've seen you. Well . . .

—*Artforum,*
December 1985

The Last Broadcast

As the number two British punk band, the Clash began as the Rolling Stones to the Sex Pistols' Beatles, but good and bad were reversed in punk. As the Beatles, as those who set the terms of the new game, the Sex Pistols demanded everything and damned everything—knowing they would be left with nothing, they played and sang as if they didn't care. The Clash criticized, always leaving an opening: the Sex Pistols were wreckers, they were partisans. The Sex Pistols were symbolist, with every meaning left open and uncertain, utopia and hell in a single, unstable body; the Clash were rhetorical, voice to flesh. If the Sex Pistols—or anyway Johnny Rotten—truly were committed to the destruction of rock 'n' roll not only as myth but as fact, the Clash were committed to changing rock 'n' roll, to taking it over, to becoming the Number One Band in the World ("The Only Band That Matters," their American label said, after the Sex Pistols disintegrated). The explanations the Sex Pistols offered when interviewers asked them why-are-you-so-angry turned into the Clash's songs, songs about boredom, autonomy, lust, power; the Clash took the true anarchy and the real nihilism the Sex Pistols offered and rationalized it, made it seem almost reasonable.

The Clash latched onto received ideas, but they soon made those ideas their own, and were changed by them—or anyway Joe Strummer was. It was never clear if he wanted to be a star or if he wanted everyone to hear him: in the rock tradition Strummer was so tied to, the difference between the one and the other was never clear. With a giant multinational corporation behind them, the Clash toured the U.S.A. (1977: "I'm So Bored With . . .") again and again.

In 1982 they finally cracked the American Top Ten: made it twice, with *Combat Rock* on the album charts and the indelible "Rock the Casbah" on the singles list. Most assumed that the Clash were working for nothing else, that the heresies of 1976 London punk were merely the old clothes of bad dreams, but the band's success seemed to shock Strummer. If the Clash had scored their hits, if large numbers of people were finally happy to listen to what the band had to say, Strummer seemed to have decided that that meant the Clash were no longer saying anything. With work on the boards, he disappeared in Paris, then reappeared with his head shaved. Drummer Topper Headon quit; the group was unraveling. Strummer called a meeting, got bassist Paul Simonon's vote, and kicked guitarist Mick Jones out of the band.

Jones had been a founder; *he* had asked Strummer to join *him*. As guitarist, singer, and cowriter, many saw him as far more central to the Clash's success than Strummer, but in a way that was the point. Jones's noisy love songs ("Train in Vain," "Should I Stay or Should I Go?") had been the Clash's most effective bids for mainstream airplay before "Rock the Casbah" (a sardonic, up-from-the-Muslim-streets reply to the Ayatollah Khomeini's ban on music in Iran, and written by Topper Headon); Jones's voice lacked Strummer's rough edges, his promise that any song could go in any direction, anytime. Strummer detected a spiritual flaw behind the style: despite the punk attempt to destroy the star system, Strummer announced, a pop star was all Mick Jones had ever wanted to be. He was a fake, a revisionist; he had to go.

Strummer and Simonon recruited three new members: drummer Pete Howard, rhythm guitarist Vince White, and lead guitarist Nick Sheppard, the latter both twenty-three-year-old "ex-punks" who affirmed they'd grown up on Clash music. As a band ("The Clash") they played a few shows; hope against hope, their American label even brought them back to the U.S.A.

It was, for a night, a trip worth taking. "This isn't *white* reggae," Strummer shouted, introducing "Police and Thieves." "This is punk *and* reggae. There's a *difference*. There's a difference between a ripoff and bringing some of *our* culture to *another* culture. You hear that, Sting?"

It was 21 January 1984. It had been eight years since the Clash formed, six years and one week since the Sex Pistols played their last show in San Francisco, and the Clash were back in town not as "The Only Band That Matters" but as the only punk band left. "What we play now is what we can do," Strummer had said in 1979. "It wouldn't be fair to do ranting music because we've mastered a time change. So there's just no point." "We started to think we were musicians," he told Joel Selvin, a San Francisco critic, before the New Clash show. "When we made the first record we knew we weren't. It's a bad thing to think; it's irrelevant, not to the point."

To a happy, not quite sold-out crowd in a dumpy, medium-sized hall, the Clash played ranting music. Keeping Strummer's promise to Selvin, they "went back to where we went wrong, and then forward again." Against an industrialist backdrop and eight television sets flashing images of present-day social disaster, Strummer shook, scowled, smiled, and sang as if he and his audience had a life to make within a world they'd already lost.

The band was ragged, Nick Sheppard played too many Mick Jones licks, and such rock-star flimsy as leaps from the drum riser or floodlights in the crowd's face was still part of the show. The only identifiable new song was the hopeless "We Are the Clash," which only added credence to the old rumor that the favorite song of Bernard Rhodes, the Clash's original and now returned manager, was "Hey, Hey We're the Monkees." Still, I'd never seen Strummer more exhilarated, or more convincing. In 1978 in Berkeley, "I'm So Bored with the U.S.A." was a gesture of contempt to a bourgeois audience; this night it was offered to the audience as their own, and they took it. Some of *our* culture to *another* culture.

Still, almost everyone was sure it was the end of the road. As time passed, Strummer gave increasingly confused interviews about "rebel rock," changing the world, the special role he had to play in that change, England's turn to the right under Margaret Thatcher, the collapse of the punk community and the possibility of reinventing it, social injustice, fascism, the end of the world, and when there might be a new Clash album. He wasn't saying anything terribly different from what he and many more had said in 1976 and '77—but in London in '76 and '77, the old rock 'n' roll dream of "taking over the world" hadn't meant topping the world's charts, it was supposed to mean making the charts irrelevant, and then proving that the charts and graphs and ledgers that governed the structures of everyday life—the hierarchies of education, work, family, bureaucracy, politics—could be made just as irrelevant. Now, though, with Thatcher's brutal, popular Tory rule, the oppressions punk had fought when it gave birth to itself—the oppressions of false leisure, false work, false entertainment—seemed like the playthings of childhood, and Strummer sounded like a crazy old man.

In May 1985, in the U.K., the new Clash, the five of them, showed up in a parking lot outside of a hall where the Alarm, a newly popular group, were playing a sold-out show. Strumming acoustic guitars and tapping drumsticks against each other, they were busking—playing for small change. Before 1976 Strummer had been a subway singer, a thick-fingered guitar banger—that was where he got his name. In interviews in the 1980s, he talked often about "going back to the roots," but no one could have guessed he'd meant going back so far. It was a bizarre reversal, and a testament to how desperate Strummer was to dramatize that punk had meant what it said when it said it would destroy all heroes. On their early tours of the U.K., the Clash sometimes brought their fans back to their hotel and let them sleep in their rooms; now, playing the Isley Brothers' (or the Beatles') "Twist and Shout," their own "Garageland" (from the Clash's first album), or "Stepping Stone" (the Monkees again—the Sex Pistols had tried it, too, once), the Clash asked the curious who gathered to hear them if the fans could, you know, put them up for the night. In this moment you could see Joe Strummer's whole future: on some dank London corner, the drunken bum calls out to passersby. "Hey, you wanna hear 'Rock the Casbah'? It was a hit, it was a hit in, ah, in . . ."

As the band chanted in the parking lot, you could see the Clash's past. On the back sleeve of "White Riot," the Clash's first single, there was a rough collage of photos (ugly public housing blocks surrounded by rubble; cops; a band) and words. Along with quotes from the Brighton Beach youth culture riots of the mid-1960s (a Mod: "I haven't enjoyed myself so much for a long time. . . . It was like we were taking over the country"), one could read something more suggestive:

that there is, perhaps, *some* tension in society, when perhaps overwhelming pressure brings industry to a standstill or barricades to the streets years after the liberals had dismissed the notion as "dated romanticism," the journalist invents the theory that this constitutes a clash of generations. Youth, after all, is not a permanent condition, and a clash of generations is not so fundamentally dangerous to the art of government as would be a clash between rulers and ruled.

The explanations of

Out of this blind fragment of a found manifesto, the Clash had made a career. In advance of any sort of pop career, the words took in the inevitable dismissal, or failure, of any attempt to use rock 'n' roll to dramatize a clash between rulers and ruled: as far as almost everyone was concerned, no band could signify more than a transient clash between generations, a present-day (now long past) version of a sixties beach riot between Mods and Rockers, new fans of the Who and the Small

Faces beaten bloody by fans of Bill Haley and Gene Vincent, Teddy Boys who kept the faith, relics whose whole lives were based on the conviction that they had heard the truth and would kick in the faces of anyone who suggested it might be incomplete.

In other words, with that old manifesto now playing against the idea that an old band could make itself new, Strummer, well into his thirties—as he spoke, as the new Clash made noise for coins, and then made a new record and asked people to buy it— was precisely the old fart punks had dumped when "White Riot" first hit the stores. *Cut the Crap*, the new Clash album was titled, and the words were thrown back in Strummer's face. *You* should talk, said the British reviews. Go away! Who wants to hear what a dead man has to say! Stop reminding us of what you failed to do the first time around!

On the terms punk set for itself, it would change the world or it would be nothing. In a certain sense, Strummer was never a real rock 'n' roller, because he trusted neither fun nor money; thus the chart success of the Clash had to mean nothing to him. You could draw two different conclusions from the failure of punk to change the world and its sometime success on the charts: you could conclude that the punk critique of everyday oppression and spectacular entertainment was wrong—or you could conclude that it was more correct, and the enemy more invisible, than even the most conscious punks had dared to think. Drawing the first conclusion, you would, if you were Strummer, try to find a place in the record business; drawing the second, you would try to find a new way to say the same old things. And of course it is the second path Strummer has chosen.

Cut the Crap seems to be set in a riot—not the idealized "White riot/ Wanna riot of my own" of the Clash's 1976, not their "LONDON'S BURNING WITH BOREDOM NOW!," but a far more prosaic affair, tired, too familiar, the everyday bad news of the New Britain. A new kind of riot: as the strict redivision of British society into capitalist and serving classes proceeds, it becomes plain that redundancy and civil disorder are not merely costs of this project, but linchpins. Under Thatcher, redundancy is not simply economics: it is social exclusion organized as spectacle. Those who are cut out of organized social life make up a third class, which is used to terrorize those who still retain their places into a thank-god-it's-them-instead-of-me acquiescence, which is silence, and that silence has no force without some noise in the streets.

This is power as culture: a form of speech that has answered all questions in advance. Behind the Labour government of 1977, which administered What Is as a final social fact, punk could discover a negative: welfare security as spiritual poverty. With Thatcher, who administers What Could Be (you can be anything, she says, which means, you can lose everything), oppositional culture can only discover an affirmative. It can only agree, and agreement is a further silence. As the redundants riot, the ranter grabs a passing clerk by the collar and tells him the truth: "You could be next!" "Right, mate," says the clerk. "That's why I'm keeping my nose clean. Hey, aren't you Joe Strummer?" As public speech, both the riot and the Clash's new music have been contained before the fact.

Thus the Clash's new riot, too, sounds like a kind of silence: an exhortation in place of drama, inspirational music for "rebel rockers." "CLASH COMMUNIQUE OCTOBER '85," it says on the inner sleeve. "Wise MEN and street kids together make a GREAT TEAM. . . . but can the old system be BEAT??. no . . . not without YOUR participation. . . . RADICAL social change begins on the STREET!!. so if your looking for some ACTION. . . . CUT THE CRAP and Get OUT there." The new songs, the new music, aren't much more convincing. A wash of ambient mass media noise, an old-fashioned punk guitar sound communicating not as a revival of a period style but as a new discovery, an occasional rhythmic jump—too soon, it all seems lost in a shoving match between skimpy lyrics and football-match chants of vague slogans. More than anything, *Cut the Crap* sounds like a transfer from the Clash to Big Country—a band that scored a good, rousing hit with the self-titled "Big Country," a teary approximation of early Clash—back to the Clash again. *Cut the Crap* sounds less like failed "rebel rock" than like failed pop music.

And out of this comes one true moment, "This Is England." Released as a single, it had a strange jacket: on the front, a Mohawked punk couple wander through Piccadilly Circus, blank-eyed and scared of the sleaze, country mice finally arriving in the big city to find out what punk is, seven years too late: "24 HOUR ETERNAL SUNSHINE STRIP STRIP STRIP," "SEX STYLE SUBVERSION," "DISCUSSION DISCO." There's no one else on the street. On the back, there are lots of people on the streets, black-and-white shots of 1950s men and women finally shrugging off the privation of the postwar period and shopping, buying, smiling, "IT'S NEW," "GET IT," "LAST FEW DAYS SALE," and, square in the middle, a collage from old painted postcards, Buckingham Palace, the Queen in her carriage, a hand raised to hide her face.

"Who will buy my potatoes?" asks the voice of a small child; a drum machine kicks in, slowly, firmly; synthesizer chords lift the music, hold it in, refuse to let it move through any melody, to find any rhythm; a punk buzzsaw guitar rides down, sounding wonderful, alive, free, then beaten. Strummer begins to sing, to talk, walking through the riot like his own tour guide, nearly mute for all his words. As the riot takes place it's already over; he is singing the ruins, and the passion in his voice, the despair, the plain desperation to make you understand, is like blood frozen on a corpse. The corpse is the singer; it's the country. "This is England," an anonymous male chorus says over and over, and again and again Strummer comes off the chorus to try and tell you what it is: "Land of a thousand stances." Images of random violence, of official murder, pass by; nothing connects. The singer flees; he's trapped. An incident comes to life with detail, then vanishes as allegory.

> On a catwalk jungle
> Somebody grabbed my arm

A voice spoke so cold it matched the
Weapon in the palm
This is England
This knife of Sheffield steel
This is England
This is how we feel

England is a nowhere, but all possibilities of feeling seem
present in the way Strummer sings that last line, here in the
voice of another, throughout the rest of the song in his own.
"THIS IS ENGLAND," echoes the chorus, and then Strummer is
solitary, bearing down on the following words so hard he makes
them vibrate, the solitary "we" so painful and strange, pressing
with such force that all that's come before, the Clash's whole
career, all the great songs, your favorite, seems trivialized by
this quiet, still negation, the patent, physical gap in the "This"
of "This is how we feel," a frightened hesitation between the
"th" and the "is," a break in time that carries the full weight of
what Strummer is saying: carries it, and suspends it, leaving
you hanging, unready for the fact that after a few minutes the
record, like other records, simply fades out.

—*Village Voice,*
    31 January 1984;
    Music Magazine (Tokyo),
    January 1986;
    Artforum,
    February 1986;
    revised January 1992

Postscript: Shortly after the release of *Cut the Crap,* the three new members quit the band; it never re-formed.

King of Nebraska

O n *King of America*, Elvis Costello moves through a world made out of old pop songs, postcards of the royal family, waiting rooms, cocktail lounges, alcoholics' bed-sitters, and half-remembered friends, lovers, chance acquaintances—it's a world of detritus. Within a single tune the time frame may range from the forties to the present, but it never holds still; time folds in on itself. A reference to Madonna's "Material Girl" can sound as dated, as faded, as one to "Smoke Gets in Your Eyes."

In the same way, the stories Costello is telling move from England to America and back again; each place is an axis of the album, but neither quite comes into focus. They stay in the distance, like old movie sets—more detritus. The music carries an undercurrent of some controlling social fact—some great social dislocation—but you can't grasp its purpose any more than Costello's characters can. Mostly they don't bother to try; their gestures are weighted, tired, bitter. In the way Costello sings their words, his people speak like exiles: in their shifting tones of voice more than in any particular lyric, they seem always to refer to something that isn't there.

The mood is rarely dramatized. Taken as a whole, the details Costello offers merely make a landscape, a flatly unnatural landscape. When violence erupts it's usually self-contained, a joke or a simile: "Well you try to love her/ But she's so contrary/ Like a chainsaw running through a dictionary." As a singer, Costello makes nothing of that last line. He slides away from it, and that's why it works as music. The line is just another line—or would be, if *King of America* didn't center around a song about the dissolution of language. The real ugliness of the moment may take time to surface: the record is disturbing, but easy to listen to. Quiet or noisy, arrangements are kept simple. They chug or float, and it takes no effort to enter the sound, which opens up, reveals itself, without the listener necessarily noticing the change. At first a forest, the landscape becomes a stand of trees, which turn into signposts, which become speakers: people talking, muttering, swearing, people who then turn back into trees, and fade back into the landscape.

The delicacy of communication here rests partly on the quality of the compositions—"American Without Tears," "Sleep of the Just," "Our Little Angel," and "Little Palaces" are exquisite songs, as good as any Costello has written—and partly on the care that has gone into their recording. Working with producer T-Bone Burnett, Costello has dropped the ornamented orchestrations and clogged melody lines of 1984's *Goodbye Cruel World* and 1982's *Imperial Bedroom*, moving often into the space cleared by the studied, subtle sound he used during that period on his pseudonymous "Imposter" singles, "Pills and Soap" and "Peace in Our Time"/"Withered and Died." The result is his enfranchisement as a singer.

Costello has no bel canto gifts to draw on; his timbre will always be moral. Throughout *King of America*, he lets his voice quiver at the end of a line, suspends it in the air, makes you aware that he is trying to get something across. There are little cracks and tears in Costello's voice when he brings it up to meet a chorus; the struggle to communicate becomes its own subject matter. You can't rest with the perfect gentleness of "Sleep of the Just," with the forgiveness in the way Costello sings "If you must, you must." What is communicated is a conviction that a form of speech is a form of morality; as the notion rises up within the music, it can begin to make you nervous.

The soft "Our Little Angel" rolls out with vaguely country accompaniment, but the beat somehow pulls against itself. It tenses up, and Costello doesn't have to make anything of "Like a chainsaw running through a dictionary"—the violence is already there, quietly turning nice girls into prostitutes, parades into funeral marches, outdoor gatherings into public executions, love into dirty pictures. When that violence is finally given a field—on "Little Palaces"—it shoots out in all directions.

The number is built out of the cadences of an ancient Irish anticonscription ballad—suspicion, dread, and rage are all but coded in its melody. It's the sort of illegal song that was meant to be sung on the street, and as Costello begins, edging up the stepped scale, he might be calling to you from an alleyway, ready to run at the first sign of the King's troops. The instrumentation is minimal but deep; just a mandolin counterpointing the immediacy of Costello's harsh acoustic guitar with a circling pattern, which carries a sense of timelessness, which against Costello's doomstruck guitar means only dust to dust. But it's the voice that cuts, that hurts: a voice of absolute powerlessness.

The social dislocation that has been taking shape in the other songs, the shadowy homelessness of every one of the characters, is inescapable here. The singer cries out against some great wrong, but while he makes the song impossible not to understand emotionally, the exact nature of the great wrong evades him, forcing him into poetry, away from the plain speech the Irish ballad was made for. Is "Chocolate Town" Hershey, Pa., or a black ghetto, or something else? Are the "little palaces" the blank blocks of English public housing, the "council tenancies" that Johnny Rotten damned to begin the punk critique which, in London in 1977, turned up Elvis Costello? Probably that's what they are: "It's like shouting in a matchbox, filled with plasterboard and hope," Costello sings; "Like a picture of Prince William, in the arms of John the Pope"—and how is that like what?

The bits and pieces of the story Costello is telling in "Little Palaces," and all across the lp—a story, it seems, about a class

struggle that has decayed into a dull resentment, relieved by
the glow of royalty—jar more than they register. The tale of
dislocation is itself dislocated. "They're moving problem families, from the south up to the north," the singer tells you, but
the agony in his voice, and the death sound of his guitar, carry
the conviction you won't hear him. In "the kingdom of the invisible" the class war goes on, but the old ballad form has been
defeated: it's as if the King himself has come to Ireland to recruit the troops for his next war, and who would say no to the
King himself? In such a world, nothing is real; the reality of any
place, any person, any emotion, is dissolved by the reality of
power, which casts itself as love; Princess Di is Margaret
Thatcher with a human face.

The mandolin spins the song to its end. Just as revolt is
coded in its melody, so is acceptance, the acceptance of the
powerlessness of its own voice. "I suppose, you need the sleep
of the just," Costello sings as *King of America* closes—sings it
slowly, beautifully, as if the thought had cost him something—
but while it's clear that everyone on the album needs that rest,
it's also clear that no one deserves it.

—*Artforum*,
March 1986

Flat, Toneless and Tiresome

In Stan Ridgway's songs, the man who's speaking suggests a character who uses his voice mainly to talk to himself. At first he can sound like a jerk; it's easy to imagine a life for him, a life reduced to a series of meaningless transactions. Even the most commonplace exchange taxes his ability to say what he means, so even "yes" or "no" comes out off-key, dubious, too eager to please. Maybe he has a job, so he says what he has to say to his boss and the people he has to work with; maybe he has a wife, so he says what he has to say to her. He buys what he has to buy when he has to buy something and he's polite about it: "Thank you very much." But you can hear him listening to himself as he says it, as if he's rehearsed the line a dozen times on his way to the counter. The tone of the man's voice carries a disquieting edge of stupidity. Something is disquieting about it, anyway.

"The American voice is flat, toneless and tiresome," Raymond Chandler once wrote, but he also watched Americans, and one of those he saw "was a man who liked to make small neat inconspicuous motions with his hands. These motions neither had, nor were intended to have, any meaning. But the making of them gave him a quiet sense of his own grace and competence." The second time through *The Big Heat*, Ridgway's first album since he left the Los Angeles punk band Wall of Voodoo, you can begin to hear this private dance of secret gestures in Ridgway's voice. Yes, he's listening to himself, but he's less rehearsing his words than playing with them, playing with words as if they were social sounds, disconnected symbols of social reality. The songs hold great floods of words; the pleasure of putting them together almost outruns whatever stories are being told. Ridgway is playing with the possibilities of the deadpan tone Chandler identified, looking for the money in it— he's looking for the way, as Chandler also wrote, that American language comes "alive to clichés," seeks naturally to make them, to make a language everyone can understand without a second thought. In "Pick It Up (and put it in your pocket)," a song about money cast in the form of an occult rumor spreading through the economy, Ridgway gets it: "Now I don't wanna seem to say that the time ahead won't be ok, but the scale is loaded down with the weight of sixteen tons—and the ones that have tell the ones that don't to tell the ones that can't about the ones who won't, and there's no place left here 'round to run. Pick it up and put it in your pocket—or somebody else will."

Speech that on a first listening to *The Big Heat* might have seemed dead in the mouth is now moving nearly too fast to follow. With a stuttering beat, the song takes clichés as tests of its ability to come to life ("sixteen tons," which as a reference to Tennessee Ernie Ford's wage-slave ballad sticks out as clumsily as would a quote from Karl Marx; the loser's sentimentality of "no place to run"; the catchphrase moral of the last lines). Picking up speed out of the rest of the performance, "the ones that have tell the ones that don't to tell the ones that can't about the ones who won't" can blindside a listener. The string of words sounds like a cliché but it's not; you seem to have heard it before but you haven't.

What's happening can only be called poetry. Here, words find each other in a certain social context, and, in their new unity (the tension between the obvious "ones that have" and the concomitant "ones that don't" snapping forward to reveal the mysterious "ones who won't"), that social context becomes flesh and blood. You begin to hear panic behind the matter-of-fact plainness of the voice, then plain fact behind the panic. "The ones that have tell the ones that don't . . ."—the words might fall apart when you try to analyze them, but heard of a piece they make the sort of line you recognize instantly, under-stand intuitively, as if it's been hiding between headlines for the last six years, just waiting for someone to find it.

The Big Heat is a storyteller's album; it's no accident that on the lyric sheet the words are set as blocks of prose. Detectives and the man they're after, laborers working on a pile driver, carnies, a man dumped by his wife, soldiers on a lost patrol, a cabbie and his fare, a traveling salesman—together they make up a gallery of nobodies. These are people who have learned not to dramatize their lives, gestures, or voices, who know they have no claim on anyone else's attention—people who, if they want anything out of language beyond the management of com-monplace transactions, want only to explain their own predica-ments to themselves. So they speak in that flat tone: "Old Mr. Johnson turns blue and starts to choke," Ridgway sings in "Can't Stop the Show," the carny tune. "Somebody slap 'em on the back." The way he says "slap 'em on the back," he might as well not have said it at all. The stories are made ordinary as dirt—and yet *The Big Heat* is probably the most compelling portrait of American social life to appear on a rock 'n' roll lp since Bruce Springsteen's *Nebraska*.

For Ridgway, the story goes back to "Lost Weekend," a number from Wall of Voodoo's 1982 *Call of the West*. With deadly simplicity, with a perfect feel for the vague, tortured rhythms of a conversation in which no sentence is ever com-pleted, he played a husband and wife driving back to Los Ange-les from Las Vegas, where they'd lost all their money. He never raised their voices, barely allowed them a sigh; with the band meandering behind them, the piece nearly screamed with all that wasn't being said. *The Big Heat* is not so extreme: the arrangements and accompaniments are easy to catch, and sometimes they turn unusual hooks and riffs into a pro-grammed commercial bounciness that pulls the numbers away from where they mean to go, breaking Ridgway's desire to cap-ture real talk by forcing him into singsong. The music is smart at best, too often merely decorative, occasionally obfuscatory, and almost always secondary to Ridgway's voice and his words: his dramaturgy.

What one really hears on *The Big Heat* is a style of natural-ism that calls attention to itself as an artificial construct. All across the record, Ridgway's goal might be to assume the flat tone of American speech as a disguise, and then to discover just how much can be expressed, how intensely what needs to be said can be said, before fear or fury burns up the disguise from inside. He wants to go no farther; he wants to find the limit, not cross it. The disguise is crucial, one side of the American thing itself—without that disguise, there could be no private dance of secret gestures. *The Big Heat* is a set of stories from people who have no reason to expect anyone to listen to them, and so they tell their stories as if no one else is listening: without that flat voice there would be no story.

—*Artforum*,
May 1986

Hum-drum

At least once a month, sometimes once a week, when I tune in to the local college radio station, I hear a sound that makes me stop, turn around, think twice. What's that?

Whistles, yelps, squeaks, shouts, a rhythm that moves like a fall down a flight of stairs; every time, it's Liliput (or Kleenex, the band's name before the company made them change it). It's "Ain't You" or "Hedis Head" from their first single, made in 1978; "You (friendly side)" or "Ü (angry side)," a 1979 single; "Split" from 1980; the apocalyptic "Eisiger Wind" from 1981. The band is gone, and this music is five, six, almost ten years old; it sounds as if it were being made tomorrow. I know these songs, each time they come on I try to remember what comes next, what words, what noise, and I never can. The tumbling "woo woo woo woo!" in "Split" is always a shock, the "eee-eee!" in "Hedis Head" an ambush; the tear through "Eisiger Wind" is always too fast for memory. Each time, in these records, there is a surprise—and that sense of surprise always lasts as long as any of the records. It doesn't matter what's being played before or after, if it's Little Richard or Frank Sinatra: the band escapes whatever context the radio might make for it.

Kleenex/Liliput was from the beginning an all-female punk group (later, a male or two briefly came and went): if the Sex Pistols could do it, guitarist Marlene Marder said, saying the same thing so many people said after 1976, so could we. Do what? Let's find out. Listening to the records, you can hear echoes of the first London female punks: the Slits, Poly Styrene and Lora Logic of X-ray Spex, and Marder's favorite, Souxsie of the Banshees (Marder still has her fan club card). But while those performers opened up the free street Kleenex/Liliput would make on their own, they soon abandoned it. Sooner or later, usually sooner, those performers lost their nerve. The group Marder and bassist Klau Schiff (who is also the painter Klaudia Schifferle) founded with vocalist Regula Sing and drummer Lislot Ha (Sing would leave after "You"/"Ü," Ha after "Split") was the only female punk band—maybe the only punk band of any description, save for the Sex Pistols—to grow more extreme as they continued their quest to find out what it was they wanted to play. Chrigel Freund replaced Sing, Astrid Spirit replaced Freund, drummers and saxophonists arrived and departed, but the essence of the band, the thrill it wanted to discover and communicate—its idea—never changed.

The music was first of all fun: funny, with a buried edge of rage, an impulse that first shaped a song with "Ü" and roared to the surface with "Eisiger Wind." Kleenex/Liliput played with the possibilities of freedom; they practiced freedom as play. From one point of view, each of their singles can sound like a manifesto; from another, like a mud fight. These people were interested in noises they had never heard on record before, interested in words without apparent meaning, phonemes, holes in the language: they sang as if they were making up language from the beginning. You can imagine that every time they went into the studio, they asked one question: if we can say anything, what do we want to say? How about "Whh-hyyyrrr"? If not that, perhaps "Wheeep"? The songs were about autonomy and pleasure, verbal nonsense and emotional facts, comradeship and isolation, resentment and pleasure, avoiding rape and getting drunk, city streets and feminist pride: fragments of everyday life thrown together with determination and abandon. There is no analogue for this music in the records of any other pop group. To find a real match for its spirit you have to go back to the Berlin dada collages of Hannah Höch: from 1918 through the twenties she cut women's heads and bodies out of newspapers and magazines, cut them up again, pasted them together as grotesques, and somehow put a twinkle in the eyes of every strange face. You can hear it happen in "Heidis Head."

On their singles, Kleenex/Liliput almost always sing in English (on their albums, *Liliput* and *Some Songs*, they used French, primitive Chinese, imaginary languages, but almost never their own language, Swiss-German). Klau Schiff, who wrote many of the words, knew English, but she knew it the way the band knew how to play their instruments—she discovered how to write English as she wrote it, just as the band discovered how to play as they played. In the music, a bassist's mistake can turn into a new theme; Schiff's uncertainty with English syntax might lead to wordplay for its own sake, trip her off the main road of her song and into an alleyway. In "Split," the lyrics are both random and a strict game: "Hotchpotch, Hugger-mugger, Bow-wow, Hara-kiri, Huz-za, Hiccup, Hum-drum, Hexa-pood, Hell-cat, Helter-skelter, Hopscotch—Yesterday was a party! Yesterday the drinks were strong!"

Do you hear the party or the hangover? Sung, shouted, screeched and chirped on the record, you can barely understand the words (what is "Hexa-pood"?); the women trip over them. From song to song they work as if they'd walked into a wall and smiled, as if they'd just missed getting hit by a car and swore, as if they'd gone into a conversation with compassion (or cynicism) and come out of it with cynicism (or compassion), and then said: why not make a tune out of it? They played and sang as if they didn't know what would happen next, and didn't care. Something would happen; it might be interesting, and it might not be. Anything was possible: in 1980 I was absolutely convinced the words "Hara-kiri" in "Split" were actually "Hello Kitty"—referring, that is, to the Japanese toy company. I still hear it that way, and I still think the association makes sense: as revolutionaries, Kleenex and Liliput always sounded as if they wanted to storm the playground, not the palace.

—preface to *Kleenex/Liliput:*
Das Tagebuch der Gitarristin
Marlene Marder, 1986

Sand in Your Mouth

Sonic Youth tries to start fires in a field of corn. Their name is pure corn; their new signature tune, "Expressway to Yr. Skull," combines corny punk misogyny with sixties psychedelia, and nothing could be cornier than that—when I first heard the song, the words drowned in nightclub acoustics, I thought it might be a cover of the Amboy Dukes' 1968 Korn Klassic, "Journey to the Center of the Mind." The way "Expressway" trails out of a noise rave-up with quiet feedback drifting into silence is as corny as the surge of suspense music when the detective stumbles on the body in a third-rate murder movie.

Rather than trying to lead an audience into a suspension of disbelief, cornball artists who get their own joke hope everyone will play along, or anyway enjoy the joke, which suggests that successful corn involves a suspension of embarrassment, or else a revel in it. Cornballs who don't get the joke insist on meaning when it's patent only clichés are present; in the supper club or the performance space, corn of this grade seeks transcendence in a heaven of pretentiousness. Sonic Youth can be pretentious, they can be embarrassing, and yet for all the corn in their music it's never merely corny. Clichés are almost always present, and so is the sense that whatever is set before you can blow up at any time. Corn is not unstable; Sonic Youth's music is.

There was a moment in a show I saw last year—one moment only—when the music blew up. It was obvious the band members—guitarist and singer Thurston Moore, bassist and singer Kim Gordon, guitarist Lee Ranaldo, drummer Bob Bert (since replaced by Steve Shelley)—were trying to make it hap-

pen; moving out of a conventional rock-song structure, Moore
was down on his knees hammering his guitar with a stick,
Gordon was bent double. It was corny, and then it wasn't. It
was shocking, and purely musical: you forgot the contortions of
the performers and felt the room fly apart. Bits of sound turned
into objects; there was one great explosion, and a thousand specific explosions inside of it.

You could see it happen in the air. This is what the Big Bang
must have been like, I thought; every sound leaped away from
every other. It was scary, it was thrilling, and it made the rest
of the show a disappointment. No band can make this happen at
will—create a moment in which everything is present, and
nothing holds—but I think this is what Sonic Youth is after.
Their five-year career as a pop group (or a downtown New
York "noise-music" band) (or an arty punk quartet with a fixa-
tion on Charles Manson) can be seen as a pursuit of absolute
moments of dissolution supported by a conventional structure:
the postpunk version of the music business, which at best
means hard-to-find records on small independent labels, tours
in clubs, radio play on college stations, cover-story interviews
in former fanzines now struggling toward regular publication
schedules, sub-rosa hits on dubious charts. The Sonic Youth album that made the U.K. indie top twenty this spring illustrates
just how uncertain any pursuit launched in this pop half-world
has to be.

The record at first suggests—any ephemeral, absolute moments aside—that Sonic Youth has arrived: the packaging of
this double live lp is gleaming, by far the classiest the band has
ever had. On the outside covers, full-color jack-o'-lanterns refer
to the band's spring single, "Halloween," and to the sleeve of
the previous Sonic Youth album, *Bad Moon Rising*, which featured a scarecrow topped with a burning pumpkin head; the
motif is continued on the four disc labels, turning it into a logo.
From the photos on the inside sleeves to the intricate, imaginative liner art, the production strikes a perfect balance between
the cultish and the deluxe. Distribution, too, seems better than

with the band's earlier records: you can find this set from California to the Midwest to Boston. There are only two problems: (1) it's impossible to know what the album is called, let alone who issued it (the title might be *This Time, the Last Time, and Here's to the Next Time,* or *The Sonic Youth Sound Experience,* or *Not 1 (But 2),* or *Walls Have Ears,* which might also be the name of the record company, which might also be oh-whoa-yo), and this is because (2) the album is a bootleg, illegal, released without the knowledge or consent of the band. Since it comes in a numbered edition of two thousand, with all further pressings barred by legal action on the part of Sonic Youth, one can conclude the album became a hit on the British independent charts by virtue of selling approximately fifty copies a week.

The package speaks in tones of glamour and success; it turns out to have ephemerality coded in its gloss. Yet both as package and as music, this is the most complete and vivid picture of Sonic Youth available. The melodrama of those blazing pumpkins gives the corn in the grooves a momentary, first-spin authority; it's up to the rest of the music to validate it, and it does. The bootleg tapes can't capture the complexity, or define the intentions and accidents, of a moment in which Sonic Youth make a room fly apart, but they can capture the band's negating impulse, its will to function as a sort of sonic corrosive—and that may be as much of itself as Sonic Youth will ever get on record.

You can hear this best—hear it as a corrosive drama—on side "not 2 B." First there's "Expressway to Yr. Skull"—as corn, this is the field, which is a potential field of action. Then comes "Spahn Ranch Dance," one of two versions of "Death Valley '69," Sonic Youth's Manson song. Now the band begins to reach for dissolution; they press hard, and fall short. The violent interjections of confusion and glee—("I had to hit it") ("I couldn't go faster") ("You had sand in your mouth") ("Sadie, I love it!")—seem to come straight from the dead souls of the Mansonoids, you're in the death room with the bodies at your feet, but the song is too well made to fragment; you're never

unaware that the power in the performance is an effect someone decided to produce.

" 'Blood on Brighton Beach' " is the realization, or antireal-
ization, of all that's gone before; it wouldn't hit half so hard
without the progressively successful failures that precede it.
This is the worst-recorded number on the album: all you can
catch is a guitar and Kim Gordon's sore-throat voice far behind
it, pulling away from it—but just as onstage Gordon-as-bassist
seems to center and direct the other musicians, she dominates
here. The pace is fast, scattered. Reserves of doubt, loathing,
terror, and perversity are summoned, exhausted, and superseded: you can't understand more than a stray word, and while
it's plain something extraordinary is happening, you don't know
what it is. Every moment is strong enough to make you wonder
how another can follow it; it doesn't make sense that the performance can be sustained even for the few minutes it lasts. Limits burn up: the jack-o'-lanterns on the package grin like canni-
bals. What they eat is whatever expectations you brought to
the music.

The strangest aspect of this remarkably constructed album,
taken from perhaps a dozen different concerts taped surreptitiously in the U.K. over the past year or so, is not musical at all.
On song after song, the band members are closing a show:
"Thanks, goodnight." "The power's off, see ya." "That's it,
goodbye." "See you again." "This is the last song." This may be
the bootlegger's joke; repeated over and over, it becomes a
blankly consistent theme of the record itself, until it both de-
flates the performances and throws them into a very queer
light. After " 'Blood on Brighton Beach' "—all across the baleful
surfaces of the album—it can shock you into realizing that what
you've heard was just a show.

—*Artforum*,
Summer 1986

U.S.A. Combat Heroes

"I am holding in my hand a document which transcends and seals all the shame of this age and would in itself suffice to assign the currency stew that calls itself mankind a place of honor in a cosmic carrion pit," wrote the Vienna critic Karl Kraus, in 1921, about an ad for a package tour to the battlefields of Verdun. Lately I think I know how he felt. There are some objects of criticism that are immune to criticism, before which criticism can only fall back in wonder and awe, disarmed and stupid, and such objects seem to come in packs. See one, and soon enough you're seeing them everywhere. It's the spirit of the times, the taste of the currency stew; you can't get it out of your mouth.

I was buying a paper in a hotel gift shop early in the year when I noticed a new title in the paperback carousel: *America 2040*, by Evan Innes, "Volume 1 in an Exciting New Series from the Creators of Wagons West." Nothing special about the cover: red, white, and blue, three indomitable types standing in front of the flag. I turned the book over, and read:

AMERICA'S NEW FRONTIER. It stretches out beyond the planets to the vastness of infinite space. The time has come for America's best and brightest men and women to again become pioneers, to carry freedom's precious message to a new wilderness.

Okay, I thought, I've heard that before. I ran my eyes down to the next block of promo type.

THE MISSION. It will determine America's destiny. Locked in a final deadly struggle with the Soviets, the free world trembles on the brink of nuclear holocaust. But whatever the Earth's fate, the spirit of America must not be allowed to die. The dauntless courage of those

Wait a minute, I said out loud (the woman at the counter looked up, alarmed; we were the only people in the shop): you mean that "the spirit of America" is more important than the EARTH ITSELF, that the . . . uh-huh, that's what it said. I was dumb-struck. What would *God* think of that, I wondered; *Why d'ya think they call it God's country, buddy?*, something answered. Feeling unclean, I bought the book, never meaning to read it, and I never have; I knew it was a talisman.

   Through the events of the months that followed, the book stayed with me—through the orchestration of grief over the space-shuttle disaster, an orchestration that didn't at all seem cynical, hierarchical, but like a natural, self-orchestration, what-ever that means, an orchestration that by the end of the first few days had turned into a kind of celebration; through the continuing apotheosis of Ronald Reagan as the test of all work-ing ideas of the good, and the buildup to the Statue of Liberty centennial (the event was all in the buildup). I took *America 2040* out again and again, reread the message, and I still had no answer to it, no reply. Of course, that back-cover copy wasn't serious, wasn't *sincere:* it was a simple commercial calculation *(Given the mood of the country and the shit market we're aim-ing at, this ought to sell)*, just a stir of the currency stew, but it also opened up the carrion pit. As a crude commercial calcula-tion, those few words made a real social fact.

   I think I held on to this $3.95 Bantam paperback as proof that this was as far as it could go—as far as the spirit of our time and place could celebrate itself, shame itself, parody itself, fuck itself to death. As Kraus wrote of the Verdun vacation, the book seemed to prove that the age had "nothing left but the naked truth of its condition, so that it has almost reached the point where it is no longer capable of lying." But then, a few weeks ago, in a local drugstore, I saw a $2.50 Warner Publisher Services magazine. *U.S.A. Combat Heroes,* read the title: "Killing Machines. RAMBO III its here. CHUCK. Commando. America's Greatest Heroes. RAMBO strikes as COBRA."

I picked it up the way I would have picked up a porn magazine. I opened it: "Rambo fights for every American who suffers from Commie tyranny. He is America's force for freedom." Big deal, I thought. Then I turned to the section on Chuck Norris, star of *Invasion U.S.A.* Caption to a two-gun Norris pose: "Chuck Has Killed More Commies and Terrorists Than Any Other American Hero." Text:

The Great American Hero has always been a loner. Whether he was a cowboy, a soldier, or a private eye, he walked alone down his mean streets—or across his war-torn battlefield, or beneath the wide, blue Western sky.

A slew of defense mechanisms went into action. "He walked alone down his mean streets" was a rip-off of Raymond Chandler's paean to Philip Marlowe: "Down these mean streets a man must go," Chandler said ("who is not himself mean," he added). But those were probably the worst words Chandler ever wrote—the most pretentious, the most sentimental. Who's to say they haven't found their rightful place in *U.S.A. Combat Heroes?* But so what, so what, I was evading the real action, which was in the caption. I read it again; it still said the same thing. "Chuck Has Killed More Commies and Terrorists Than Any Other American Hero." No, I said to the magazine, "Chuck Norris" is a *fiction,* he/it never killed a single "Commie" or "Terrorist"—it was all I could do to stop myself from running into the parking lot and buttonholing other shoppers, like the people hawking petitions to Save the Waterfront, Fight the Insurance-Crisis Fraud, Preserve Rent Control: *Look! Look at this! You won't believe it! This is all—*

I dropped the magazine and went home, but I couldn't get it out of my mind. Whenever I went back to the drugstore I found myself peering at it, surreptitiously, as if I were afraid it would notice, talk back. One day I read a letter to the editor in the *San Francisco Chronicle*: the writer was railing at the hypocrisy of Sylvester Stallone's refusal to attend the Cannes Film Festival. According to the writer, and the gossip columns, the muscle-bound coward was afraid of Libyan terrorists. ("So the KHADAFYS and other terrorists around the world better watch their step, because every American is a RAMBO," read the first page of *U.S.A. Combat Heroes*.) John Wayne would have gone, the letter-writer said. Yeah, right, RamboRockyCobra-StalloneSlywhateveryournameis, I thought, but I still felt shadowed—and somehow a letter appearing a few days later, noting that John Wayne too was a phony, that he sat out the Second World War pretending to fight on-screen while other actors did the same thing in, uh, what's it called, "real life," didn't bring the world back into balance either. Anything I had to say doubled back into nothing.

Criticism is the bringing of the terms of x to bear on y: it is an analytical juxtaposition that forces a certain tension, a certain friction, and the result is up for grabs. But what if the object of criticism is at once a shark and a jellyfish, transparent and opaque, an object that for all its obvious falsity, contrivance, and insincerity is still the emblem of an age, simultaneously empowered by the age and empowering the age itself? "Writing is always somehow an expression of powerlessness, or the fruit of frayed nerves," the Czech novelist Ludvík Vaculík once wrote. "It betrays complexes, or a bad conscience."

It took me weeks to work up the nerve to buy *U.S.A. Combat Heroes*. Finally I paid my money and took it home; now I run my hands over it. I wonder what it means. I wonder how it talks, why I can't talk back to it. I wonder what it has to do with pop music, the ostensible subject of this column, and if the answer isn't in *The Edge of the World*, the latest album by the Mekons. It's an odd record: it seems to be set sometime after a war, in an England that has been turned into an American army base. It seems to have taken the critical immunity of objects like *America 2040* and *U.S.A. Combat Heroes* for granted, to be suffering it, to be living it out. The Mekons are playing with the speech that has left me mute.

—*Artforum*,
September 1986

The Return of King Arthur

The Mekons: currently six to ten members, including fiddler and accordionist. On stage they wear cowboy hats and sing "Help Me Make It Through the Night." Founded 1977, Leeds, England—first punk band in town, now the last.

Two or three original members remain; dozens have come and gone. Lacking anything that could be called a hit, their very persistence across a decade marginalizes them. As pop stars who never were, they have nothing to revive; "Tenth Anniversary of Punk" retrospectives ignored them. As an anachronism, though, today they are gaining strength. *Fear and Whiskey* may have been the best pop record of 1985; *The Edge of the World* may be the best of 1986. The two discs in one: history is a nightmare from which the Mekons are trying to awake, and when they do they're still drunk.

To the first Mekons, "punk" meant collective self-realization through playful art against a backdrop of social strife. It meant an unfinished utopia in which the freedom to say everything would lead to the freedom to do everything. The present-day Mekons are like any casualties of a defeated revolution—nervous, on good terms with oblivion, filled with rage and guilt. A celebration of the values that keep them alive can turn instantly into a curse; mocked by each day's news of the adventures of the powerful, those values rob the Mekons of peace of mind. They're like any losers who've won the gift of history: in a crucial public moment, they found themselves, but, as A. J. P. Taylor said of the revolutions of 1848, it was a moment when "history reached its turning point and failed to turn." So now they live by their humor, and their humor is what used to be called "survivor's humor," before "survivor" became a reference to someone between jobs.

A Mekons song begins from the premise that the singer is oppressed by everything that is empowered. It includes the corollary that the world could care less: self-pity becomes sardonic self-hate. When the Mekons rail from the stage against U.S. funding of the Nicaraguan contras, they mean it, of course, but it's also a hopeless joke, and the joke's on them, and they know it—that's part of what they mean to say. The denunciation is real, but what its tone dramatizes is less outrage than powerlessness.

By the same token, a Mekons bad joke, even a cheap play on words, can change into a moment of passion, of resolve. There's something irreducibly stirring about "Hello Cruel World," the mournful stomp that opens *The Edge of the World*—it's in the drums secretly building the beat, the accordion picking up the melody and running with it, the drone of the guitar vibrating like an autonomous wire, in the way the self-parody in the voice of the man singing falls away as the story he's telling takes on flesh. The song is set in a war, or a raid, or a riot; the singer has to step over bodies to reach the woman he wants to sing to. The world is cruel because it's just a meaningless assemblage of empowered facts—this broken body; that one—facts so powerful they limit one's choice of response to acceptance or denial: "Ignore these trembling hands/ Don't think of this as blood/ I know it is." The notion of action, of will and result, seems meaningless. "Hello, cruel world," the man says dully; "It's a cruel world," trills the woman, with the sympathy of reason: 'twas ever thus. "Come on, cruel world," the man says, suddenly turning the song around as the music fades, opening up the struggles, doubts, retreats, and occasional joys played out on the rest of the album—"show me what you've got."

The paradox of the Mekons' music is that their pathetic oppression—their reports on the wasteland Thatcherism has made of their England, their fantasies of Reaganist holocaust, their cultivation of their powerlessness, of their self-proclaimed status as isolates, reprobates, ranters, exiles, castaways (by the sound of their voices, they only have to set foot in a place to make it a desert island)—is never solipsistic. Every song pointedly dramatizes a listener; every song is an attempt to find someone to talk to. The conversation may be blocked, imaginary, hopeless, pointless, or even refused; that does not make it false. Mekons records are an attempt to make the falsity of a choice between acceptance or denial real—as they say onstage, "Do you want to be part of the crime, or do you want to be part of the punishment?" The records are also an attempt to escape that choice: to live not as an object but as a subject of history, even when history has passed you by. The records are a dramatization of the wish to make history, to live as if something actually depended on what one says or does—even to the point of "Garage d'Or," which I take to mean "garage door," in the sense of what you have to close when you're going to asphyxiate yourself: the song, a woman's monologue, is a suicide note.

More than ten years ago, writing about the Band, I said that many young Americans had spent the years preceding the group's 1968 *Music from Big Pink* teaching themselves to feel like exiles in their own country, and that the Band's music, fashioned out of old styles, out of what had endured, was made as a way back into it. The Mekons are a lot like the Band in their seamless melding of rock 'n' roll, old country music, and ancient British folk music—here, a Celtic fiddle piece calls up Bob Dylan's "A Hard Rain's A-Gonna Fall," Wire's "I Am the Fly," Richard Thompson's "Withered and Died," and turns out to be Hank Williams's "Alone and Forsaken." The dedication of *The Edge of the World* to the Band's Richard Manuel, this year a suicide, makes the connection explicit: "See you down the road," the sleeve reads. But the world has changed. *Music from Big Pink* left community in its wake; the Mekons, as a small, unstable group of coworkers and friends, may be seeking community through dramatization of what it means to feel like an exile in one's own country.

As a listener, as a fan, by "one" I mean myself. One is exiled in one's own country not when one cannot understand the language, but when one cannot bring oneself to speak it. Last month in this column, I tried to confront a language I couldn't bring myself to speak: the language of *America 2040*, a sci-fi paperback based on the premise that the nuclear extinction of the planet would be OK so long as a spaceship carrying representatives of "the American spirit" got off in time, and the language of *U.S.A. Combat Heroes*, a new magazine celebrating the cinematic exploits of Chuck Norris and Sylvester Stallone as real history. I argued then, and a month later I still believe, that this is the language of our time and place: an empowered oppression, no matter that the language is born dead, that it can't develop beyond the syntax of a T-shirt slogan: "JOIN THE MARINE CORPS / VISIT FOREIGN LANDS / SEE RARE AND EXOTIC PLACES / MEET NEW AND UNUSUAL PEOPLE / AND KILL THEM."

Remember that one? In 1968, in the Vietnam era, the slogan appeared on antiwar bumper stickers: it was an irony, an attempt to negate what it described. With opposition to the Vietnam War growing by the day, the bumper-sticker irony was empowered: talking backward, it said what it meant. Today, worn by marines on whorehouse leave from their foreign bases, the slogan only speaks forward; now it is an affirmation. Now the irony empowers—absolves—those who may do the killing. The joke is on the antiwar activist who, long ago, invented the slogan.

Context is all: because the world has changed, one old slogan has its meaning reversed; an older slogan simply comes back to life. Consider this T-shirt motto, much favored by Americans working with the Nicaraguan contras: "KILL 'EM ALL, LET GOD SORT 'EM OUT." The derivation of this T-shirt (no doubt soon to be marketed in the back pages of *U.S.A. Combat*

Heroes) is interesting. In 1209, at the beginning of the Albigen-
sian Crusade, Pope Innocent III's war of extermination against
the Cathars of southern France, a Catholic commander asked
how he might distinguish believers in the true Church from the
heretics. "Kill them all," came the reply: "God will recognize
His own." The new language may be born dead, as a language;
as power, it only has to kill to stay alive.

So here we are, almost a millennium later, in Nicaragua, or
in a San Francisco nightclub with the Mekons onstage, the fiddler draped in a Sandinista T-shirt bearing an old Spanish Republican slogan: "NO PASARAN" (they shall not pass). The
Mekons make clowns of themselves; some of them are too thin,
some are too fat; their cowboy regalia looks ridiculous. For
Richard Manuel, they play the Band's "The Shape I'm In"
("Save yourself, or save your brother/ Looks like it's/ One or
the other"). There are perhaps fifty people there (half of them
on the guest list); the critic for the local daily passes on the
show. But the show is alive; it is funny; it is warming. There
are moments of terror, when a void opens up and the musicians
seem ready to dive into it, but when they play "King Arthur"
("His mind was filled with memories/ Of friends long gone by/
. . . Scattered all over from Newport to Leeds/ People hiding,
people like bees/ Talking of unity, crippled by fate/ Divided and
lonely, too weak and too late"), the feeling isn't so scary as it is
on *The Edge of the World*, because there are other people there.
The voices are as thick as the words are corny; both feel like
real talk.

Maybe all winning is simple, all losing complex. The language of *Fear and Whiskey* and *The Edge of the World* is as
uncertain as the language of *U.S.A. Combat Heroes* is plain.
The Mekons can say anything, and do nothing; Chuck Norris
and Sylvester Stallone can say nothing, and do anything. As the
Clash once sang, the language of Norris and Stallone "is
the currency"; the problem is, there's nothing I want it can
buy. The Mekons are a reminder that there is something else:

in a world ruled by a language one refuses to speak, they are a reminder there are still people one might want to meet.

—*Artforum*,
October 1986

Free Speech, #2

At the Caesars Tahoe hotel in Lake Tahoe there's a booth where you can cut a tape of yourself singing along to instrumental versions of your favorite songs. Naturally, the results are often pretty funny; the concession operator likes to make copies of performances that strike him as particularly ridiculous, and recently he passed a few of his anti-chart-toppers on to a local radio show. The unqualified hit was some guy stretching his lungs to Billy Joel's "Uptown Girl."

Listening to it was unsettling. "Uptown Girl," more or less a tribute to the Four Seasons ("Dawn," "Rag Doll," "Big Girls Don't Cry," etc.), is a tricky number; those ascending wo-wo-wo-wos almost defeated Joel himself. This singer, whoever he was (I imagined him short, overweight, about forty, sweating like mad, sort of Billy Joel without the money), didn't come close: I mean, he wasn't in the room. You had to laugh; it was hard to figure how the guy kept from laughing himself.

As the tape kept playing, though (and it kept playing—the backing track seemed about twice as long as the record), the fact that the singer never flubbed a lyric began to seem interesting. The fact that, hopelessly out of breath, he somehow stood straight and tall for the flat self-affirmation demanded by the blunt last line of each verse (". . . downtown man/ *That's what I am*"), began to seem remarkable. There was no way around it: as a shower singer the man was drowning, but he was also moving. The poor-boy/rich-girl story line of the song, which in Joel's hands came off as the sort of thing you write when you're working up a Four Seasons tribute, now seemed to count for something. The singer in the booth was desperate, tortured by the arrangement, Sisyphus rolling up the wo-wo-wo-wos, and yet he put all of his panic into the story he was trying to tell: he wants an uptown girl, but he's a downtown man. You heard the guy trying to smile through his boundless incompetence; you heard the pride Joel wrote the song about, but never quite gave it. This Tahoe tourist, probably drunk, changed the song, at least for one listener: I'll never hear Billy Joel sing "Uptown Girl" again without thinking of how little it must have meant to him, compared to what it meant to somebody else.

Such an incident defines the pop song as a gift, and it defines the pop process as a medium of exchange which elicits gifts in return. Billy Joel makes a record, sends it out into the world, and it comes back to him in various forms: as money, as fame, as approval, scorn, indifference. But should he have found himself in the right place at the right time, his radio tuned to the right station, it would have come back to him in a form he could have never anticipated: in the form of a fan who, returning the gift, took the song away from the man who made it.

Weird, huh? Well, it's just idle speculation, Billy Joel will probably never hear the Tahoe tape, so we can forget about it, but Roy Orbison is going to see what's been done with his "In Dreams" in David Lynch's film *Blue Velvet*, and what's he going to think? The same thing that happened in the Caesars booth happens in Lynch's movie.

Though as filmmaking *Blue Velvet* is your basic work of genius, as the dramatization of an idea—the primeval pit of corruption simmering beneath the bland surface of middle-class life—it's your basic work of corn. As Pauline Kael once said of *Citizen Kane*, it's a shallow masterpiece. That may be why none of the critical raves the film attracted are half as convincing as the movie itself; if you read them after seeing the movie, they can make you doubt the power of what you've just seen. The writers are trying too hard to say what *Blue Velvet* means, what Lynch's message is, certain that anything so aesthetically

strong must mean something socially, even philosophically, profound. Thus they make the movie more than it is, ultimately
making it seem less; they fetishize *Blue Velvet*'s fetishes, refusing to let them remain as ordinary as Lynch made them. So far
I've read that the plastic mask the Dennis Hopper character
clamps onto his face each time he's about to commit an act of
sex or violence contains helium, cocaine vapors, ether—as if
mere oxygen were just too tame. But *Blue Velvet* is a movie of
sensations, not ideas. The horrible roar that rises out of the bed
when the clean-cut kid and the mystery woman fall together
just after she's made him hit her—it's the voice of Grendel's
mother—is an event, a breach, not a thesis on sexuality or phe-
nomenology.

What *Blue Velvet* dramatizes is displacement—not, it would
seem, because Lynch finds displacement socially significant, but
because he finds it thrilling. There's no other reason for what
he does with "In Dreams"—the song creates the most pointless
moment in the film, the most perverse, and the most elegant. It
adds nothing to the plot, nothing to characterization. It's as if
Lynch simply loved the song, as if he'd waited since it hit the
charts in 1963 to find a way to reply to it, as if, in the middle of
making *Blue Velvet*, he simply decided he'd waited long enough.

Dennis Hopper, the fiend, forces the clean-cut kid and the
mystery woman into his car and drives them across town to a
scummy whorehouse. They're greeted by Dean Stockwell, the
whoremaster. The mood is cruel, but not exactly menacing;
there's a lassitude in the way the villains move that almost
freezes the scene, as if they've run through their cheap bullies'
gestures for so many years they can't imagine how to get more
pleasure out of them.

Hopper stands silent, smiles, then screeches, but the kid
and the woman know this is just the way he talks. What scares
them is Stockwell: you can sense them trying not to look at
him. He's a pervert beyond gender; the makeup on his face is so
thick you can't believe there's skin underneath. Everyone is

waiting around, waiting to leave, waiting to think of what to do, waiting for something to happen, and then suddenly "In Dreams" is playing, and Stockwell is posing in an archway, miming, performing, a little entertainment, the song coming out of his mouth, perfectly. You don't know what's going on, where the music's coming from (a cassette machine, but that's not shown right away), why it's there at all.

As Roy Orbison songs go, "In Dreams" is bland, even vague —shapeless. Here it's distinct, demanding, beautiful, horrible: you have to look at Stockwell, you can't bear not to. A terrific tension builds up in an instant: the song is expanding, and it's going to blow up at any second. The whole movie is going to blow up, right here, for no reason. At the same time, the movie has become irrelevant; as a story, the viewer isn't even in it anymore, and neither are the other characters.

Maybe this is just the Stockwell character's favorite song. Maybe he'd been waiting around all night for someone to show up so he could put it on and pretend to sing it. Who knows? His performance is as revolting as it is fascinating, and to keep from seeing what you have to look at you listen harder, and the music takes on a clarity it never had before. But you might as well be catching the sweat that drips out of Stockwell's makeup in your mouth: as a conventional romantic ballad the song vanishes, turning into a wash of loathing, of hatred, of vileness. It becomes a threat, what it means for Stockwell to commit an act of sex or violence. It's all too much to take in; Dennis Hopper walks over to the tape recorder and cuts the song off.

"In Dreams" is now changed. As a conventional romantic ballad it now contains extremes a punk rant about rape and gore could not begin to suggest. Presumably, David Lynch has gotten pleasure from "In Dreams" for years. It appears on his screen as a moment of pleasure, at once empty and overwhelming. As a director, Lynch speaks through actors; no less than the man in the booth at Caesars Tahoe, he's singing a song he likes, just singing it. Like the man in the booth, he's returning a gift, giving something back to the song—something, in this case, it never wanted, but now has to accept.

—*Artforum*,
December 1986

1987–1992

Born Dead

For every new art form there's someone to come along and pronounce it dead, but rarely has an art form been born dead—as is the case with rock video, and its major outlet, MTV. MTV is the pornography of semiotics. Available around the clock, a closed system where nothing outside its frame of reference is ever allowed to intrude, it most closely resembles the lowest porn commodity, the loop: a continuous, circular repetition of signs whose meanings have been frozen long in advance. Promising pleasure through immersion in a seamless collage of visual and aural surprises, delivering instead the stupor of reification, the contradiction running twenty-four hours a day on MTV is so ugly, so directly productive of aesthetic and moral shame, as to be fundamentally obscene.

"Obscene," the dictionary says, means first of all "offensive to the senses"—the senses, not the rational, socialized intellect. Obscenity is a violation, felt in the gut before it is organized by the mind. Of course obscenity is subjective: one man's meat is another woman's poison, and all that. But there is an objectivity, a formalism, at work in it too: to watch and hear what is frozen is, eventually, to begin to freeze. Like pornography, MTV can glue you to the screen—at least until the split between what ought to be fun and what is in fact oppressive becomes intolerable. Glued to the screen, you can start to feel like Lot's wife.

Shame is an interesting emotion; as semiotic pornography, MTV lets you decipher your responses. Turn it on: along with the medley of Whitney Houston's greatest hits, which glamorizes insincerity to the point where no other emotion seems real (the look on Houston's face when she hugs her mother at the end of "The Greatest Love of All"—self-love—would scare Machiavelli), along with the interchangeable female models gliding through male singers' videos, their makeup so pristine they dissolve the reality of whatever situations they are gliding through—along with everything else MTV has to offer, you see, perhaps, Big Country's "One Great Thing."

This is an elaborate, ambitious piece of work. The key lines of the song are, "If there's one great thing to happen in my life/ Let it be a time for peace"; to dramatize the idea, the video presents dozens of ordinary-looking people, grouped by gender, class, and vocation (nuns, grocers, bankers, bodybuilders, doctors, etc.), posed as if for school club photos in a yearbook. They mouth the words to the song as, on the soundtrack, Big Country—a male U.K. rock combo known for rousing tunes pushed by a guitar that sounds like a bagpipe—performs it. The premise is simple: all people want peace. The subpremise is patent: all people, wanting the same thing, are basically the same. We live in one world. But it's a queer exercise, and the queerness isn't simple.

The people in this video aren't lip-synching—pretending to sing. They're not like the contestants on the TV show *Puttin' on the Hits*, or Mickey Rourke miming Bob Seger's "Feel Like a Number" in *Body Heat*. When you lip-synch you take over the song, or vice versa; you actively respond to someone else's creation and, if only for a moment, you change yourself. The process is fun, and the result is something new.

What goes on in "One Great Thing" is so far from fun it's morbid. You see separated, segregated groups of people stolidly, blankly forming their lips around the word "peace" as you hear the word coming out of Big Country's mouths. The feeling is creepy. Halfway through the video, you're watching not an intended dramatization of the truism that everybody wants peace, but an unintended dramatization of alienation—which feels like the shame, the obscenity, the pornography of everyday life. What you see is that these people (real nuns, real actors, who knows?), who were presumably told to look serious (peace is a serious matter), are not, as they mouth words that signify a good thing, having a good time. Why not? Maybe because they were told to say what they're saying; maybe because what they are portraying, or what they're living out, is not freedom, pleasure, or even advocacy, but the stupor of reification. What's most intensely dramatized—the social fact that overwhelms the notion of "peace"—is not, finally, the idea that all of these putatively separated groups of people want the same thing, but separation itself. Watching, you anticipate a finale where the nuns mingle with the bodybuilders (What would happen? Would the nuns finger the bodybuilders' biceps, or the bodybuilders lift the nuns' wimples?), but it doesn't happen.

Intercut with the groups of "real people," Big Country is shown onstage playing "One Great Thing." The band performs as the voice of all people; the crowd cheers; the singer emotes. But the band helplessly orchestrates its absolute statement of right thought as if it were a song about anything else, performed by anyone else. Very quickly, the performance is not about peace; it's about MTV.

Everything you see is second-hand, third-hand—received and reified. To highlight a solo, the singer leans on the guitar player's shoulders as the guitarist thrashes out the notes. Within all-male rock bands, this is a gesture so tired, so stereotyped, as to be no longer capable of signifying what it's supposed to signify: camaraderie, fraternity, solidarity, or simply the delight of making physical contact. All the gesture signifies here is that the guys in Big Country know what male rock stars are supposed to do onstage. They're not touching because they want to, because the music drove them together, or because a gesture of solidarity symbolizes peace, but because it's in the male-rock-performer script, and that's signification enough: the movement just says that these people are, in fact, rock stars. It walks like a duck, it talks like a duck, it must be a duck. The semiology is circular, but that's all there is to MTV semiology: the only course it can describe is a loop.

Just as all people want peace, and male rock musicians lean on each other's shoulders, most male rock singers on MTV are now supposed to wear shoulder pads. ("Populist" performers like Bruce Springsteen and his epigones don't have to.) Within MTV's closed frame of reference, this bizarrely unnatural style is meant to seem natural: you're not intended to notice the pads, merely to register them subliminally, to understand without thinking that rock-stars-wear-them, non-stars-don't. It's useful: watching MTV, you can automatically tell the stars from the other people. But the pads on the Big Country singer are impossible not to notice: they look like tumors.

The Big Country singer fidgets behind his rock-star poses; he seems uncomfortable, as if his clothes don't fit him, because they don't. As fashion, the shoulder-pad style was designed to make one look larger than life, powerful, aggressive, invulnerable. But when everybody has to wear shoulder pads, all they can signify is that one-is-wearing-shoulder-pads—at best, that one is in fashion, and can afford to be so. But fashion is a dictatorship—and the Big Country singer is performing as a citizen of that dictatorship far more than as a member of the community of people who want peace. The longer you look, the more his grinning, grimacing face seems to match the unhappy, stiff expressions of the nuns and bodybuilders mouthing his words a few seconds on either side of his performance inserts: they're all doing what they're told to do. The singer isn't wearing shoulder pads; they're wearing him. Invented to signify power, they now signify that whoever wears them has none—not even the power to choose his own clothes.

Or, anyway, they signify that he's a rock star on MTV.

That's something, even if they make him squirm. He'll get used to it, or he'll be off the air. Such are the pleasures of an art form born dead.

—*Artforum,*
January 1987

The Return of Iron Butterfly

Wire: *Snakedrill*. Active in London from 1977 to 1980, this foursome sometimes played songs lasting under a minute, but even the longest were as gnomic as that gesture. A wash of repetition disguised careful sonic choices, and the edge of the music, and the moment, was never reduced, merely removed from the obvious: "I am the fly—the fly in the ointment" was Wire's version of "I am an antichrist." On this EP, the group's first recording in years, neither the sound nor the role-playing has changed. "'A Serious of Snakes'" starts off with some punning on "In-A-Gadda-Da-Vida," and the title tells you who the Gardener is; weaving a dramatically modulated melody around the conceit, Wire seems as implacable, as mysterious, and as new as it did a decade ago. I take this to mean not that Wire was ahead of its time, but that Wire caught its time, and that time has stood still—that the chiliastic voice found in London in the first year of punk has hardly been answered, let alone superseded.

—from "Real Life Rock Top Ten," *Village Voice*,
13 January 1987

Judgment Day

November 1986, Election Day: I was thinking about Lino A. Graglia, a law professor at the University of Texas. Earlier in the year President Reagan had submitted his name to the American Bar Association for preliminary approval before nominating him to the Federal Court of Appeals; the ABA, in its own measured way, had thrown up. "It is doubtful that the net contribution of the Constitution to our national well-being has been positive," Graglia had written in 1984. "The ultimate source of authority is simply force, physical force." The nomination had been shelved, but there were more where he came from. It was a lovely day, the Senate was up for grabs, this was what was at stake.

Thinking about Lino A. Graglia, I was trying not to think. Gunning the motor, looking for a good song, I wanted to surrender to the claims of the weather, but instead, as if drawn back to a screen memory, I thought for perhaps the hundredth time of a word Elizabeth Drew, Washington columnist for the *New Yorker*, had used in her wrap-up on the 1980 elections. The new Republican senators swept into office then, she had said (all of them, save for John East of North Carolina, who had killed himself, standing for reelection this November 4), were "nihilistic."

What was Drew talking about? She's famous for her reasonableness, her blandness, for numbing transcriptions of interviews and cherry-blossom reports, and as a violation of her normal discourse this word made no sense. It was loud and violent, but like the crash of a falling tree nobody hears. The word was a hole in her pages; she didn't explain what she meant. I don't think she knew. I wasn't sure, six years later, that I knew. But her loss of her professional voice was the sort of moment that can stick in the mind: a little media shock. For an instant, it seemed, she found it impossible to simply do her job. "Nihilism": if in art it can mean a clearing of the ground, a preparation for something new, a wellspring of creation, in politics its only meaning is the acceptance, or the pursuit, of someone else's death. In the world of affairs, a belief in nothing means that no one is anything and everyone is expendable.

I was trying not to think about this—about whether or not, by the end of the day, Drew's nihilists would remain in place to confirm the president's next crop of Graglias—when I changed stations and happened upon the first phrases of Laurie Anderson's "O Superman." It was a surprise: usually, if you hear "O Superman" on the radio, you hear it late at night—it's that sort of record.

It was disabling. I pulled over, turned off the motor, and tried to find the perfect volume. I no longer wanted to surrender to the day; I wanted to surrender to the specter Anderson would become by the end of the song. Since 1981, when it was first released ("Special Thanks" to, among others, the National Endowment for the Arts), I'd played the song as many times as I'd returned to Drew's "nihilistics"; it should have had nothing left to say. But this was Election Day, and "O Superman," like Lincoln's Second Inaugural Address, or the Gettysburg Address, is a portrait of the Republic.

Anderson shares something of Lincoln's tone—his somberness, his Puritan sense of sin, his expectation of Judgment—but not, of course, his context. "O Superman" is a dream about imperialism—about a supernation that has had done with the rest of the world and has turned back to colonize itself. Beginning, as dreams do, in triviality, the song becomes a totality: an impenetrable whole made out of private life (Mom calls up and leaves a message on the answering machine), public life (mail delivery, summoned in the motto—"Neither snow, nor rain, nor heat, nor gloom of night . . ."—that makes it the embodiment of national will), and natural life (birds singing, a cat meowing). Once the piece catches you, you can't get away: it touches all bases, there's nowhere left to go.

"O Superman" is a very simple production, yet it's hard to think of a recording that's more carefully made. The eight minutes and twenty-one seconds go by very quickly, partly because "O Superman" works out of slowness, time cut up and ordered, each moment both segmented and connected (the constant "ah-ah-ah-ah" in the background—a cricket's chirp, or a last breath infinitely extended). The crucial temporal mode is an implacable, hysterical hesitation: hesitation as a form of anticipation. In the nation "O Superman" describes, what one never believed would be now is: you fill in your own nightmare, but it has something to do with "freedom," with a world where quotation marks have to be put around the word. One must say yes to that world, say yes or say nothing, and to say nothing is to cease to be, to become a hole in the fabric of the "Republic," and so the singer says yes.

The woman who's singing presses the message button on her answering machine: she hears her mother, and then the voice of the facts of life, the world-historical, which has a sense of humor, but which talks in a whisper like a sex pervert, and then you don't know if it's still the world-historical that's speaking, or if the woman has taken that voice into her own throat. Finally a chord comes down, softly, hard (what is the right volume?): "So hold me now."

In the music of the last six years, is there another line, another harmonic shift, another rape victim's calculation that to say yes might be to live and to say no is probably to cease to be, that bears so much weight? The singer, the rape victim, the citizen of the Republic, explains what Elizabeth Drew didn't explain: "When love is gone/ There's always justice/ And when justice is gone/ There's always force/ And when force is gone/ There's always Mom (Hi Mom!)," and now Mom is not only the first voice on the answering machine, but the second: the world-historical, the facts of life.

"O Superman" is a love song: a love song to power. Power in "O Superman" is invisible, but patent, omnipresent: as present in chirping crickets and buzzing answering machines as in the arms the singer asks to hold her, Mom's arms, her "petrochemical arms," her "electronic arms" (a complex, curling rhythm in the way Anderson speaks those words), her "military arms." The mood is so quiet, so seamless, that not even the interjection of shibboleths breaks it. The dream remains a dream, but a dream, as an Australian parable has it, "that is dreaming us."

There's no sense of choice in "O Superman." It is in fact "nihilistic." Sure, it's an ironic depiction; certainly, it's a yes that's really a no—but what I mean is that to hear "O Superman" in the right place at the right time is to feel the quotation marks lift off the word. Nihilistic.

It was a vision of a future of stone. It was impossible not to recognize it, not to feel at home there. The last moments of the song are so beautiful, the shifting tones a caressing whirlpool, so full of dread, so welcoming, it's painful to know that the music is about to end. And I was almost sorry, hours later, watching the returns, that most of the nihilists were sent back where they came from: sorry that the song had lost its moment. Almost sorry.

—Artforum,
February 1987

Music

Released in 1977, Fleetwood Mac's "Go Your Own Way" was the initial single from *Rumours*, which eventually sold more than twelve million copies. As the first shot by the group since their quadruple-platinum *Fleetwood Mac*, "Go Your Own Way" should have been an automatic smash, no matter what it sounded like, but it surfaced a few times and then vanished, quickly replaced by "Dreams," a soft ballad, which sailed easily to number one. "Go Your Own Way" was rough, harsh, hard to follow. From its opening notes it was a maelstrom, excitement and nothing else. It was an assault, a hammering, the singer moaning and threatening, pleading and damning; it didn't let up for a second.

Coming two thirds of the way through the performance, the requisite instrumental break should have provided a rest; instead it raised the stakes. When Lindsey Buckingham dropped his words for a guitar solo—a shattered, severed solo almost drowning in a dozen more overdubbed guitar parts, the off-beat rhythm chasing his lead, then overtaking him, then seeming to wait for him to catch up, which he never quite did—the song began all over again. Ten years later, I flinch every time it comes on the radio, knowing what's coming, knowing that no matter how completely I can predict what's going to happen, *I* won't be able to catch up: the instrumental passage supersedes not only the singing that precedes it, but the ability of memory to enclose it. And the record got its due: "Dreams" hasn't been on the air since it dropped from the charts, while "Go Your Own Way" has never been off the air.

Well, what's going on here? Why is what ought to be a

"break"—a relief, a respite—a charge of even greater energy? This happens all the time in rock 'n' roll—often, maybe most often, the charge isn't sustained, the lift is all in the shift, but that can be enough. It's as if some sort of promise is being made, some vision of possibility opening up, if only for a second; to glimpse it is to reach for it. But to reach, finally, for what?

A person writes a song. On the page, the words are probably banal; sung, accompanied by instruments, they come to life. They seem new, perhaps even prophetic; the musical dimension enshrines the verbal dimension. The process works in the other direction too: words, perhaps just a title ("One title is worth a million lyrics," says Mike Watt of the Minutemen), suggest a meaning for music, make sense of it—but because the words would be little or nothing without the music, the music finally rebukes the words. Building in any successful rock 'n' roll record is a sense of the power of the singer to say what he or she means, but also a realization that words are inadequate to that task, and the feeling of fulfillment is never as strong as the feeling of frustration. The singer goes as far as he or she can go; the singer even acknowledges the quandary, gives in to its tension, abandons words and screams. But the singer still comes up short; the performance demands the absolute lucidity it has already promised, a promise from which it is already falling back, and so an instrument takes over. It is a relief: a relief from the failure of language. The thrill is that of entering a world where anything can be said, even if no one can know what it means.

You can hear this happen, appreciate it as a deliberate piece of drama, in Elvis's "Jailhouse Rock": there's a slur of "rockrockrock," then a perfectly placed cymbal smash. The ensemble means to sweep you off your feet, and it does. The tactic is a little more complex in "Hound Dog." The first guitar solo is terrific, but its function turns out to be to set up the second solo, which exists, it sometimes seems, only to supersede the first—to show you how ordinary it was, to show you what the extraordinary really is. Scotty Moore takes the fluid notes of the first break and smashes them, cuts them up, then leaps over the empty spaces. He says, "You thought that was the truth, but I was only kidding. I'm not kidding any more."

But the same kind of thrill can be delivered without any setup at all—and that's the real claim of such a moment on musical time. In the original version of "(What's So Funny 'Bout) Peace, Love and Understanding," which Nick Lowe recorded in 1974 with his band Brinsley Schwarz, the song is a joke on sixties pieties, so full of irony you can feel the stuff oozing out of the speakers. In Elvis Costello's 1978 version, he sings with apparent conviction, but given his then still-controlling "revenge and guilt" persona, you know it has to be a joke— a dialectical joke, maybe, given the strength of the music, but nevertheless an account of world-historical dopiness. Then Costello shuts his mouth and plays chord changes on his guitar that are so rudimentary they can't even be called a solo; the band presses down just slightly; and everything is different.

Suddenly, all the context, all the pop knowledge one might have brought to the performance (the hard-edged punk rejection of hippie naïveté, etc.), is dissolved. Not only is the built-in hokiness of the tune diverted, the irony is boiled off; the guitar notes don't neutralize the pathos of the lyrics, they validate it. What's so funny about peace, love, and understanding? Now, nothing. For an instant, the search for peace, love, and understanding is what life is all about. You come back to the ordinary world, the world of ordinary language, with a wonderful story: "I saw it! I heard it!" "What was it?" everyone asks, and you open your mouth, and begin to wave your hands in the air.

—*Artforum*,
March 1987

More Bad News

Elvis Costello: "I Want You" (San Jose Civic Auditorium, April 16). Quietly diseased on record, drawing poison no one else knew was there out of Howlin' Wolf's "Goin' Down Slow," the Beatles' "I Want You (She's So Heavy)," and god knows what else, on record this is a horror movie that doesn't need special effects: *The Servant*, maybe, or *M*. The words "I want you" alternate every other line with collapsing scenes of torture, flagellation, remorse, bloody glee; at first you're convinced it's all happening in the singer's mind, next that it's happening in the flesh. "I want you/ And when I *wake up*," Costello sang, just as he does on his *Blood and Chocolate* lp—and then he pulled the string. Hanging onto the end of it were Dionne Warwick and Aretha Franklin, who came tumbling into the song like new victims: "—and put on my *makeup*/ I say a little prayer for you/ Because I *want* you. . . ."

—from "Real Life Rock Top Ten," *Village Voice*, 5 May 1987

Groovy Hate Fuck

In college, I learned about Plato's ideal Forms, and mused that if there were Forms of justice, eros, agape, and the like, there really ought to be a Form of rock 'n' roll—an Essence, preexisting what we benighted prisoners of the cave of illusion 'n' reality called the music's "form" and certainly outlasting it. I didn't have to think too long to be convinced. Transposed into the vulgate, this was an argument rock 'n' roll had been making about itself from Chuck Berry's "Roll Over Beethoven" to the Showmen's "It Will Stand," and on, and on. If these people were reaching for something, even if they couldn't grasp it, wasn't that proof it was there?

Faith in such a notion may explain why I never went on to logic class, but I thought of it again recently, reading Bill Flanagan's *Written in My Soul*, a book of interviews with rock songwriters. "The only thing that rock & roll did *not* get from country and blues was a sense of consequences," Flanagan says to Neil Young. "In country and blues, if you raised hell on Saturday night, you were gonna feel real bad on Sunday morning when you dragged yourself to church." "That's right," says Young. "Rock & roll is reckless abandon. Rock & roll is the *cause* of country and blues. Country and blues came first, but somehow rock & roll's place in the chain of events is dispersed" —and what an amazing remark that is! Young is saying that while as forms blues and country preceded rock 'n' roll, as spirit rock 'n' roll preceded blues and country, which came forth precisely to control that spirit. Penned in and locked up, the spirit achieved shape, emerged as form, and thus revealed the existence of the Form itself.

Among other things, Young's line can undercut fear of the current wave of rock censorship—the actions of Tipper Gore's PMRC, the banning of many lps and rock magazines from chain stores, major labels pressuring their acts to dispense with certain cover art and lyrics. Official government action would be another story—and since Tipper Gore's husband is running for president, and the FCC is cracking down, we may get it yet. But no matter how disgusting, corporate censorship is part of the marketplace in which rock 'n' roll has chosen to take its stand, and citizens' groups denouncing songs they don't like as depraved are engaging in public speech no less than the performers they might prefer to have locked up.

The opposition itself may not be bad for the music. Rock 'n' roll thrived in the fifties, when censorship was taken for granted; restrictions and limits, out in the open, can lead the music to reinvent itself, to discover secret languages, to come up with a communication that doesn't bounce off a listener's head but burrows into it. Certainly, if there is a Form of rock 'n' roll—if the Showmen were right in 1961, and Neil Young is right today—this is what ought to happen. The real problem may be harder to escape than social or even political censorship: self-censorship. As the late Alexander Trocchi once wrote: "We have to attack the 'enemy' at his base, within ourselves."

Self-censorship is never simply a response to outside pressure. One kind of self-censorship has to do with what Eric Alliez and Michel Feher call "the luster of capital," with the alienation of the artist from the commodity he or she produces. Another kind is rooted in the artist's need to trap a spirit in the form, to make a wish obey rules supposedly guaranteeing its realization. The Sex Pistols were a reaction against the first sort of self-censorship, which by 1976 had almost completely taken over rock 'n' roll; Pussy Galore, a new punk band from New York, may be working in reaction to the second.

"New punk band" sounds like an oxymoron. After more than ten years, punk has become an old story—a collection of received ideas, borrowed attitudes, stale gestures. If you say no enough times, you're saying yes. When I first saw a Pussy Galore record I laughed at the title, *groovy hate fuck*—gosh. I was in the studio of a college radio station, and the program director had written play/don't play instructions on the jacket: "Pretty good 'I hate everything' stuff, can air last cut (instrumental)." A few weeks later I heard "Cunt Tease" on the radio, from the same record, and on the same station that had tried to restrict airplay to the instrumental. The song made you notice it: lead singer Jon Spencer pressing the theme, guitarist Julia Cafritz chiming in after every verse with a delighted "FUCK YOU!"—a delight in the chance to say the words, and mean them. The tune was ugly, and it was funny.

"What do you do?" a sixtyish businessman asked me. "I'm a rock critic," I said. "My son's in a punk band," he said, throwing his arms wide: " 'Fuckfuckfuckfuckfuck.' " And that's what Pussy Galore say. By now such spew ought to be a harmless cliché, but somehow it isn't, not as Pussy Galore use it. What you hear on their records—on *groovy hate fuck*, on the recent *Pussy Gold 5000*, on the group's bizarre cassette recording of the whole of the Rolling Stones' *Exile on Main Street* (the first before-the-fact answer record, issued in response to Sonic Youth's oft-proclaimed intention to rerecord the Beatles' white album)—is a search for the utterly heedless. You hear, if not Neil Young's reckless abandon, an argument that today reckless abandon has to be searched for.

Pussy Galore are two women and three men. They scream at each other—on songs, between songs, as numbers begin wrong and end off the mark. Listening to their shouts and curses, some seemingly desperate to achieve form, others seemingly as driven to throw it off (it's as if you were listening to a rehearsal tape they forgot to erase), you can imagine that you're hearing the first steps of a definite project: an attack on self-censorship with the crudest tools. The project is the attempt by a small group of people to discover what it is they most want to say. How do you do that? Well, you can start by trying to expose your own self-censoring impulse. What is it that I think I most *don't* want to say? What would happen if I said it? What would happen if I got it across? FUCKFUCKFUCKFUCKFUCK.

It's all in the tone, what happens: in the singers' tone of voice, in the tone of the band's playing, in the huge, corrosive growl from the guitar that ambushes Cafritz the moment she begins "Spin Out" on *Pussy Gold 5000*, a sound that comes out of nowhere and goes back where it came from as soon as you register it. In a punk context, where the certainty that every-thing is permitted has come to mean that nothing is true, once-forbidden words, now commonplace and meaningless, regain the power they had when they were used only in oaths, when they meant what they said, when people were rightly afraid of them. They begin to recover their forbidden content, their for-bidden spirit—and that spirit is no less forbidding today than it ever was. The words cut; the tone hurts; both thrill. They go far enough to put you in Tipper Gore's shoes. As a listener, no matter how enlightened, you're forced to ask: should this be allowed?

For Pussy Galore, the creation of a musical incident strong enough to raise such a question may be merely a means to the discovery of what it is they want to say—and there's no way of knowing if they'll ever make that discovery, or if it'll be worth hearing about if they do. For the moment, their no remains a no, and it will do. When rock 'n' roll no longer produces a ver-sion of itself worth banning, none of it will be worth listening to.

—*Artforum*,
Summer 1987

Punk Is Where You Find It

Absolut Vodka ad: *New Yorker*, 21 December 1987. You open the four-page insert, pull a strip at the fold, and out comes the melody of "We Wish You a Merry Christmas." Taking the pages apart, you find a sort of music box, about the size of a hearing aid, but much thinner; while the sound it makes isn't loud, it seems to travel through floors. The machine is efficient: mine has been playing for more than forty-eight hours.

There are here possibilities for the creation of disturbance, for the promulgation of aesthetic displacement and social uncertainty, far beyond the obvious brutalism of beat boxes or the street-art critiques of Barbara Kruger and Jenny Holzer. The mechanics can't be that complicated; it ought to be easy to copy, program, and disseminate. Imagine tens of thousands of undetectable music boxes, coded with "Summertime, Summertime," "Come on in My Kitchen," "Jump," all secreted in the crevices of skyscrapers, in the cracks of telephone poles, stuck under bus seats, rugs, desks (in your office, in the Office of Management and Budget, behind the presidential seal the next time there's a televised White House news conference). Imagine "You Are My Sunshine" and "When a Man Loves a Woman" turning the whole country into one vast theater for the aural itch of a song you can't get out of your head, but now *every* song, a different one every few minutes, every few steps, people saying, "God, what *is* that, I know it, I just can't—"

Who knows, there might be a lot of interesting new con-

versations. There might be rioting in the streets. It might
be the end of civilization as we know it. You read it here
first.

> —from "Real Life Rock Top Ten," *Village Voice*,
> 19 January 1988

An Echo

The Clash: "Complete Control," from *The Story of the Clash, Volume 1*. The purpose of this conventional two-record retrospective, complete with unreadable life-on-the-road notes by the group's self-titled valet, seems to be to certify the Clash as a conventional rock band. The fact that there was something more at stake in the Clash's career than a career is suppressed by the exclusion of idiosyncrasy, playfulness, and despair ("The Right Profile," "Brand New Cadillac," the broken, empty-handed "This Is England," what was left after Thatcherism erased the last traces of the white riot) in favor of rebel-rock shtick and chart hopes ("The Guns of Brixton," "Lost in the Supermarket," "Stay Free," "Should I Stay or Should I Go?").

Given the shape of the package, the numbers on side three —all from 1977–78, when punk was still an idea seeking its field —send a nearly incomprehensible message of disruption, desire, and fear. Even less explainable, now, is that at the heart of this side is a performance that as pure sound stands as the greatest rock 'n' roll recording ever made. Oddly, it's about the Clash's career, at least on a literal, lyric-sheet level: their label-sanctioned protest single about the same label committing the atrocity of releasing an earlier single without the band's permission. So what. Yet from this flimsy soapbox they fly to a dramatization of autonomy, community, personal identity, and social contestation, and with a few scattered slogans ("THIS MEANS YOU!") make those usually abstract notions as real, as dangerous, as any moment governed by love or money, hate or war. Across more than ten years of listening to "Complete Control," one reaction has always come first: disbelief. Disbelief that mere human beings could create such a sound, and disbelief that the world could remain the same when it's over.

> —from "Real Life Rock Top Ten," *Village Voice*,
> 31 May 1988

The Assassin

E lvis Costello: "Tramp the Dirt Down," from *Spike*. This ode to the death of Margaret Thatcher—no metaphors, Costello names her—recalls his "Pills and Soap," "Little Palaces," and "Sleep of the Just" in its arrangement; anchored in hate and regret, it also begins in Bob Dylan's "Masters of War," "With God on Our Side," and "The Lonesome Death of Hattie Carroll." There is a lot of death here, in the deliberate cadence of the first verse, in the rage that follows, in the way Costello forms the words "cheap," "maimed," "pitiful," and especially the phrase "subtle difference"—the "subtle difference," in Thatcher's Britain, "between justice and contempt." To make true political music, you have to say what decent people don't want to hear; that's something people fit for satellite benefit concerts will never understand, and that Costello understood before anyone heard his name.

—from "Real Life Rock Top Ten," *Village Voice*,
21 February 1989

Chapters from History

The Mekons: *The Curse of the Mekons*, and Wallace Shawn: *The Fever*. Their fourteen years as a transhistorical punk band have become the Mekons' subject, but not in terms of career. Rather their subject is their quarrel with history, and their growing conviction that it means to leave them behind; Sally Timms, so quietly soulful that against her Rosanne Cash can sound strident, sometimes makes this story seem fated, but it still hurts. In Wallace Shawn's one-person perform-anywhere play, the subject is the impossibility of escaping from history, and there is no relief, no humor. There is simply the scream of a bourgeois sorcerer (to quote Marx, and the Mekons quoting Marshall Berman quoting Marx) who cannot get free of his own magic, cannot break the contract that ties his comfort to torture, his priceless individuality to the facelessness of the poor, who must be made to "understand that the dreamers, the idealists, the ones who say that they love the poor, will all become vicious killers in the end, and the ones who claim they can create something better will always end up by creating something worse. The poor must understand these essential lessons, chapters from history. And if they don't understand them, they must all be taken out and shot."

The Mekons are always good for a laugh, whistling in the dark, but this is tough stuff, no fun, sleepless nights: to be left behind by history is to have never existed at all. "Funeral," a song about the collapse of Marxism—which on *The Curse of the Mekons* means any resistance to capitalism as the measure of all things—is "a dinosaur's confession": "This funeral is for the wrong corpse." Shawn's nameless tourist enjoying his cheap holiday in other people's misery has a ticket to the funeral, but he doesn't want to go: "Cowards who sit in lecture halls or the halls of state denouncing the crimes of the revolutionaries are not as admirable as the farmers and nuns who ran so swiftly into the wind." Listen as you read, read as you listen, and you might be back in Bob Dylan's "Memphis Blues Again": "Now people just get uglier/ And I have no sense of time."

—from "Real Life Rock Top Ten," *Artforum*, September 1991

yglg

Not long ago I came across a proposal for a documentary film on great rock concerts. The concept was simple. Starting with the greatest concert of all time—Woodstock—you'd show all these legendary gatherings, most involving at least one dead hero, and each segment would end with its host, a current movie or music star, grinning into the camera: "You shoulda been there, man."

Recently people who weren't there have been having fun replying to this tyrannical imposition of '60s nostalgia, which is really a way for middle-aged '60s people to protect their own identity by discouraging others from making their own history. In the strangled lines from the Youngbloods' '67 anthem "Get Together" that open Nirvana's "Territorial Pissings," you can hear unmitigated contempt for this project, along with a gleeful realization of how stupid it is. *Comeonpeoplenowsmileon-yourbrothereverybodygettogethertrytoloveoneanotherrightnow* —Chris Novoselic sounds nuts, completely Mansonoid, and also thrilled to deliver a new punch line to a bad joke.

Even better is a moment in "Liar," a tune by Bikini Kill, a three-woman, one-man (all in their early twenties) band from Olympia, Washington, and Washington, D.C. A furious march through the song suddenly breaks off, and instead of railing curses singer Kathleen Hanna is crooning: "All we are saying/ Is give peace a chance . . ." Behind her, though, are the most amazing female screams—wrapping around the old words like snakes. They're the screams of a talking doll under torture. You get the feeling you'll never hear *that* bit of pop holiness again.

Trumpeting the Bikini Kill slogan REVOLUTION GIRL STYLE

NOW—also the title of their homemade eight-song cassette—this group's way of making their own history is to act as if they have no ancestors, musically or politically. Of course, there's a way in which Hanna, drummer Tobi Vail, bassist Kathi Wilcox, and guitarist Billy Karren *are* starting from zero. The plain-speech feminism in their Bikini Kill fanzines ("It is not our responsibility to explain how boys/men are being sexist any more than it is our responsibility to 'prevent ourselves' from getting raped") might not have been surprising in 1972; after twenty years of I'm-not-a-feminist-but, talk like this communicates directly. People who've heard it before might find it depressing that the list of ten favorite male put-downs of feminism in the Bikini Kill fanzine *Girl Power* could have appeared in the '70s in the feminist journal *Off Our Backs*: "1. You Take Things Too Seriously. . . . 3. You Know, Some Women Manage to 'Go Beyond' Sexism. . . . 9. But I Know a Girl Who Lied About Being Raped. . . . 10. Complain, Complain, Complain. . . . At Least You Don't Have It As Bad As a) women used to b) people of color c) women in other countries." But read the Bikini Kill analysis that follows each heading and you'll find an energy, a sense of delight, that only comes when it seems like you're doing something for the first time.

It's the same with Bikini Kill's music. It's the purest, crudest punk, and testament to a crucial cultural truth: when you get down to the bones and teeth of the punk form—the desire of people who *can't* to *do*—punk is never "revived," but always rediscovered. Kathleen Hanna may not high-step with the same force Poly Styrene of X-ray Spex found in London in 1977 with "Oh Bondage Up Yours!," but the sense of a person finding herself is just as strong. The two women are speaking the same language. In the background of "Oh Bondage Up Yours!" teenage saxophonist Lora Logic trips, stumbles, and falls, and seizes the music; Bikini Kill set "Daddy's Li'l Girl"—a vocally complex song about incest—to what is more or less "Batman Theme." In both cases you wonder what's going on, why it's so hard to keep up, why the dumbbell can't-play simplicity can support such a rich conversation.

"Candy," a tune about sex and degradation, opens with a chant that's on the verge of collapsing into a whine ("Complain, Complain, Complain"). Just as you might be ready to dismiss what you're hearing as secondhand noise, yesterday's papers—some kid's mother's old issue of *Off Our Backs*—a fuzztone solo rises out of nowhere and invests every word of Hanna's can't-sing drone with irrefutable emotional credibility.

After a while, then, you begin to hear what is new in Bikini Kill's music: a certain harshness, a blank ugliness, a disgust you can find as well in Mary Gaitskill's fiction, or Jayne Anne Phillips's, but that you might not have heard before in music. FUCK DAD OR DIE runs a line on a page of lyrics in Bikini Kill's *Color and Activity Book*: song by song, the band takes that as a manifesto in reverse, a negative principle. You can hear the line—really, it's no less a slogan than REVOLUTION GIRL STYLE NOW—in the voice Hanna finds for the song "Suck My Left One," the first female equivalent I've ever heard to the worldwide chart-topper, "Suck My Dick." It's a gurgling, vomiting, triumphant croak, Medusa in sound. But it's not merely a no: sometimes Hanna snaps off the last word, "one" hitting the wall, and sometimes she makes a world out of the word, drifting off into whatever melisma she can find in it. Maybe it's a protective fantasy ("Daddy comes into her room at night/ He's got more than talking on his mind/ My sister pulls the covers down/ She reaches over flicks on the light, she says to him/ Suck—"); it sounds like freedom.

Listening now to X-ray Spex, what's surprising is how far they go. X-ray Spex and Poly Styrene were unusual in that their music grew stronger, more fierce, and funnier as they went along. The world they took on got bigger; more detail emerged. So many bands arrived with one great shout, a fabulous clatter—the Au Pairs with "You" and "Kerb Crawler," the Raincoats with "Fairytale in the Supermarket," the Slits with

"A Boring Life"—and though they became more musical, more accomplished, more self-referential, they never again made such a grand claim on anyone's attention.

Bikini Kill practice a kind of public clandestiny. They sing about forbidden things; they fill their fanzines with suggestions of a "secret society" ("Each separate yglg sect will have its own particular reading list") and coded gestures ("Okay," runs an infinitely suggestive passage, "so I propose that those girls who wanna change things start writing stuff on their/our hands. . . . it will just be a way for pro-revolution girls to identify each other"). Bikini Kill cannot simply get bigger any more than they can simply get better. To make the music, to talk the talk, to make the history still only implied on the *Revolution Girl Style Now* cassette, they may have to get more extreme.

—*Interview*, September 1992

Three Premature

Endings

The Return of the Ranter

The Buzzcocks: *Spiral Scratch* and *Time's Up*. In the summer of 1976, in Manchester, England, the Buzzcocks formed on the model of the Sex Pistols; in October, with Howard Devoto as singer, they went into a local studio and for something under a hundred dollars' worth of mike time cut their songs. Released in February 1977, the EP *Spiral Scratch* was only the third U.K. punk disc to be issued; more than that, it was the first independent, do-it-yourself U.K. punk record; and more than that, it was definitive. "Boredom" ("I'm living in this, uh, movie," Devoto snapped, "but it doesn't move me") was an instant anthem, or rather a fragment of an anthem floating away to be caught by its listeners. It set the tone: sarcastic (many of the band's tunes had their genesis in a notebook where Devoto had set down all-purpose, lumpen-surrealist insults), distracted, thin, spidery, and most of all in a hurry. Carl Perkins's "Blue Suede Shoes" was about taking a stand; "Breakdown," "Friends of Mine," and the rest (bootlegged as *Time's Up* again and again over the years, and only now officially released) were about evading an enemy more sensed than defined, and then turning up at its back, then disappearing. The feeling was anonymous—a dare taken and won.

Devoto went on to more ornamented music with his groups Magazine and Luxuria; led by guitarist Pete Shelley, the Buzzcocks made sharp, poppy punk through the decade (reformed, they tour the clubs even today). But October 1976 was their moment. With "Lester Sands (Drop in the ocean)" they caught an ancient snarl, blindly retrieving the voice of the Ranters along with echoes of their cosmology ("Every creature is God," it was written in 1646, "every creature that hath life and breath being an efflux of God, and shall return to God again, be swallowed up in him as a drop is in the ocean"). Blasphemy edged out of the Buzzcocks' blank complaints; ambition rose from the songs and came down as vengeance.

"History is made by those who say 'No,'" Jon Savage writes at the close of *England's Dreaming*, his re-creation of the Sex Pistols' era, "and Punk's utopian heresies remain its gift to the world." On these recordings that gift was offered as everyday life, pinched and tensed; since the music was made the world has changed little enough that, putting on the discs today, it can seem as if the gift is being opened for the first time.

—from "Real Life Rock Top Ten," *Artforum*, December 1991

The End of the 1980s

The decade was owned here by a man who simultaneously incarnated Mickey Mouse and Pinochet: a "vile tyrant" (so wrote Walter Karp, the brave political critic who died in 1989), the Great Cretinizer. All that is left of the mirage is the wreckage of the legacy: a political landscape where what were once republican institutions have been replaced by rackets, and speech by silence. The present-day ruler may believe in nothing, but for him and for the country that void now functions as a principle of freedom: a craven bully, he has learned to slip all accountability, and so have former citizens, now consumers at best, private criminals otherwise. This is nihilism, and as nihilists dance around the abyss of values they trace a circle, complete it: when you can't get what you want you kill everything around yourself. When in the early 1960s a man named Hollis Brown shot his family and himself, the event was so remarkable, so anomalous and strange, that Bob Dylan felt moved to write a song about it, but today such occurrences are everyday news, worthy only of a shrug. *San Francisco Chronicle*, 9 December 1989: "A gunman described in a psychological examination as unlikely to harm his ex-wife burst into her house in Spanaway, Wash., early yesterday and killed her, their two daughters and her new husband before killing himself . . . In Belleville, Ill., a man identified as 48-year-old Kurt Steibel shot and killed his wife, daughter, and 1-year-old grandson, then shot at firefighters before committing suicide." Will those who certified the first killer sane and harmless publicly apologize and quit their jobs? Not in this country. The U.S.A. has less need of Japanese industrial techniques than of sanpaku.

The legacy is a realm of private violence, have-it-all, what's-in-it-for-me taken to its limit. The country is dead, and only a revival of public violence—a refusal of circumstances that, as in the first days of the civil rights movement, physically interposes itself between corrupt institutions and their everyday functions—can bring it back to life.

"That couldn't happen here go the reassuring passwords," Howard Hampton wrote of the U.S. press coverage of the events in Tiananmen Square: "the massacre or the uprising?" Our tyranny is bland, hard to find, hard to fight, fragmented, a morass of seemingly trivial private humiliations and insults, nobody else's business, no public speech for it. In the United Kingdom, the ruler privatizes industry and water; here the very ideas on which the country was founded—life, liberty, and the pursuit of happiness—are privatized. We look in wonder, or we turn away as if from a conversation in a foreign language, at the story now being told on the other side of the world: in Poland, Hungary, Czechoslovakia, East Germany, Romania, the Soviet Union. But it's not our story. As cultures these places may be much older than ours, but as countries, and as political entities, they are far younger, jerry-built out of a tyranny that was never bland, that never possessed a shred of the of-the-people legitimacy our kind of tyranny still feeds on. So these places are reinventing themselves out of immediate desire and distant memory, the "mystic chords of memory" Lincoln spoke of; they are making history. We aren't; we're eating what history we've already made, the history that is no longer ours to make. "The Declaration of Independence makes a difference," Herman Melville wrote; he was talking about the freedom of the mind, the freedom to invent, to create, to say what one meant without blinkers or even conscience. But today that difference has passed to other places.

There is no question that our example, as a people and as a polity, inspired those who in our time make history, from Tiananmen demonstrators justifying themselves with images of

Woodstock to the constitutional details of the agreements being hammered out between Communists and New Forums as I write. But our example, put into practice, come to life and on the move, is now a foreign language to us. It's a conversation that we, as a polity, as a society, as a country, can't understand, and, finally, none of our business. The last decade promoted a nihilism we live out as if it were real life, which is to say that we are now a backwater, happy as a pig in shit and precisely as capable of saying what we mean.

—*LA Weekly*,
5–11 January 1990

The Return of the Antichrist

C olin Hughes: "Search for Antichrist leads soldiers astray," *The Independent* (London), as covered in the *San Francisco Examiner*, July 23. "Five men and one woman, all of whom worked with the 701st Military Intelligence Brigade . . . [and] belonged to the End of the World Group . . . went AWOL on July 9 from their station in Augsburg, West Germany. The disappearance of soldiers who all had top security clearance and access to confidential information triggered an automatic counterintelligence investigation by the Army. . . . The soldiers set off for Florida in search of the Antichrist but apparently failed to find the biblically prognosticated evil one before being arrested last Sunday in Gulf Breeze, Fla. Now, they are awaiting court-martial on desertion charges at Fort Benning, Ga." Reached in Los Angeles, John Lydon, former singer for the rock group the Sex Pistols and one time self-professed "Antichrist," had "No comment. Probably they just wanted to go to Disney World. The media always lie. Anyway, I wasn't in Florida. Ha ha ha ha ha."

—from "Real Life Rock Top Ten," *Village Voice*,
28 August 1990

EPILOGUE
A Brief Return of the 1960s:
Real Life Rock Top Ten
Spring 1991

1. Bob Dylan: at the Grammy Awards, 20 February 1991. Thirty years after arriving in New York from Minnesota, Bob Dylan stepped forward to be honored with a Lifetime Achievement Award. With the Gulf war in progress, the blanket of acceptance that had been draped over the show was so heavy the WAR SUCKS T-shirt New Kid on the Block Donnie Wahlberg wore to the American Music Awards a few weeks earlier would have been forbidden here; maybe that's why Dylan sang "Masters of War," from 1963, and maybe that's why he disguised it, smearing the verses into one long word. If you caught on to the number, the lyrics did emerge—"And I'll stand o'er your grave/ 'Til I'm sure that you're dead"—but lyrics were not the point. What was was the ride Dylan and his band gave them. With hats pulled down and dressed in dark clothes, looking and moving like Chicago hipsters from the end of the fifties, guitarists Cesar Diaz and John Jackson, bassist Tony Garnier, and drummer Ian Wallace went after the song as if it were theirs as much as Dylan's: a chance at revenge, excitement, pleasure. You couldn't tell one from the other, and why bother?

With this career performance behind him, Dylan took his trophy from a beaming Jack Nicholson; he squinted, as if looking for his mother, who was in the audience. "Well," he said, "my daddy, he didn't leave me much, you know he was a very simple man, but what he did tell me was this, he did say, *son*, he said"—there was a long pause, nervous laughter from the crowd—"he say, you know it's possible to become so defiled in this world that your own father and mother will abandon you and if that happens, God will always believe in your ability to mend your own ways."

Then he walked off. He had managed to get in and out without thanking anybody, and this night it really did seem as if he owed nobody anything.

2. Rolling Stones: "Highwire." There's a helplessly celebratory cast to the flabby, crowded, let's-hope-for-the-best closing choruses of this Desert Storm disc, but the action is up front, in the open sound that drives the verses (built around "Get up, stand up" and "Catch a fire," old revolutionary slogans from Bob Marley and the Wailers), in the amazingly cynical snap Mick Jagger uses to break up every line. Recorded just before the air war began, hitting the radio just as the ground war was ending, the song's timing made it simultaneously moot and dangerous: it came off as a cheap exploitation of the last war and as a setup for the next.

3. Enigma: *MCMXC a.D.* For the nearly twelve minutes of "Principles of Lust," which includes the worldwide Gregorian chant hit "Sadeness," probably the best heavy-breathing number since Jane Birkin and Serge Gainsbourg's 1969 "Je t'Aime (Moi Non Plus)"—which enjoyed a certain revival after Gainsbourg's March 2 death in Paris, though Conservative leader Jacques Chirac said it was Gainsbourg's tune "Harley-Davidson" that was "engraved on my heart."

4. Oliver Stone, director: *The Doors.* Nothing could be easier than to write this movie off, but there are currents of empathy at work throughout that bring you face to face with "the sixties" as a true curse: no grand, simple, romantic time to sell to present-day teenagers as a nice place to visit, but a time that, even as it came forth, people sensed they could never really inhabit, and also never leave. Stone catches this displacement in the concert sequences near the end of the Doors' career. He makes a terrific noise out of instruments, fans, booze, nudity, fire, feedback, and history, but as he moves the visual noise on he makes the sound stop. All you can fix on is Val Kilmer's Jim

Morrison, in a moment of complete suspension, caught between wondering how he got where he is and accepting that he can't go forward and he can't go back. It may not be the story the band set out to tell, but it's what the movie has done to

5. The Doors: *The Doors* (1967). It didn't cost much to listen to "Take It as It Comes" ("Time to live/ Time to die," etc.), "The Crystal Ship," or the last, quiet minute of "The End" when they were new, but now you can hear an ugly momentum in the band's first music, the music's urge to catch up with the people who made it. Forget the soundtrack album, forget best-ofs and greatest hits; this is all you need and, maybe, all there ever was.

6. Randy Newman: "Lines in the Sand." Not for sale, distributed only to DJs, and no surprise most didn't play it. Against the piety of "Voices That Care," the Hollywood tribute-to-the-troops number (they should have called it "We Are the War"), this was an elegy in advance: a cold, defeatist funeral march.

7. Gang of Four: *Mall.* Where you don't pick up pennies because you don't want anyone to think you have to.

8. Eleventh Dream Day: *Lived to Tell.* Made by a four-piece Chicago band, this is a record to get lost in, with vocal action that's hard to catch hovering over grinding, growling guitars like a heat mirage on a highway no one's driven for years. Guitarist Rick Rizzo does most of the singing, but it's drummer Janet Bean, rushing in at the end of a verse like Exene Cervenka ambushing John Doe in X, who nails song after song. Words emerge in fragments in a floating aural setting; the whole, once you glimpse it, is exhilarating and bleak, the exhilaration of people saying what they mean, even if they wish they could mean something other than their fear of loss, defeat, and exile. The music holds an inner drama, summed up in lines from Bean: "There's this thing, lately/ Where the sound of tearing fabric/ Is louder than the traffic."

9. Rolling Stones: "Gimmie Shelter," as licensed for a public

service announcement for the American Red Cross. What a fine
conceit: as the number storms in the background, we're introduced to a paramedic squad as a band, with, among others, Paul
Shaffer of the David Letterman show "on keys" (at a blood-
drive computer), and Carly Simon "on lead," heroically guiding
some kids to safety with the same expression of celebrity no-
blesse oblige that Jean-Luc Godard and Jean-Pierre Gorin
spent a whole film critiquing with the 1972 *Letter to Jane*. It's
no use saying the song deserves better; a commercial for home
insurance would be better.

10. Pink Floyd, Julie Christie, the Small Faces, David Hock-
ney, the Marquess of Kensington, etc.: *Tonite Let's All Make
Love in London* (1968). To end our mini-sixties survey, this
weird artifact: the augmented CD soundtrack to a forgotten
Swinging London movie by Peter Whitehead. Pink Floyd offer
nearly half an hour of intriguingly vague psychedelic music; one
Vashti sings bits of the charmingly innocent "Winter Is Blue";
and various people talk about various aspects of the New
World, from Edna O'Brien on sex to Mick Jagger on his plans to
go into politics to Michael Caine and Lee Marvin (what's he
doing here?) on miniskirts: Marvin is pro, Caine is con. It's a lot
of fun, and pathetically trivial: people trying to describe the
enormous energies of change and having a hard time thinking
of anything to say. But then you run into Whitehead's liner
notes, written in 1990: "Never forget that what that time
meant to the people who were responsible for creating that
whole period and mood . . . was the love of freedom, in the
profound sense, the hatred of fascism, in every sense. . . ." He
goes on: "It was a time of anarchy, yes, but also a time of sow-
ing . . . seeds of hope and the future. Those seeds are continu-
ously sprouting in the most unexpected places, and there are a
lot of them still under the soil. . . . Keep an eye on those
verges at the side of the concrete road . . . those margins at
the side of that colossal text, that thrust of rationality and falsi-
fication. . . . Be ready when it comes—the flood—Salome
dancing again—the demise of history."

I found it hard to gainsay a word; I put the disc back on and tried to make it give up even a hint of what Whitehead was talking about. It didn't. Someone was crazy, but I don't know who.

—Artforum,
April/May 1991

I am a cliché

Y ou'd feel bad too if every time you fucked someone he had to die. I don't even get to pick them, the eunuchs do it. They dope them up so they babble all night long. Some of what they say is pretty interesting. But it's not like they're ever talking to me, if you know what I mean.

I remember what happened with this one. I did the trick on him: that's when I cut a little hole in the sac of his balls, put in a tiny plastic straw, blow air through it until the scrotum swells up like a balloon, cover it up fast with a Band-Aid, and then suck him off. Usually it makes them shut up for a while. This one vomited all over me. The eunuch got up from his stool in the corner but I made him go back. This had never happened before and I wanted to see what would happen next.

He asked me who I was. That had never happened before either. The drug they give them just makes them talk about themselves, starting when they're about three years old, and by the time they kill them in the morning they're still children.

I didn't know what to say. What was I supposed to say? I'm a princess and you've died and gone to heaven? Ha ha. I told him it was a test.

He seemed to understand that. He began to run his hands over my breasts. He didn't notice the vomit. I've been waiting for something like this, he said. Are we still in Italy? How long have you been with them, you don't look old enough. Do you do this all the time? Does everyone take a turn?

Then he fucked me. It took about a minute. When it was over he sat up, grinning, proud of himself, as if he'd passed. That's not it, I said. I pointed to the eunuch. You've got to do it to him.

He looked at a tattoo on the inside of his left thigh as if he were wondering how it got there, then as if he remembered. A double crescent with letters in a script I didn't know. Then he rubbed the tattoo, not hard, but the way he'd touched me, and went over to the corner where the eunuch was sitting. The eunuch pulled his knife and this one kicked it out of his hand, hit him in the face, and kept hitting him until he stopped moving. Then he went through the eunuch's clothes and found the syringes. He brought them back to the bed, the knife, too, and put it all down between us. I held out my arm and he shot me up. Then I shot him up.

We could barely move, and we couldn't stop talking. I remember all of it, but I don't always remember when it was him talking and when it was me. It was like we were in each other's minds, or like our minds were down between us with the needles and the knife and we didn't have anything to do with our minds, we were just watching them talk.

It started out like this: which was worse, hot or cold, would you rather burn to death or freeze to death, he said freeze to death. And if you had to die how would you want to die, and if you were going to kill yourself how would you do it, I said jump. Who would you kill if you could kill anyone in the world and get away with it, and how would you do it, and would it be better to do it so no one would ever know, drop the person in a lake in Canada, or send the head through the mail to someone whose face you'd want to see when they got it, except whoever

that would be probably doesn't open his own mail, he has someone else do it, a secretary, or a guard, because of the letter
bombs. The drug was wearing off so I removed the Band-Aid
and blew him up again and made him move the knife in me
very slowly while I made him come. I'd read about that in a
book.

He began to act very manly, in charge. He got on top of me
even though he was still soft and told me that no matter how
beautiful it was between us we'd never be able to see each
other again, not at least until it was over, and when I asked him
what *it* was he just kept talking about how the work was more
important than any of us. I really began to wonder where
they'd found this one.

The eunuch got back up then but I waved him away. I want
to give you a tattoo to go with the one you've got, I said. I took
the knife and reached into the drawer of my bed table for some
heroin.

He pulled away. There can be *no others*, you *know* that, he
said. He was looking around the room for his clothes, he didn't
remember that he'd been brought in naked. I waved for the
eunuch and he came over and grabbed this one from behind. I
held the knife on him. Alright, he said, alright. It doesn't matter and I've done it before. The eunuch let him go and bent
over the bed. This one sniffed a little of the powder and then he
fucked the eunuch. I cut into his back as deep as I could without getting sick and I rubbed more of the powder into the
blood. All I could think of to make was a cross.

I felt very romantic. Now you'll always have something to
remember me by, I said. The eunuch got up and went back to
his stool.

Usually I leave the room in the morning and then they take
them somewhere else and kill them. This time I said I wanted
to watch, and I wanted them to do it here. All they did was give
him another shot. So I smeared the rest of the heroin between
my legs, took a bath, and was about to get dressed when my

mother came in. I jumped. I didn't want her to see the vomit around the edges of the tub.

I have feelings just like everybody else. Of course my mother knows what I do, or what is done to me, or what *happens*—I don't know how to say it. Sometimes I think what happens is only to make her forget what my father did, while she watched, her hands buckled to the wall, her eyes held open with tape, then with stitches, so she couldn't close them for as long as it took.

I didn't want my mother to see the vomit, you wouldn't either. I collected it from the side of the tub and rubbed it once more over my body and watched it wash off and eddy again to the side, and as I ran toward her I wished it all away. For her.

Of course, I don't really know her. I've seen the pictures— not the Palace pictures, not those, I've seen those too, but I mean the old pictures, with those wonderful men, they're al-

most all dead now, but not *because* they were with her, she was so perfect! She was everything a woman can be to a man and yet she gave up nothing.

But because my father was not my real father, she has never been able to act as if she were my real mother. It was the same with all of us: he watched while someone else fucked her. People fucked her until it took. When she was pregnant he loved her, touched her, cooed over her, he talked to her.

When we were little we were given drugs to weaken our skin, so it could be shaped to make us look like him. It didn't last long. We had to go every week to the room for what they called massages. When we were old enough to fuck—old enough to bleed, old enough to butcher, one of them said once when I fucked him—we had plastic surgery to make us into his children. I read once about the Man in the Iron Mask—whoever our fathers were should have been so lucky.

After I ran down the hall to meet her, my mother took me into my father's room. She has to know! she said, as if we didn't. As if the eunuchs didn't talk, as if cutting off their pricks were the same as cutting out their tongues. We can lick their asses and make them tell us anything. It's time! my mother said. She's not your daughter! She's a human being!

My father screamed back. He made his mouth into the O that I remembered from when he sucked the dildo he fucked me with, the special one with the button I had to push when he said Yes that made the come come out, real come, I don't know where they got it.

My mother was fat. She was not my mother anymore, not the woman in the pictures. She looked less like her than I ever will. So she stood there screaming at my father, who stood there sucking his invisible dildo, and I felt like I was sucking it, I felt my mouth close around it.

Finally he sat down behind his desk. He masturbated into a wineglass. She watched. I didn't, after I saw what he was do-

ing. I ran. The last thing
I heard him say: she'll
want to be my daughter.
But I already was, I
knew it.

It must have started
with my father's secret
police.

"Those morons," the
first man would have
said. "I told the Palace—
when was it?—that we
would provide the lov-
ers. I still cannot understand why they insist on
providing their own. The princess has had congress with one of
the terrorists. We can't keep them out.

"She is only a receptacle—a receptacle for anonymous scum
and whatever words go with it. You've heard the tapes, you
know what nonsense the drugs make them talk, but this time it
didn't seem to work, and it was the worst time for it not to
work."

"We have the film," the second man would have said. "You
saw her take the same medication he was given. She's not used
to it, she can remember nothing."

"You're a fool. I am a fool. This palace was established as a
publicity stunt. Our neighbors favor us our borders because
they believe we can maintain them. If they learn we cannot,
their police will follow, and their police will stay. The princess
is not a human being, she is a set of blown fuses, and she could
say anything. It was all new to her last night. She watched him
die. *They talked to each other.* We cannot be sure she will not
blow one last fuse, and talk to everyone else."

"Do you think," the second man would have said, "that she would *join* them?"

"There is no chance. They would never have her. They know an animal when they see one. They are careful. They are serious. They are not like the American insects who took the Hearst *prostituta*. They'd kill her the minute she contacted them."

"So, then we—"

"No. We replace a scandal we cannot manage with one we can."

I wasn't afraid. I knew they had orders. Scare her. Find out what she knows.

In fact I knew a lot. I knew that last one was a killer. I knew who he wanted to kill, how he wanted to kill them, how he was going to kill them, how he wanted to die, how he thought he was going to die.

First they brought the woman over in front of me and tortured her. While they were cutting her they tried to make me eat her. They put her liver in my lap and her womb in my mouth. I threw up. I shocked them, I could tell. They'd never seen a princess throw up. I had.

Later I found out what everybody thinks they know. Headlines about PRINCESS DISAPPEARS, TERRORIST INVOLVEMENT FEARED. All of it made my father look good. It put my mother's death on the back page. I'm sure you remember.

They never physically hurt me, they never raped me, never even threatened me. In a funny way it was silent. They just did what they did. A lot of drugs, a lot of bodies, a lot of organs, a lot of children who'd been told to beg me for their lives and who I had to watch getting cut up.

I have feelings just like anybody else. I didn't want to see what happened to them, I didn't want it to *happen*. But that wasn't the point. There was nothing I could do. The point was to keep me safe. I'd heard them talking when they thought I'd be too crazy to listen: we're not to touch her. We're to let her go when it's over. *Let* her talk. The Palace went too far and now we are to go farther still. Let her talk, she's *supposed* to talk: no one will believe a word of it, and no one will believe anything else she says either. We will fill her with impossibility.

I knew it was because of that last one. I thought about him. He told me the idea was to kill a lot of people so that whoever would live would really live. The death of a few means that few will die—and the dead will be passéists, and passéists are already dead. If you had to die how would you want to die, he said eat myself to death: he wanted a table covered with oysters, pasta with anchovies and wild mushrooms, mussels stuffed with goose liver, a whole calf's head with the top cut off so you could scoop the brains out with a spoon, the eyes removed and baked with garlic and parsley, a bottle of Bâtard-Montrachet, a bottle of Margaux, a bottle of cheap brandy that smelled like kerosene, a baron of rabbit, a haunch of venison with risotto

and morels, peaches in fresh cream with little wild strawberries around the plate, then chocolate poured all over my body, and into it, so he could lick it off my breasts and out of my cunt. I didn't tell him he was getting his wish.

But he said that wasn't how he was going to die. He was going to die with a lot of other people. He said Europe was dead. We would make it live. He wouldn't see it happen, but maybe I would. So maybe I saved him from that.

I didn't save the children. I was ready when they held my eyes. I thought about other things. When they gave me the pieces I tried not to throw up again but I couldn't help it.

Christ, it wasn't so bad! I knew they couldn't hurt me. They didn't understand what I'd already seen, what I'd already done. I'd left a thousand warm corpses in my bed. I'd had the sperm of a thousand dead men in my throat. I'd had a thousand dead babies between my legs. There was nothing they could do to me.

Even though I knew his body was somewhere in the Palace I couldn't help looking for it at the railroad station. I ripped my clothes and smeared some of the blood from the walls on my face and arms, I didn't want to look out of place.

It was easy getting to Bologna. They had tied me to a chair and left me in the room with the pieces but the ropes were loose and the doors were unlocked. I was supposed to wander out in a daze, be found, be taken back to the Palace, have the doctors come, tell them and my parents and anyone else whatever I had to say, get well, pose for pictures, marry someday. You know I did. It's not like I had anything else to do. But first I wanted to see what it was like to fuck someone I picked for myself.

The first car that stopped for me was a big truck driven by a woman and her son. I told them I was running away from home and that the border guards would be watching for me, I don't have much of an imagination. They laughed and gave me some wine. They said I needed a bath. Near the border they stopped, got out blankets, laid them down across the engine, had me lie on them, closed the hood over me and tied it down with twine. A few minutes later we were out of that phony country and into Italy.

I hadn't even thought to ask where they were going and before I knew it we were in Florence. I got out and a few minutes later three rich boys in an Aston Martin picked me up. I didn't care where they were going and I didn't ask.

Did I want to go to a party, they said. Did I like to dip donuts, ha ha. When I didn't say much they switched back and forth between Italian, French, English, German, Spanish, and even Latin.

In Milan I decided to get out. They gave me money, about 50,000 lire, and said I'd have much more fun in Como, where they knew how to get cocaine. They blew me kisses. They hadn't touched me except to take my hand as I got in and out of the car, and I don't think they were gay. I'd had a thought of having the small blond one do it to me in the ass, but not all three of them, and not in the car.

I had three days to get to Bologna. I was tired of traveling. Milan is dull. It looks dull, it feels dull. The sky was yellow. It was just right. I sat in cafes in the cheap shopping districts, rode the bumper cars at night in the amusement park, walked down the streets to see how long it would take to find one that ran both ways. I spent two days getting lost, usually ending up a block from where I started.

The last night at the park I met a man at the cars when I smashed him head-on and nearly knocked him out of his seat. He chased me around the divider until the ride was over and then as if we'd had it all planned we both ran to get more tickets and kept at each other. After a few more rides he winked at me, pointed at a car with two spinsters in it, and we smashed it together from both sides.

He was about forty, well dressed—everybody else was in work clothes or dowdy. I was a mess but he didn't seem to notice. We had a drink and he said he had to leave, he was due in Bologna the next day for a lecture. He was a college professor. I said I'd like to hear him lecture.

I fell asleep in the Fiat. It was already light when I woke

up. His right hand was under my dress. I let him. Do it, he said. I took off all my clothes and rode naked. He told me to turn so my ass was facing him and he shoved his forefinger in. Then I saw him push in the cigarette lighter. He hadn't smoked since I'd met him.

I pulled the lighter out and threw it out the window. He kept his speed steady and unzipped his pants. I reached for his prick and he hit me. *It's mine*, he said, it's none of your *business*. Then he drove along as if nothing had happened. In a moment he came without ever touching himself. I put my clothes back on. In Bologna he stopped just outside the university, thanked me for a wonderful evening, and said he hoped we might see each other again sometime. The torturers should have been so weird.

I went to the railroad station. My idea was to go in just before, wait, see what it looked like when it happened, and die or not die. I didn't *not* care. It was the biggest choice I could think to make. I'd wanted to choose who I wanted to fuck and so far I hadn't found anyone I wanted to fuck or could. So I chose this.

At the entrance to the station I saw one of the men from the torture room and two men I'd seen once or twice from the Palace. So I went to look for another entrance and the bomb went off. Then there must have been ten more. He'd only mentioned one. They seemed to come from everywhere. I ran back to the front entrance and it was completely blown apart.

Inside there were bodies all over, people all over, people screaming, strange moans coming from the corners. But it was like the room for me. For me it was so quiet. I went up to a boy who was reaching out to me and his arm came off in my hand. I gave it back to him and kept walking. It was too late to choose anything. I saw a woman's foot and put it in my purse. A man was going through the crowd of bodies. He had a gun. Three times he stopped, found someone, poked him, and if he moved, shot him in the forehead. When the troops arrived he threw

away the gun and lay down on the floor with his arms out. I saw him clench his jaw and fake blood poured out of his mouth. When I walked by him he caressed my ankle and laughed at me.

I'd had enough of Italy. The last one hadn't been in the station. Sometimes I could almost convince myself everything had been a play, that he'd left the Palace alive and gone where he'd said he was going. But I would have found him. And when I'd found him I would have walked right past him.

On the edge of the city I buried the foot. I got a ride from a man in a green Mercedes. He was about fifty, bald, fat, an American tourist on his way to Marseilles for the bouillabaise. In Genoa he stopped at a hotel and asked if I wanted to sleep with him. I said yes.

We laughed all night. Everything we did was like playing. I stood on his stomach and giggled when the fat rolled out and then he squeezed his sides and pitched me off. The bed was soaked with our sweat. He came in my hair and then washed it himself with Head & Shoulders shampoo. He asked had I ever been to Seattle. He said I was better than squid.

We crossed into France the next day. When I asked him to hide me in the trunk he didn't say a word. I got in and he broke the lock. The border guards didn't bother him and a few kilometers later he pried the trunk open with a hammer and we rode on in the front. In Marseilles he said he was meeting his son and I would have to go my own way. He gave me 300 francs—for squid, he said, and a new purse.

I felt like I owned the world. I walked through the streets into every neighborhood. The whores glared at me as a straight and I knew they'd never know half of what I knew. Downtown women looked at me as a whore and I felt like a princess for the first time in my life.

I went into a restaurant and ordered squid three different ways. I bought a picture postcard and sent it to the Palace: having a wonderful time, wish you were dead. I signed it with a smile face. I bought scissors and cut my hair in a museum bathroom. I met a punk and went back to the place where he lived with a dozen other boys and girls and fucked him once. When everyone was asleep I took clothes from all over the room and left.

You know what I liked about punk? It's that song "I Am a Cliché." I AM A CLICHÉ, it ought to read. Bigger than that:

I am a cliche!

It was one of the first ones. The other side of "Oh Bondage Up Yours!," which I like too but I don't sing it to myself all day. It was by X-ray Spex, really two girls called Poly Styrene and

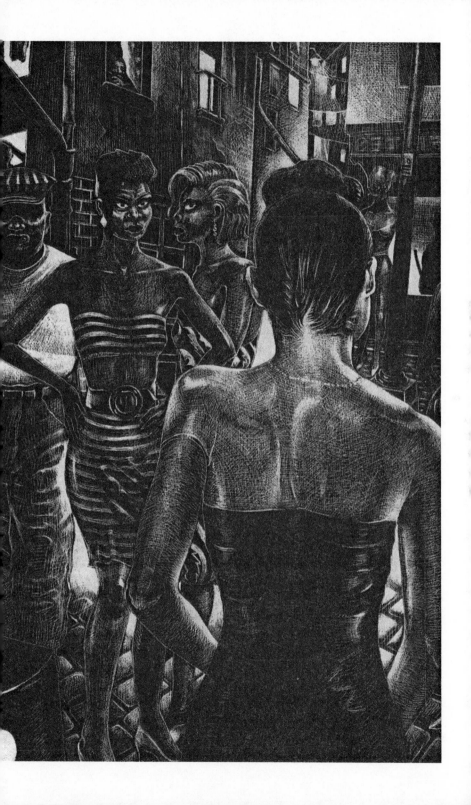

Lora Logic and some boys. They were younger than I was when I heard it. They're Hare Krishnas now.

I heard it walking down a street near Saint-Sulpice in Paris. There's a little punk record shop and the sound was coming out of the doorway. I went in and bought it before it was over and made them keep playing it. Then I took the record out of its jacket and walked down the street tossing it up in the air and catching it. By the time I got it back to my room it was all scratched and dirty. I didn't care. I didn't have a record player anyway. I was so happy.

It was so *funny*. I'd never heard anybody talk like that before. *I am a cliché*, I don't even exist, there's nothing you can do to hurt me, I am a zero, I can start from *nothing*, you made me up out of your fantasies and now reality is up to *me*. I leaned my head out the window and screamed it to the wall.

I went to Paris because the punks in Marseilles were stupid. I liked the clothes. The punks were stupid in Paris too. All the freedom was in the music and that was better than nothing.

For the first week I just rode the Métro. I'd never been on it before. Of course I'd been to Paris all my life. From our floor in the Meurice we'd go to Maxim's and then we'd go back to the Meurice.

I collected money for the singers in the Métro corridors and kept half. Joe Strummer used to sing here, one of them kept saying to the people, comprenez-vous? C'est moi! I didn't know who Joe Strummer was. When I got enough money I'd spend it. Once I thought of going back to Maxim's in my leather and studs and green hair and demanding our table and signing for the check but the food there always made me sick: having to watch my father eat. One night I walked down the river to the Tour d'Argent and looked up at the lights in the dining room and remembered the little metal tag they'd given me when I had to eat pressed duck. Mademoiselle, you are the recipient of the tenthousandmillionbullshiteth duck to be served by this establishment, and we are proud to offer you this token of the event. I am a cliché. I had a lot of money that night and I walked up the block at the beginning of the Boule Saint-Germain and into a little noisy place with friendly waiters and people having fun. They made fun of my accent, they had a liquor bottle with a dead snake in it and platters of pigs' feet that I couldn't eat. They had écrevisses fried in so much garlic and butter you bit right through the shells and ate everything. When someone at another table tried to eat them with a knife and fork all the waiters stood around his table and acted like he was from Mars.

I went home with one of the youngest waiters. He was about twenty-five and gay. He showed me how to put my hand and then almost my whole arm up to the elbow into his ass. I felt like a doctor. I felt like a torturer. He wanted to do it to me but I made him stop at the hand. He kept asking me if I could come. When I woke up he was gone and I trashed his apartment and left.

I stuck my tongue out at the *Mona Lisa*, which was the only thing I'd ever seen in the Louvre with my parents. I found Alfred Jarry's address in the rue Cassette and spent days in the Jeu de Paume. I stole a bicycle and worked as a messenger. I was raped three times in the street and killed the fourth man who tried with the knife I'd bought after the third one cut a line between my breasts. I cut out his heart and carried it until I found a dog to throw it to. One day I bought ten copies of my favorite record and scratched off the labels and left them on doorsteps.

I went into a cinema called Studio Cujas and saw a movie that lasted an hour and a half and all it had was a white screen when people were talking and a black screen when they weren't. There were about twelve people in the theater which maybe had room for a hundred. I think everyone was asleep after twenty minutes. On the soundtrack, men and a woman

spoke like they were
tired of being bored but
couldn't think of any-
thing else to be.

The poster said it
was made before I was
born, the most radical
film of all time. It caused
riots here and in Lon-
don. *To see this film is to
prove one's courage*, said
the poster. I was sur-
prised more people
weren't there, maybe
they already knew it was
a joke. But it was new to
me.

I liked it. After a while, I began to look forward to the
change from silence and black screen to talking and white
screen, or even vice versa. The pieces were all different and
halfway through it was suspense when the change would come.
At first I was sure it was a mistake, the projector had broken
and the man in the projection room was too wiped out on
Quaaludes to notice, then I thought it was building up to fucking or a mushroom cloud, then I went along with it. It was
about Paris, before I was born. It was about me. *We were going
to make the bridges jump*, one of the men said, *but the bridges
got their own back*. I saw people jumping off the Seine bridges,
even though you can't kill yourself that way. I saw people *prac-
ticing* suicide and still meaning it. There was nothing on the
screen, just white, then black. The last lines came down like a
cloud: *We're living like lost children, our adventures incomplete*. The screen went black again and after ten minutes it was
still black. I got up to leave and then sat down when there was
no FIN. I sat there another quarter of an hour and then the film

ran out, the lights came up, and the usher went down the aisles shining his flashlight in the faces of the rest. The cleaning woman said I could sleep in the office and I did.

I was alone in Paris. I was alone for the first time in my life. I had my own room and I could earn money anytime I liked. Once I brought a boy back to my room and talked for hours and told him to leave and he did. Once I brought a boy back to my room and fucked him the minute we closed the door and told him to leave the minute it was over and he did. Once I wrote a long letter to my father telling him everything I thought and sent it. Once I wrote to Poly Styrene and Lora Logic and sent it to their record company and they wrote back saying that abortion was a crime against Krishna. But I'll never need one anyway.

One day I walked past the Meurice and I wanted a soft bed. I wanted a massage. I wanted flowers in my room and chocolates on my pillows and a man who would be dead in the morning. I went into an alley off the rue du Temple and stuck my finger down my throat and made myself throw up but I couldn't help walking past the hotel and wanting it all.

In three days I fucked fifteen men and ten women. Nothing helped.

I spent all my money and walked up to the first person I saw in the rue St. Honoré and asked her for a hundred francs and she gave it to me and patted me on the head and said Dear, I can tell you're from a good family, you're going through a phase, wait until it's over, and go back to them. I had never felt so much like dirt, not even the first time they brought the first dead man. I waited until night and found a bum passed out drunk and undid his clothes and sucked him and sucked him and couldn't even make him hard. Two days later I was back at our border. I sat there in my punk clothes and looked at the guards and they looked right through me. Finally I went up and told them who I was and they made phone calls and they came and got me and that was it. You know the rest.

———

I've been back for years and I've tried to tell the truth but you still don't know what happened. Having a wonderful time, wish you were dead. I am a cliché. I still don't have a record player and the new ones still wonder what I'm saying when I come.

—*RAW* #7,
1985

CITATIONS

Individual sound recordings are listed by performer; books by author or editor; movies and various-artists sound recordings by title.

Adolescents. *Adolescents* (Frontier, US, 1981).

Adorno, Theodor. *Minima Moralia: Reflections from Damaged Life* (1951), trans. G. F. N. Jephcott. London: Verso, 1978. Pp. 15, 16.

Anderson, Laurie. "O Superman (For Massenet)" (One Ten and Warner Bros., US; WEA, UK, 1981). Also included on *Big Science* (Warner Bros., US; WEA, UK, 1982).

Anemic Boyfriends. "Guys Are Not Proud" (Red Sweater, US, 1980).

Arendt, Hannah. "Organized Guilt and Universal Responsibility" (1945), in *The Jew as Pariah*, ed. Ron Feldman. New York: Grove, 1978. P. 233.

Au Pairs. "Diet"/"It's Obvious" (021, UK, 1981).

———. *Playing with a Different Sex* (Human, UK, 1981).

———. "You"/"Domestic Departure"/"Kerb Crawler" (021, UK, 1981). Their first recording.

Bailey, David, and Peter Evans. *Goodbye Baby & Amen: A Saraband for the Sixties*. New York: Coward-McCann; London: Condé Nast/Collins, 1969.

Bangs, Lester. *Blondie*. New York: Fireside; London: Omnibus, 1980.

Beat (in US, "English Beat"). *I Just Can't Stop It* (Go-Feet, UK; Sire, US, 1980).

————. "Stand Down Margaret (Dub)" (Go-Feet, UK, 1980).

Beefheart, Captain (a.k.a. Don van Vliet). *Doc at the Radar Station* (Virgin, 1980).

————. *Trout Mask Replica* (Straight, US; Reprise, UK, 1969).

Big Country. "One Great Thing" (Mercury, 1986).

Bikini Kill. *Revolution Girl Style Now* (K, 1992).

Blue Velvet—Original Motion Picture Soundtrack. Music composed and conducted by Angelo Badalamenti (Varese Sarabande, US, 1986). Includes "In Dreams." See Orbison, Roy.

Bonzo Goes to Washington. "Five Minutes" (Sleeping Bag 12″, US, 1984).

Booth, Stanley. "Blues for the Redman" (1973). Collected in *Rythm Oil—A Journey Through the Music of the American South.* London: Jonathan Cape, 1991; New York: Pantheon, 1992. Pantheon edition omits a portfolio of William Eggleston color photographs.

Brains. "Money Changes Everything" (Gray Matter, US, 1979). Different version on *The Brains* (Mercury, US, 1980).

Brinsley Schwarz. "(What's So Funny 'Bout) Peace, Love and Understanding," on *The New Favourites of . . . Brinsley Schwarz* (United Artists, UK, 1974). See Lowe, Nick.

Buzzcocks. *Spiral Scratch* (New Hormones, UK, 1977; rereleased as 12″ and CD on Document, UK, 1991).

————. *Time's Up.* 1976 sessions originally bootlegged on Voto, 1978 (Document, UK, 1991).

Cale, John. *Sabotage/Live* (Spy, US, 1979).

————. *Vintage Violence* (Columbia, US; CBS, UK, 1970).

Carter, Carlene. *Musical Shapes* (Warner Bros., US; F-Beat, UK, 1980).

Clash. *The Clash* (UK, CBS, 1977). US version is a botch and should be avoided.

————. *Clash on Broadway* (Epic Legacy, US, 1991). 3 CD retrospective covering 1977–82. Omits anything from *Cut the Crap.*

——. *Combat Rock* (Epic, US; CBS, UK, 1982).

——. "Complete Control" (CBS, UK, 1977).

——. *Cut the Crap* (CBS, 1985).

——. *Give 'Em Enough Rope* (Epic, US; CBS, UK, 1979).

——. *London Calling* (CBS, UK, 1979; Epic, US, 1980).

——. "A Night of Treason" concert poster. Collected in Paul Grushkin, *The Art of Rock*. New York: Abbeville, 1987. P. 476.

——. *The Story of the Clash, Volume 1* (Epic, US; CBS, UK, 1988).

——. "This Is England" (CBS 12″, UK, 1985).

Costello, Elvis. *Armed Forces* (Columbia, US; Radar, UK, 1979). UK version omits "(What's So Funny 'Bout) Peace, Love and Understanding" in favor of "Sunday's Best."

——. *Goodbye Cruel World* (Columbia, US; F-Beat, UK, 1984).

——. "I Want You" (Demon, UK, 1986). Also on *Blood & Chocolate* (Columbia, US; Demon, UK, 1986).

—— (as the Costello Show). *King of America* (Columbia, US; F-Beat, UK, 1986).

——. "Less Than Zero"/"Radio Sweetheart" (Stiff, UK, 1977). His first release.

——. "Let Them All Talk (Extended 12″ Remix)" (F-Beat, UK, 1983).

——. *My Aim Is True* (Stiff, UK, 1977; Columbia, US, 1978). U.S. version adds (and unbalances original configuration with) "Watching the Detectives."

—— (as the Imposter). "Peace in Our Time"/"Withered and Died" (Imposter, UK, 1984). Inferior version on *Goodbye Cruel World*. "Withered and Died" is a Richard Thompson composition on the level of Hank Williams's "Alone and Forsaken."

—— (as the Imposter). "Pills and Soap" (IMP, UK, 1983). Different version on *Punch the Clock* (Columbia, US; F-Beat, UK, 1983).

——. *Taking Liberties* (Columbia, US, 1980). Released in

very different form as *Ten Bloody Mary's and Ten How's Your Fathers* (F-Beat, UK, 1980).
———. *This Year's Model* (Columbia, US; Radar, UK, 1978). U.S. version replaces "Night Rally" with "Radio, Radio" and omits "I Don't Want to Go to Chelsea."
———. "Tramp the Dirt Down," from *Spike* (Warner Bros., US; WEA, UK, 1989).

The Decline . . . of western civilization. Directed by Penelope Spheeris. Slash Films, 1980.
Delta 5. "Anticipation"/"You" (Rough Trade, UK, 1980).
———. "Mind Your Own Business"/"Now That You're Gone" (Rough Trade, UK, 1979).
———. *See the Whirl' . .* (Pre, UK, 1981).
———. "Try"/"Colours" (Rough Trade, 1980).
Descendents. *"Fat"* (New Alliance, US, 1981).
Diamonds. "Little Darlin' " (Mercury, 1957).
Doors. *The Doors* (Elektra, 1967).
The Doors. Directed by Oliver Stone. Tri-Star, 1990.
Drabble, Margaret. *The Ice Age.* New York: Knopf; London: Weidenfeld & Nicolson, 1977.

Eleventh Dream Day. *Lived to Tell* (Atlantic, US, 1991). A bitter, shamed embrace of exile and retreat. Janet Bean's drumming is loud, stoic; you can stretch out on Rick Rizzo's long, tensed guitar passages as if they were a rack. Slipping into lines that establish "It's Not My World" as a set of stray fragments about how people are failing, are falling through the cracks, are finding that all doors open onto blank walls, you hit a chorus with no narrative connection to the bar talk you've been overhearing, just an absolute spiritual connection. The lyric jumps from third person to first, the singing is no longer conversational but stately, heavily cadenced, a curse read from some ruined pulpit: "Over and over/ By and by/ Living by habits/ To get by," the chorus begins, two people singing, but separately, as if they'll never meet, don't need to, don't want to. "The world might be changing/ Outside my door/ But that's not my world/ Anymore."

Enigma. *MCMXC a.D.* (Charisma, 1990).

Ellis, Bret Easton. *Less Than Zero.* New York: Simon & Schuster, 1985.

Essential Logic. *Beat Rhythm News* (Rough Trade, UK, 1979).

———. *Essential Logic* (Virgin, UK, 1979). Includes original recording of "Wake Up." See Red Crayola; X-ray Spex.

Faithfull, Marianne. *Broken English* (Island, 1979).

Flanagan, Bill. Interview with Neil Young. In *Written in My Soul—Rock's Great Songwriters Talk About Creating Their Music.* Chicago: Contemporary, 1986; London: Omnibus, 1989. Pp. 128–129.

Fleetwood Mac. "Go Your Own Way," from *Rumours* (Warner Bros., US; WEA, UK, 1977).

———. *Tusk* (Warner Bros., US; WEA, UK, 1979).

Flipper. *Album/Generic Flipper* (Subterranean, US, 1982).

———. "Sex Bomb"/"Brainwash" (Subterranean, US, 1981).

Fripp, Robert. *Exposure* (EG/Polydor, 1979).

Frith, Simon. *Sound Effects: Youth, Leisure, and the Politics of Rock 'n' Roll.* New York: Pantheon, 1981; London: Constable, 1983.

Funky 4+1. "That's the Joint" (Sugarhill 12″, US, 1980).

Gang of Four. "At Home He's a Tourist"/"It's Her Factory" (EMI, UK, 1979).

———. *A Brief History of the Twentieth Century* (Warner Bros., US; EMI, UK, 1990). A retrospective through 1983.

———. "Damaged Goods"/"Love Like Anthrax"/"Armalite

Rifle" (Fast Product, UK, 1978). Their first release, with conversation between bull and matador on sleeve.

———. *Entertainment!* (EMI, UK, 1979; Warner Bros., US, 1980).

———. *Mall* (Polydor, 1991). Actually, a Gang of Two—Jon King and Andy Gill—and one of the more ambitious and quietly realized discs of its year.

———. *The Peel Sessions* (Strange Fruit, UK, 1990). Radio broadcast from 1979, and very hard. Augmented as *The Peel Sessions Album*, a CD adding broadcast from 1981 (Strange Fruit, UK; Dutch East India Trading, US, 1990).

———. *Solid Gold* (Warner Bros., US; EMI, UK, 1981).

———. *Songs of the Free* (Warner Bros., US; EMI, UK, 1982).

Germs. *Germicide* (ROIR cassette, Bomp/Mohawk lp, US, 1981). Live recording of group's first performance, at the Whisky in Los Angeles in June 1977, introduced by former Germ Belinda Carlisle.

Gilmer, Jimmy, and the Fireballs. "Sugar Shack" (Dot, 1963).

Girls at Our Best! "Politics"/"It's Fashion" (Rough Trade, 1980).

Gladiolas. "Little Darlin' " (Excello, 1956).

Go-Go's. *Beauty and the Beat* (I.R.S./A&M, 1981).

Grandmaster Flash & the Furious Five. "The Adventures of Grandmaster Flash on the Wheels of Steel" (Sugarhill 12", US, 1981).

Green, Peter. *In the Skies* (Sail, US; PVK, UK, 1979).

Harrison, George. *I Me Mine.* Guildford, Surrey, UK: Genesis Publications, 1980. Reissued New York: Simon & Schuster, 1981.

Hebdige, Dick. *Subculture—The Meaning of Style.* London and New York: Methuen, 1979.

Henderson, David. *Jimi Hendrix—Voodoo Child of the Aquarian Age.* New York: Doubleday, 1978. Reissued in condensed and revised form as *'Scuse Me While I Kiss the Sky —The Life of Jimi Hendrix.* New York: Bantam, 1981; London, Omnibus, 1990.

Holden, Stephen. *Triple Platinum.* New York: Dell, 1979.

Imposter, the. See Costello, Elvis.

Innes, Evan. *America 2040.* New York: Bantam, 1986.

Iron City Houserockers. *Have a Good Time (But Get Out Alive)* (Cleveland International, US, 1980).

———. *Love's So Tough* (Cleveland International, US, 1979).

J. Geils Band. "Love Stinks" (EMI America, US, 1980).

Joel, Billy. "Uptown Girl" (Columbia, 1983).

Joy Division. *Closer* (Factory, UK, 1980; Qwest, US, 1989).

———. *Still* (Factory, UK, 1981; Qwest, US, 1991). Collection released after suicide of lead singer Ian Curtis; includes Joy Division version of "Ceremony" from their final performance.

———. *Substance, 1977–1980* (Factory, UK, 1980; Qwest, US, 1988). Anthology; includes "Love Will Tear Us Apart" and US 12″ version of "She's Lost Control."

———. *Unknown Pleasures* (Factory, UK, 1979; Qwest, US, 1989).

Karp, Walter. "Coolidge Redux." *Harper's,* October 1981.

Kleenex. "Beri Beri"/"Ain't You"/"Hedis Head"/"Nice" (Sunrise, Switzerland, 1978). Issued as "Ain't You"/"Hedis Head" (Rough Trade, UK, 1978).

———. "You (friendly side)"/"U (angry side)" (Sunrise, Switzerland; Rough Trade, UK, 1979). See Liliput; Marder, Marlene.

Lauper, Cyndi. *She's So Unusual* (Portrait, US, 1984).
Lennon, John, and Yoko Ono. *Double Fantasy* (Geffen, US, 1980).
Lennon, Julian. *Valotte* (Atlantic, US; Charisma, UK, 1984).
Liliput. "Eisiger Wind" (Rough Trade, UK, 1981).
———. *Liliput* (Off Course, Switzerland, 1993). Collects all Kleenex/Liliput releases plus many fugitive recordings.
———. *Liliput* (Rough Trade, UK, 1982).
———. *Some Songs* (Rough Trade, W. Germany, 1983).
———. "Split"/"Die Matrosen" (Rough Trade, UK, 1980). See Kleenex; Marder, Marlene.
Lindley, David. *El Rayo-X* (Asylum, US, 1981).
Logic, Lora. See Essential Logic; Red Crayola; X-ray Spex.
Lowe, Nick. "American Squirm"/"What's So Funny 'Bout (Peace, Love, and Understanding)" (Radar, UK, 1978). See Brinsley Schwarz; Costello, Elvis.

Marder, Marlene. *Kleenex/Liliput: Das Tagebuch der Gitarristin Marlene Marder.* Zurich: Nachbar der Welt, 1986.
Mekons. *The Curse of the Mekons* (Blast First, UK, 1991).
———. *The Edge of the World* (Sin, UK, 1986).
———. *Fear and Whiskey* (Sin, UK, 1985).
———. *it falleth like the gentle rain from heaven—The Mekons Story, 1977–1982* (CNT, UK, 1982).
———. *The Mekons* (a.k.a. *Devils, Rats and Piggies—A Special Message from Godzilla*) (Red Rhino, UK, 1980).
———. "Never Been in a Riot"/"32 Weeks"/"Heart and Soul" (Fast Product, UK, 1978). Their first recordings.
———. *Original Sin* (TwinTone, US; Sin, UK, 1989). Collects *Fear and Whiskey* and other Sin recordings from 1983–86, including the abortion-rights anthem "Chop That Child in

Half." From the liner notes: "These days you don't have to leave home to be in exile."

———. *The Quality of Mercy Is Not Strnen* (Virgin, UK, 1979).

———. "Where Were You?"/"I'll Have to Dance Then (On My Own)" (Fast Product, UK, 1978).

Morrison, Van. *Common One* (Warner Bros., US; Mercury, UK, 1980).

———. *Into the Music* (Warner Bros., US; Mercury, UK, 1979).

Newman, Randy. "Lines in the Sand" (Reprise promotional cassette, US, 1991).

New Order. "Ceremony"/"In a Lonely Place" (Factory, UK, 1981).

———. *Substance* (Factory, UK; Qwest, US, 1987). Recordings from 1981–87.

Nig-Heist. "Walking Down the Street" (Thermidor, US, 1982).

Nirvana. *Bleach* (SubPop, US, 1989; Tupelo, UK, 1991).

———. *Nevermind* (DGC, 1991).

No Nukes. Directed by Barbara Kopple, Haskell Wexler, and Anthony Potenza. Warner Bros., 1980.

Oh Ok. *Wow Mini Album* (db, US, 1982).

Orbison, Roy. "In Dreams" (Monument, US, 1963). New version on *Blue Velvet—Original Motion Picture Soundtrack* (Varese Sarabande, US, 1986).

Pablo, Augustus. *East of the River Nile* (Message, UK, 1981).

Pennies from Heaven. Directed by Herbert Ross, written by Dennis Potter. MGM, 1981. See Tracy, Arthur.

Phillips, Jayne Anne. "What It Takes to Keep a Young Girl Alive," in *Black Tickets*. New York: Delacourt/Seymour Lawrence, 1975.

Prince. *Dirty Mind* (Warner Bros., 1980).

Public Image Ltd. (a.k.a. PiL). *Metal Box* (Virgin, UK, 1979). Released as *Second Edition* (Warner Bros., US, 1980). Reyissued in CD form in tin can by Virgin, UK, 1990.

—— (as Image Publique S.A.). *Paris au Printemps* (Virgin, UK, 1980).

Pussy Galore. *Corpse Love—The First Year* (Caroline, 1992). Collects *groovy hate fuck*, *Pussy Gold 5000*, and excerpts from *Exile on Main St.*

——. *Exile on Main St.* (Shov cassette, US, 1986).

——. *groovy hate fuck* (Shov, US, 1986).

——. *1 Yr Live* (Shov cassette, US, 1986).

——. *Pussy Gold 5000* (Buy Our Records, US, 1986). Includes "Pretty Fuck Look."

Raincoats. "Fairytale in the Supermarket"/"In Love"/"Adventures Close to Home" (Rough Trade, UK, 1979).

——. *The Raincoats* (Rough Trade, UK, 1979).

Red Crayola. "Born in Flames"/"The Sword of God" (Rough Trade, UK, 1980). See Essential Logic.

Rich, Charlie. "I Feel Like Going Home" (1973), on *Rockabilly Stars, Vol. I* (Epic, US, 1981). Not to be confused with versions released on Rich's *The Silver Fox* (Epic, US, 1974) or *Pictures and Paintings* (Warner Bros., 1992).

Ridgway, Stan. *The Big Heat* (I.R.S., US, 1986). See Wall of Voodoo.

Rolling Stones. "Highwire" (Rolling Stones, 1991).

——. *Let It Bleed* (London, US; Decca, UK, 1969).

——. *Tattoo You* (Rolling Stones, 1981).

Seventeen. Directed by Joel DeMott and Jeff Kreines, 1980–82.

Sex Pistols. "Anarchy in the U.K." (EMI, UK, 1976).

——. "God Save the Queen" (Virgin, UK, 1977).

————. *Gun Control—Winterland 1/14/78* (Ruthless Rhymes bootleg, 1978). The last concert.

————. *Never Mind the Bollocks Here's the Sex Pistols* (Virgin, UK; Warner Bros., US, 1977).

Shawn, Wallace. *The Fever*. New York: Noonday, 1991.

Sonic Youth. *Walls Have Ears* (Not 1 But 2 bootleg, 1985).

Springfield, Rick. "Jessie's Girl" (RCA, US, 1981).

Springsteen, Bruce. *Born in the U.S.A.* (Columbia, US; CBS, UK, 1984).

————. "Live at the Roxy, 7 July 1978." Several numbers from this performance are included on *Bruce Springsteen & the E Street Band Live, 1975–85* (Columbia, US; CBS, UK, 1986), but not "Prove It All Night" or "Racing in the Street." The three-CD *Hands Toward the Sky* (Lobster, Italy) may be the best bootleg.

————. *Nebraska* (Columbia, US; CBS, UK, 1982).

Stewart, Rod. *Every Picture Tells a Story* (Mercury, US; Vertigo, UK, 1971).

Strength Thru Oi (Decca, UK, 1981). Includes recordings by 4 Skins, Cock Sparrer, Shaven Heads, etc.

Summer, Donna. "Hot Stuff" (Casablanca, US, 1979).

Tonio K. *Life in the Foodchain* (Full Moon/Epic, US, 1979).

Tonite Let's All Make Love in London (See for Miles, UK, 1991). Augmented soundtrack to the 1968 film. US version on Sony omits nearly half an hour of Pink Floyd.

Tracy, Arthur. "Pennies from Heaven" (1937), on *Pennies from Heaven—Original Soundtrack* (Warner Bros., US, 1981). See *Pennies from Heaven*.

UB40. "Madame Medusa," on *Signing Off* (Graduate, UK, 1980).

USA for Africa. "We Are the World" (Columbia, US, 1985).

———

Wall of Voodoo. "Lost Weekend," on *Call of the West* (I.R.S., US, 1982). Included on Stan Ridgway, *Songs That Made This Country Great—The Best of Stan Ridgway* (I.R.S., US, 1992). See Ridgway, Stan.

Wire. *On Returning* (Restless Retro, US; EMI, UK, 1989). Original 1977–79 recordings.

———. *Snakedrill* (Mute 12″ EP, UK, 1986).

X. *Los Angeles* (Slash, US, 1979).

X-ray Spex. *Live at the Roxy Club* (1977) (Receiver, UK, 1991). With Lora Logic on saxophone.

———. "Oh Bondage Up Yours!"/"I Am a Cliché" (Virgin, UK, 1977). X-ray Spex's first release, and Lora Logic's only official studio releases with the group. All sixteen of X-ray Spex's 1977–79 releases are included on the augmented version of the group's sole album, *Germfree Adolescents* (Caroline, US; EMI, UK, 1992). See Essential Logic; Red Crayola.

Young, Neil (and Crazy Horse). *Re • ac • tor* (Reprise, US, 1981).

———. *Rust Never Sleeps* (Reprise, US, 1979).

Y Pants. *Beat It Down* (Neutral, US, 1982).

ACKNOWLEDGMENTS

My thanks for all the conversations that followed the inevitable "Heard anything good lately?" with the (for a time) equally inevitable "You mean you haven't heard . . . ?", and to all those who took part, including Dave Allen, the late Lester Bangs, Andrew Baumer, Adam Block, Bart Bull, Hugo Burnham, Barbara Carr, Art Chantry (source of the strange tale of Robert Prechter), Michael Conen and Lexy Green of Asta's Records in Oakland, the late Melanie Fechner, Donn Fileti of Relic Records, Ken Friedman, Simon Frith, B. George of the ARChive of Contemporary Music in New York, Andy Gill, Richard Gossett, Glenn Lambert, Bonnie Simmons, and Beverly Wilshire of KSAN-FM in San Francisco, Steve Goulding, Tom Greenhalgh, Howard Hampton (across a decade of epistolary friendship), Ella Hirst, Scott Kane and Robin Schorr of KALX-FM at the University of California at Berkeley, the late Walter Karp, Elisabeth Kauffmann of Elisabeth Kauffmann Zürich, Marian Kester, Russ Ketter and Doug Kroll of Rather Ripped Records in Berkeley, who sold me my first copies of *My Aim Is True* and "Anarchy in the U.K.," Jon King, my typist Nancy Laleau, Jon Landau, Jon Langford, Lora Logic, Cessie Marcus, Emily Marcus, Jenny Marcus, Steve Marcus, Marlene Marder, Dave Marsh, Jim Miller, Toru Mitsui, Juliana Muller, Scott Piering, John Rockwell, Jon Savage, Geoff Travis of Rough Trade in London, Lin van Heuit, and Anthony Wilson of Factory Records in Manchester.

I owe special thanks to the editors and publishers of those publications where the contents of this book first appeared: at *Artforum*, Ingrid Sischy, David Frankel, Robin Cembalest, Ida

Panicelli, and Anthony Korner; at *Interview*, Graham Fuller; at the *LA Weekly*, Kit Rachlis and Steve Erickson; the staff of *Music Magazine* in Tokyo; at *New West* (later *California*), Jon Carroll, Nancy Friedman, Janet Duckworth, and Bill Broyles; at *RAW*, Art Spiegelman and Françoise Mouly; at *Rolling Stone*, Jann Wenner, Barbara Downey Landau, Terry McDonell, and Paul Nelson; at *Threepenny Review*, Wendy Lesser; at the *Village Voice*, Robert Christgau and Doug Simmons.

At Doubleday I was lucky to have the support and enthusiasm of editors Martha Levin, Charlie Conrad, Jon Furay, and David Gernert, designers Julie Duquet and Marysarah Quinn, indexer Lionel Dean, and copy editor Bill Betts; at Penguin Books in London, that of Jon Riley, Tony Lacey, Rosie Glaisher, and researcher Clinton Heylin. Camille Smith of the Wendy Weil Agency was always helpful. I can promise Wendy, and Anthony Goff in London, that the next one will be a lot harder.

PERMISSIONS

Every effort has been made to locate current copyright holders of material either reproduced or quoted in this book.

"GOD SAVE THE QUEEN" (Glen Matlock, Steven Jones, Paul Cook, Johnny Rotten) © 1977/1978 WARNER BROS. MUSIC LTD., GLITTERBEST LTD. (Administered by Careers–BMG Music Publishing Inc.). All Rights Reserved. Used by Permission.

"Green Shirt" by Elvis Costello © 1978 PLANGENT VISIONS MUSIC LIMITED.

"Chemistry Class" by Elvis Costello © 1978 PLANGENT VISIONS MUSIC LIMITED.

"(What's So Funny 'Bout) Peace Love and Understanding" by Nick Lowe © 1983 Plangent Visions Music Limited.

"ANTHRAX" by Jonathan King, David Allen, Andrew Gill, and Hugo Burnham © 1979 Bug Music Ltd. (PRS) administered by Bug Music, Inc./Songs of Polygram International (BMI)/Elastic Purejoy Music (ASCAP), Hugo Burnham Pub. Designee & Bughouse (ASCAP), administered by WB Music Corp (ASCAP). Used by permission, also of Empire Music, Ltd. in the U.S.A. and Canada. All rights reserved.

"MONEY CHANGES EVERYTHING." Words and music by TOM GRAY. Copyright © 1978 by GRAY MATTER PUBLISHING. Used by Permission. All Rights Reserved.

"THE RIGHT PROFILE" by Joe Strummer and Mick Jones © 1991 NINEDEN LTD. Rights Assigned to EMI VIRGIN MUSIC LTD. All Rights for the U.S. and Canada Controlled and Administered by EMI VIRGIN MUSIC INC. All Rights Reserved. International Copyright Secured. Used by Permission.

"DEATH OR GLORY" by Joe Strummer and Mick Jones © 1991 NINEDEN

LTD. Rights Assigned to EMI VIRGIN MUSIC LTD. All Rights for the U.S. and Canada Controlled and Administered by EMI VIRGIN MUSIC INC. All Rights Reserved. International Copyright Secured. Used by Permission.

"Revolution Rock" © 1977 Fairwood Music Limited (on behalf of J. Edwards)/Panache Music (on behalf of D. Ray). All Rights Reserved.

"JOHNY HIT AND RUN PAULENE" (John Doe, Exene Cervenka) © 1980 WARNER-TAMERLANE PUBLISHING CORP. & EIGHT TWELVE MUSIC. All rights on behalf of EIGHT TWELVE MUSIC administered by WARNER-TAMERLANE PUBLISHING CORP. All Rights Reserved. Used by Permission.

"Brickbats" words and music by Don Van Vliet. Copyright © 1976, 1980 Don Van Vliet/Singing Ink Music. Used by permission. All rights reserved.

"MIND YOUR OWN BUSINESS" by Simon Best/Julie Sale/Kelvin Knight/ Alan Riggs/Bethan Peters/Roslind Allen © Complete Music Ltd. (PRS). Administered by Incomplete Music, Inc. (BMI) in USA.

"YOU" by Julie Sale/Kelvin Knight/Alan Riggs/Bethan Peters/Roslind Allen © Complete Music Ltd. (PRS). Administered by Incomplete Music, Inc. (BMI) in USA.

"PARALYSED" by Jonathan King and Andrew Gill © 1981 Bug Music Ltd. (PRS) administered by Bug Music, Inc. Published by EMPIRE MUSIC LIMITED in the U.S.A. & Canada.

"THIS TOWN" by Charlotte Caffey and Jane Wiedlin © 1981 Daddy-Oh Music (adm. by BMG Songs, Inc.) and Lipsync Music. All Rights Reserved. Used by Permission.

"Weinerschnitzel" by the Descendents. Used by Permission.

"Mansion on the Hill" by Bruce Springsteen. Copyright © 1982 by Bruce Springsteen (ASCAP). All Rights Reserved. Used by Permission.

"Used Cars" by Bruce Springsteen. Copyright © 1982 by Bruce Springsteen (ASCAP). All Rights Reserved. Used by Permission.

"Nebraska" by Bruce Springsteen. Copyright © 1982 by Bruce Springsteen (ASCAP). All Rights Reserved. Used by Permission.

"Pills and Soap" by Elvis Costello © 1983 PLANGENT VISIONS MUSIC LIMITED.

"Reason to Believe" by Bruce Springsteen. Copyright © 1982 by Bruce Springsteen (ASCAP). All Rights Reserved. Used by Permission.

Jayne Anne Phillips, "What It Takes to Keep a Young Girl Alive," from *Black Tickets*, © by Jayne Anne Phillips. Originally published in *Sweethearts* magazine. Used by permission of publisher Delacorte Press/Seymour Lawrence.

"This Is England" by Joe Strummer and Bernard Rhodes © 1991. Casbah Productions Ltd./Oddball Productions, UK. Reproduced by permission fo Casbah Productions Ltd./EMI VIRGIN MUSIC LTD., London WC2H OEA.

"PICK IT UP (AND PUT IT IN YOUR POCKET)" by STAN RIDGWAY © 1985 ILLEGAL SONGS, INC./MONDO SPARTACUS. All rights reserved. Used by permission.

"Split" by Marlene Marti/Klaudia Schifferle/Lislot Hafner/C. Freund/A. Scheitzer (All PRS). Reprinted with permission of Lipservices, on behalf of Incomplete Music, Inc. (BMI) and Complete Music Ltd. (PRS). All Rights Reserved. International Copyright secured. Reproduction without permission is prohibited.

"King Arthur" by the Mekons © Low Noise Music, 1986. Used by Permission.

INDEX